MAD MEN

The Cultural History of Television
Series Editors: Bob Batchelor, M. Keith Booker, Kathleen M. Turner

Mad Men: *A Cultural History*, by M. Keith Booker and Bob Batchelor

MAD MEN

A Cultural History

M. Keith Booker
Bob Batchelor

ROWMAN & LITTLEFIELD
Lanham • Boulder • New York • London

Published by Rowman & Littlefield
A wholly owned subsidiary of The Rowman & Littlefield Publishing Group, Inc.
4501 Forbes Boulevard, Suite 200, Lanham, Maryland 20706
www.rowman.com

Unit A, Whitacre Mews, 26-34 Stannary Street, London SE11 4AB

British Library Cataloguing in Publication Information Available

Library of Congress Cataloging-in-Publication Data

Names: Booker, M. Keith, author. | Batchelor, Bob, author.
Title: Mad Men : a cultural history / M. Keith Booker and Bob Batchelor.
Description: Lanham, Maryland : Rowman & Littlefield, 2016. | Series: The cultural history of
television | Includes bibliographical references and index.
Identifiers: LCCN 2015039815| ISBN 9781442261457 (hardback : alk. paper) |
ISBN 9781442261464 (ebook)
Subjects: LCSH: Mad men (Television program)
Classification: LCC PN1992.77.M226 B66 2016 | DDC 791.45/72—dc23 LC record available at
http://lccn.loc.gov/2015039815

∞ ™ The paper used in this publication meets the minimum requirements of
American National Standard for Information Sciences Permanence of Paper for
Printed Library Materials, ANSI/NISO Z39.48-1992.

Printed in the United States of America

For you-know-who. You know why.
—Keith

To my parents, Jon and Linda Bowen, for all your love
and support.
To Suzette, for everything and more.
And to Kassandra Dylan, as always, the center of my life!
—Bob

CONTENTS

ACKNOWLEDGMENTS

I feel fortunate to have a fantastic group of mentors and friends who I can turn to when writing a book becomes tough and needs discussion to fight through the difficulties. My deepest thanks go to Keith Booker, my coauthor on this *Mad Men* journey. Keith has long been an inspiration to me and countless other scholars. Our collaboration has helped me grow tremendously as a writer and thinker.

Others have provided so much more than I could include here: Phillip Sipiora, Don Greiner, Gary Hoppenstand, and Lawrence Mazzeno. Thank you for being wonderful role models and guides. Many friends offered cheer along the way, including Chris Burtch, Larry Leslie, Kelli Burns, Thomas Heinrich, Gene Sasso, Bill Sledzik, Josef Benson, Ashley Donnelly, Jesse Kavadlo, Sarah McFarland Taylor, Heather and Rich Walter and family, and Tom and Kristine Brown. I have been lucky to have many fantastic mentors, whom I would like to thank: Lawrence S. Kaplan, James A. Kehl, Sydney Snyder, Richard Immerman, Peter Magnani, and Anne Beirne. I benefit from a secret team of like-minded scholars: Brendan Riley, Brian Cogan, Kathleen Turner, Norma and Brent Jones, and Leigh Edwards! I would also like to thank my new Miami University colleagues.

This book launches the Rowman & Littlefield Cultural History of Television book series that I edit, along with Keith and Kathleen. We have a great lineup of books ahead that will explore and assess the role of television programming on American cultural history. Thanks to Stephen Ryan, our senior editor atRowman & Littlefield, for promoting and helping get the series launched. Stephen's constant support and friendship have been crucial. Thanks to the creative team at Rowman & Littlefield for their work on this book, especially the design team that created the outstanding cover.

My family is incredibly supportive considering what writing books means for one's time and energy. Thanks to my parents, Jon and Linda Bowen, for everything they do to make our lives infinitely better. Finally, Kassie is my inspiration, hope, and joy no matter what. I am blessed to have such a wonderful daughter!

—Bob Batchelor

INTRODUCTION: A MAD AGE

When *Mad Men* premiered on the AMC cable channel on July 19, 2007, it had already been seven years since series creator and showrunner Matthew Weiner wrote the initial script for the pilot. In the meantime, though, that script had garnered the attention of *Sopranos* creator and showrunner David Chase, leading Chase to hire Weiner as a writer for that show. *The Sopranos* not only gave Weiner an opportunity to develop his writing skills (previously he had been a writer for the Ted Danson sitcom *Becker* and some other minor television shows), but also helped to change the landscape of American television, ushering in the "quality television" revolution and helping cable television to gain an unprecedented prominence as a venue for that revolution.

    Mad Men would become a key element of that revolution, eclipsing even *The Sopranos* in terms of awards and recognition, winning the Primetime Emmy Award for Outstanding Drama Series in each of its first four seasons. (*The Sopranos* won only two Primetime Emmys for Outstanding Drama, though it does have the distinction of having been nominated in the Outstanding Drama Series category every year that it was eligible and having been the first cable series to win the award.) Fame tends to be fleeting in the world of television, of course, and whether *Mad Men* will challenge *The Sopranos* in terms of its ongoing critical reputation remains to be seen. In any case, *Mad Men*, which ran for seven seasons spanning nearly eight years (AMC broadcast the finale on May 17, 2015), stands as one of the most talked-about and written-about series of its time and seems likely to be remembered as an important part of

Don Draper, c. 1962. *AMC/Photofest ©AMC*

American cultural history long after most of its contemporaries have been mostly forgotten.

MAD MEN AND THE 1960S IN AMERICAN CULTURAL HISTORY

First and foremost, *Mad Men* drew both popular and critical attention for its vivid evocation of the 1960s, one of the most important decades in American cultural history. From the Kennedy-Nixon electoral campaign of 1960, to the Kennedy assassination of 1963, to the Chicago police riots of 1968, to the Apollo 11 moon landing of July 1969, well-remembered events of the 1960s provide vivid background to the experiences of Don Draper, Peggy Olson, Joan Holloway Harris, Roger Sterling, and the other characters of *Mad Men*, who collectively represent one of the most interesting groups to have appeared on American television since the crew of the starship *Enterprise* in the 1966–1969 airing of the original *Star Trek* (which, of course, also features in *Mad Men*). *Mad Men* engages in an extensive dialogue with the history of the 1960s, and the events of the series are keyed to contemporary events in their larger world to an extent that has seldom been rivaled in American television. Indeed, the events of *Mad Men* are so carefully synched with events in their contemporary context that the date on which the events of the series occur can almost always be located with considerable precision. However, even more important than its evocation of specific events is the general way in which *Mad Men*, which begins in 1960 and ends in 1970, clearly wants to argue that this period was a crucial turning point not only in the history of American advertising (the ostensible topic of the series) but in American history in general.

The essays in part III of this volume deal specifically with *Mad Men*'s engagement with history—and, in particular, with the ways the series addresses our ways of remembering and talking about history. Chapter 8 deals with the topic of nostalgia—and, of course, with the use of nostalgia as a weapon in the arsenal of advertisers. Chapter 9 contains a discussion of the role of the oppositional political and cultural movements of the 1960s in the series, including a discussion of the difficulties of Draper (who moves into his forties in the course of the series) in coming to terms with these movements, while chapter 10 looks at the imaginative role played by California in the series, a role that is closely related to *Mad Men*'s exploration of the American dream.

The most vivid historical memories of the 1960s, of course, have to do with the eruption of political activism that marked the decade: the women's movement, civil rights movement, and antiwar movement all sprang up in parallel during the decade, often making common cause in an outburst of idealism and utopian hope for the future. Of course, the "counterculture" of the decade included much more than these specific "issue-oriented" movements, also extending to what might be called more "lifestyle-oriented" movements, as a variety of groups (most of which came to be labeled under the general rubric of "hippies") sought alternatives ways of living that were intended to bring more satisfaction and emotional fulfillment than the dog-eat-dog, money-driven world of capitalism could offer. Such lifestyles—often described as supported by a "tune in, turn off, drop out" mentality—were closely associated with an emergent drug culture, the sexual "revolution," and a variety of cultural innovations, including rock music. There was, of course, considerable overlap between the issue-oriented movements and lifestyle-oriented movements, as when sexual emancipation (fueled partly by the introduction of the birth-control pill in, appropriately enough, 1960) was a key ingredient of the women's movement.

Mad Men contains an extensive engagement with all of these political issues and movements of the 1960s—though it is certainly possible to argue that this engagement isn't extensive *enough*, given the crucial importance of these issues and movements of the decade. Still, the women's movement is engaged in a particularly thorough, if indirect way, in *Mad Men* through the inclusion of numerous important women characters who struggle to find their way in the world amid the changing gender roles that the movement made possible. The final section of this volume is devoted to a discussion of the role played in the series by the three most important of these women characters—Joan Holloway Harris, Peggy Olson, and Betty Draper—including a discussion of what the representation of these characters has to say about the changing status of women in American society in the 1960s.

Of course, the counterculture in all of its manifestations is not the subject of *Mad Men*, which focuses on the mainstream capitalist culture itself, particularly on the evolution of American consumer capitalism through the 1960s, and even more particularly on the business (and discourse) of advertising as one of the key motive forces behind that evolution. The action of *Mad Men* thus takes place primarily in the meeting rooms and offices of Madison Avenue advertising firms, as well as in the suburban homes and urban apartments where the people who work in those firms pursue their private lives. And, while the countercultural movements that were so crucial to the 1960s (especially the women's movement) certainly impinge on these mainstream cultural spaces in the course of *Mad Men*, they generally remain marginal to the spaces that define the world that is the central setting of the series.

It is in its presentation of these latter business and private spaces (as well as in the costuming of the characters who occupy them) that *Mad Men* primarily manifests the visual style for which it has been so widely lauded. Indeed, it may be more in this visual style than for any direct engagement with the specific events or broad movements of the decade that *Mad Men* can truly be said to evoke the historical context in which it is set. One can, for example, track the progress of the action through the decade by monitoring the lengthening hair and sideburns of most of the men, along with the shortening skirts of most of the women. It is, however, in the set design that brings the spaces of the series to life that the visual style of the 1960s is most vividly re-created in *Mad Men*.

It should, however, be noted that *Mad Men*'s evocation of the look of the 1960s is heavily mediated: it is a representation not of the way the 1960s actually looked so much as of our cultural *memory*, half a century later, of the way the 1960s looked. Whether this memory is accurate is one of the issues that constantly lurks in the margins of the series, and Weiner himself has suggested that one of his principal goals in the series is to remind viewers "that they have a misconception about the past, any past" (Weiner, Spring 2014). Exactly how successful the series is in achieving this goal can be debated, but it is certainly the case that *Mad Men* is often highly successful in creating a vision of the 1960s that reminds us how different that time is than our own, while at the same time reminding us that this different time is still closely connected to our own and is in many ways more like our own time than we might care to admit. Much of *Mad Men*'s treatment of the issue of historical memory resides in the plot and characters, of course, but the visual style is a big part of this memory as well, and it is fairly clear that the visual style of *Mad Men* owes as much to well-known cultural representations of the

1960s (the early James Bond films are an obvious source for much of the look of the series) as to the physical reality of the period.

In many ways, in fact, *Mad Men* is really more engaged with the popular culture of the 1960s than with the 1960s themselves. Weiner has said that he extensively studied films and television series of the decade in developing his vision of what the period was like, and the series itself includes even more representations of the cultural products of the 1960s than of the historical events of the decade. These products include, among other things, books, which have a surprising prominence in the series, with protagonist Draper being a particularly avid reader. This prominence suggests a number of things about Draper himself, but it also suggests that books (especially fiction) played a larger role in American culture during the 1960s than they do now—one of the numerous (and not always obvious) ways in which the series reminds us of the differences between that time and ours. Television itself plays a key role in *Mad Men* as well, and (though specific individual programs factor into the series relatively little) one of the main historical arcs narrated in the series has to do with the rising prominence of television in the decade—a story, of course, that is not unrelated to that of the subsequent decline of the importance of books, especially as entertainment. Meanwhile, if Draper is a lover of books, he is even more a movie lover. His taste in cinema is eclectic and surprisingly sophisticated (many of his favorites seem to be European "art" films), and he is often shown attending films in theaters in scenes that generally include a snippet of the film being viewed as well.

Part II of this volume explores *Mad Men*'s engagement with specific forms of American popular culture, beginning with chapter 4, which discusses the role played in the series by books and reading. Chapter 5 looks at the use of music in the series, and especially at the way in which the engagement of *Mad Men* with the music of the 1960s is used to enhance its engagement with the context of the 1960s in general. Chapter 6 then details the role played in the series by movies, including Draper's use of popular films as a means of gauging the popular American mindset. Finally, chapter 7 discusses the numerous points of contact between *Mad Men* and the popular genre of science fiction, including a consideration of the ways in which the series itself might be read as science fiction.

In any case, the world of *Mad Men* is not a representation of the world that actually existed in that decade but a representation of an imaginary world that never existed in any sort of historical reality. It is, in Baudrillard's terminology, a simulacrum of the 1960s (or, in Jameson's terminology, a pastiche of the 1960s) rather than any sort of genuine representation of the 1960s. Meanwhile, in its evocation of the 1960s through cultural representations of the decade, *Mad Men* is a quintessentially postmodernist work, and one of the stories told by the series has to do with the status as a sort of bridge decade that took us from the still largely modern culture of the 1950s to the full-blown postmodernism of the 1970s. In this sense, the focus of the series on the world of advertising is particularly apt, because advertising itself was a key contributor to this cultural transformation and to the growth of a postmodern cultural climate marked by the thoroughgoing commodification of everything, including culture itself.

Draper himself seems to understand the close connection between advertising and other forms of American culture in the 1960s. Thus, he consumes culture not merely for entertainment or to stimulate his mind, but also as research for his work as a creator of advertising. Draper seems to be convinced that reading the books or viewing the films that are currently popular will give him a leg up on understanding the popular mind of America and that he can then use this understanding to craft advertising campaigns to which that mind will respond positively. One of the key ironies of the series, however, is that, despite his emphasis on being plugged into contemporary trends, Draper himself is very much a man of the 1950s who is always a step or two behind in trying to catch up to the dramatic cultural changes that marked the 1960s—or at least he is until the very last scene of the series, when (in one possible interpretation) he finally latches onto a workable (and brilliant) idea for how to commodify and sell the counterculture of the 1960s, just as we move into the 1970s.

MAD MEN AND ADVERTISING IN AMERICAN CULTURAL HISTORY

As *Mad Men* begins in 1960, advertising is still struggling to define itself amid the rapidly changing landscape of American consumer capitalism. The latter had already undergone two periods of widespread and revolutionary change in the twentieth century. As the century began, the United States was still lagging behind the rest of the Western (capitalist) world in terms of the historical progression of capitalist modernity, but that progression was already entering an important new phase. The period between the 1890s and the 1930s saw capitalism transform itself from the classic, industrial (production-oriented) form so compellingly analyzed by Karl Marx half a century earlier into the more modern form that would eventually come to be known as consumer capitalism. Struggling to recover from the social and economic consequences of the deep depression that struck Western capitalism in the final years of the nineteenth century, advanced Western nations such as Great Britain and Germany instituted a number of important social reforms, such as dramatic increases in the number of working-class individuals who were eligible to vote or to receive free public education. In addition, the basics of the social "safety net" that would become fully developed in what would later become known as the "welfare state" began to take shape at this time.[1]

As a relatively underdeveloped capitalist economy, the United States was affected less dramatically by the late-nineteenth-century depression than were most of the economies of Europe. However, just beginning to exploit its vast store of natural resources, the United States was ripe for a period of explosive growth. Moreover, as Marx himself had argued decades earlier, the United States (while economically backward in many ways) was, ideologically, already more advanced than Europe, given that the dominant bourgeois ideology of Europe still contained significant vestiges of the aristocratic ideology of the Middle Ages, while the ideology of the United States was much more purely modern and bourgeois. The United States was thus perfectly situated to take full advantage of the transformation that was under way in global capitalism at the end of the nineteenth century. Indeed, as William Leach has impressively detailed, this transformation was more striking and profound in the United States than anywhere else.

Among other things, the rise of American consumerism at the end of the nineteenth century put in place a system of perpetual revolution far more radical than the "all that is solid melts into air" famously associated with capitalism in *The Communist Manifesto*. As Leach notes, "American consumer capitalism produced a culture almost violently hostile to the past and to tradition, a future-oriented culture of desire that confused the good life with goods" (1994, xiii). And the rise of consumerism in the first decades of the twentieth century was accompanied by a vast array of changes that were designed to support and facilitate this phenomenon.

One of the most important of these (in Europe as well as in the United States) was the rapid development of advertising, as the relatively simplistic print-based ads of the late nineteenth century quickly grew in both their reach and their sophistication, while entirely new techniques began to be developed via the use of billboards, electrical signs, and show windows. And, as the new century proceeded, the new medium of radio provided unprecedented challenges and opportunities for advertisers as well.

As Leach notes, at the beginning of the twentieth century, business began, via the discourse of advertising, to pursue and colonize the imaginations of Americans in an unprecedented way (1994, 37). And the strategies of advertising began to penetrate virtually every aspect of American life. "Business," Leach explains, "flooded American culture with new symbols and images. A whole new aesthetics of color, glass, and light appeared on the American scene" (38). The onset of the Great Depression at the end of the 1920s significantly derailed the historical advance of consumer capitalism in the United States, but consumerism and advertising would remain central powers in America throughout the rest of the century.[2] Meanwhile, the mobilization of the U.S. industrial base during World War II finally brought the Depression to an end and prepared the way for that advance to get back on course in the postwar years. Indeed, consumer capitalism, fueled by a sense of urgency generated by the rhetoric of the Cold War, grew in those years with a fervor that had never before been seen. The rapid growth of the American economy during the 1950s represented the second great wave of revolutionary change in American consumer capitalism of the twentieth century, though in many ways it was simply a return to the course set by the original consumerist revolution of the first decades of the century.

The changes in American culture in the 1950s gave consumerism (and the advertising that drove it) an importance and a power that grew with shocking speed, especially with the appearance of the new medium of television, which gripped the imaginations of Americans with a rapidity and a tenaciousness never before seen in human history. It is this historical situation in which the characters of *Mad Men* find themselves as the series begins in 1960, while the next decade (during which the events of the series take place) might best be described not as a time of startling new countercultural challenges to the status quo but as a period during which the consumer culture that began to take shape at the beginning of the century became fully formed and started the process of consolidating its now-ubiquitous power.[3]

By the time the action of *Mad Men* ends in late 1970, a person such as Don Draper, born (as Dick Whitman) in 1926, would have lived in several different worlds, even if he had not undergone the kind of intentional identity shift undergone by Whitman/Draper. Born in the boom years of the 1920s, when the first wave of American consumer capitalism was reaching its zenith, Dick Whitman would have grown up largely during the hardships of the Great Depression, narrowly missing service in World War II only to be shipped off to Korea just as the American economy was shifting back into boom mode. Now transmogrified into Donald Draper, he would have returned after the war to a world of opportunities that allowed his talents to reap huge benefits.

Draper's change of identities can thus be read as a sort of allegorization of the changing national identity of the United States itself during the course of his lifetime. This changing national identity included such things as a growing global presence during the Cold War years. Domestically, though, the most important change to occur in American society during Draper's lifetime involved the growing importance of advertising and marketing at the heart of consumer capitalism, as success came to be equated with the accumulation of specific commodities—as recommended, of course, in the advertising that gained increasing penetration into the day-to-day lives of ordinary Americans.

Mad Men, in fact, invites a number of allegorical readings, as many aspects of the series—including the characterization of Draper himself—clearly mirror larger phenomena in the American society of the time. Part I of this volume explores some of these connections, beginning with a discussion of Draper's identity and of the way in which the definition of his identity comments upon the cultural identity of the United States in the 1960s. The second chapter deals with *Mad Men*'s treatment of the idea of the American Dream, an idea with which, of course, the subject of advertising is crucially involved. Chapter 3 looks at the frequent bad behavior of characters in *Mad Men* and at the way in which the representation of this behavior comments on the topic of vice in American culture at large.

The ever-growing American consumerist economy demanded that consumers buy more and more, with consumption coming to be equated with patriotism. Indeed, numerous campaigns were conducted not to sell specify products but to sell America, as the government sought to create a Cold War consensus at home and a positive image abroad. "These campaigns," explains historian Dawn Spring, "were designed to create an appearance of consensus, yet they were tightly controlled from the top down and were carefully orchestrated at every level, from grassroots activities to print advertisement" (2011, 4). In a broader sense, as part of what Stuart Ewen has called "ideological consumerization," consumerism was itself marketed as a positive good during the post–World War II era, when "mass consumption erupted, for increasing numbers, into a full-blown style of life" (2001, 208). The television set became the centerpiece of the nation's living rooms, while consumption was pursued with an almost religious zeal, with television as the new altar at which consumers could worship, reverently viewing commercials designed, crafted, and aired to sell products in ways that brought Marx's notion of the commodity fetish to unprecedented new levels.

By the 1960s setting of *Mad Men*, the United States had long been viewed as a locus of hope and opportunity, though the actual term "American dream" did not become a part of the nation's lexicon until James Truslow Adams introduced that term in the peak Depression year of 1931. For Adams, the Dream centered on individual freedom, but the idea would gradually morph more and more into a fantasy of materialist wealth and consumerist acquisition. As a result, the American Dream soon became entangled with broader notions of what it meant to be successful in a capitalist system (Samuel 2012, 3). Meanwhile, by the 1950s, America became a dreamland for advertisers even more than for consumers. Television provided advertisers with access to potential consumers that went beyond anything they previously could have dreamed of. And advertisers capitalized on this access by making advertising into a genuine art form; television commercials soon became as well-crafted and as entertaining as many of the programs, thus developing an independent following of their own. In this modern climate, "advertising has become an integral category of modern-day pop culture. Indeed, ads and commercials are often more entertaining than are the programs sponsored" (Danesi 2008, 208).

In *Mad Men*, of course, the aesthetics of advertising and the aesthetics of television programming often merge, and one of the most striking aspects of the series is the way in which its use of visuals and sound often echoes that of the commercials that are such a crucial part of its subject matter. In fact, the aesthetics and the subject matter of *Mad Men* are merged in a number of particularly interesting and profound ways that are worthy of careful examination. At first glance, *Mad Men* might be a combination of flashy set design with a soap opera plot and a collection of stereotypical characters. It is, however, one of those series that gets better and better on closer inspection, as various subtleties of its construction come more clearly into view. This volume is intended as a contribution to that project, seeking to provide not only a survey of some of the more important aspects of *Mad Men* but a guide to the genuine richness of the series and to some of the ways in which it provides a truly important commentary on American cultural history.

NOTES

1. For a wide-ranging review of these changes in their historical context (including the ramp-up in imperialism that was also a reaction to the economic crisis in Europe), see Hobsbawm (1987).

2. For an overview of advertising in the 1900s, see Batchelor (2002, 55–72).

3. For a discussion of the ways in which the 1960s were marked more by an outburst in consumerism than counterculturalism, see Frank (1998), who in fact sees the counterculture of the decade as significantly aligned with consumerism and as being largely an artifact of certain marketing strategies.

Part I

Mad Men as America

Sterling Cooper of 1960: Roger Sterling (John Slattery), Joan Harris (Christina Hendricks), Ken Cosgrove (Aaron Staton), Don Draper (Jon Hamm), Harry Crane (Rich Sommer), Peggy Olson (Elisabeth Moss), Paul Kinsey (Michael Gladis), and Pete Campbell (Vincent Kartheiser). *AMC/Photofest ©AMC*

I

WHO IS DON DRAPER?

*Why is the American man so unsure today about his masculine iden-
tity . . . because he is so unsure about his identity in general. Nothing
is harder in the whole human condition than to achieve a full sense of
identity—than to know who you are, where you are going, and what
you are meant to live and die for.*—Arthur Schlesinger Jr., 1958

*What you're watching with Don is a representation, to me, of
American society. He is steeped in sin, haunted by his past, raised by
animals, and there is a chance to revolt. And he cannot stop himself.*—
Matthew Weiner, March 19, 2014

Don Draper is a hero and villain. The things he worships—California,
cars, self-worth, movies, lasting accomplishment—symbolize postwar
America in an age when the nation's power seemed unbounded. Draper,
too, is a study in paradox, which essentially serves to make him even
more profoundly American. In creating this character, Matthew Weiner
forces viewers to reflect on Draper's life and deeds (good and bad) by
showing that aspects of him are in us all—a true everyman for the modern
world.

The extremes are always just below the surface with Don. He can lose
control in an instant. Draper is also capable of deep compassion. There
are bouts of terrifying malevolence. Often, his contempt for the shackles
of the corporate world and advertising business forces him to flee, as if
one more moment at his desk or in a meeting will yank his soul into
eternal damnation. Yet, at the same time, his zeal for what he calls "the

Don Draper. *AMC/Photofest ©AMC*

work" and the creative spark that wins him fame and fortune rarely wa-
ver. These dualities create a character that exudes everything that is right-
eous and strong about the American Dream—a kind of Superman in a
suit—but one that also typifies the nation's ugliness. As a result, there is
no easy way to answer this chapter's title question. Instead, the judgment
is pieced together by interrogating both the subtle nuance and audacious
bluntness Draper embodies.

   Similar to other outstanding fictional characters across film, literature,
and television, Draper is timeless. He symbolizes our own era, even as he
is meant to typify the chaotic 1960s. Yet, he is not simply a televised
version of John Updike's Harry "Rabbit" Angstrom, Don Corleone, Bob
Dylan, Sloan Wilson's man in the gray flannel suit, Saul Bellow's Augie
March, or Batman. He is representative but also unique, which is at least
in part why audiences are so attracted to him, despite his reprehensible
traits. Viewers can see "real life" in Don (traits of their family members
and friends), but also those drawn out of the fictional world, from suave
characters played by Cary Grant to the real or imagined John F. Kennedy.

   Draper is a composite of ideas, actions, and impulses that audiences
have proven to relish across American popular culture for decades. Like

F. Scott Fitzgerald's Jay Gatsby, for example, Don is mysterious and has difficulty attuning his two lives after assuming a new identity. Physically, Draper projects the "leading man" looks and toughness of Hollywood stars, like real-life icons Clark Gable and Gregory Peck. In playing Don, Jon Hamm flashes the same tough/tender and realist/idealist persona that many of the golden age film actors emanated. The "tough, but sensitive" personality, combined with traditional male beauty, draws viewers to the Draper character because we feel his quest, the unyielding existential angst. He is reaching for greatness but lassoed to the here and now, essentially waging warfare between these competing proclivities.

As a character, Don Draper asks audiences to contemplate his fictional life with the impulses and ideas that power the contemporary world: what role does sexism play in modern society, how much alcohol is too much, how do we treat friends and family, how might we interpret our coworkers and bosses, can we outrun the past, is the future bright. There is no doubt that some viewers take pleasure in the bad boy side of Draper's personality, particularly with booze, cars, women, and cigarettes. As the character both suffers and rejoices over seven seasons, people acquire the context to add value to their own ideas about life, the past, and avenues toward the future. The framework that Weiner created not only makes Draper an important character in television history, but also provides the show with lasting importance.

EVERYBODY'S ALL-AMERICAN

In unraveling mid-twentieth-century America, Weiner's decision to make Draper a successful ad man in New York City places him in an environment that viewers comprehend. Like the real-life Mary Wells, who Bill Bernbach dubbed his agency's "dream maker," Don is an extremely talented creative thinker steeped in American folklore but also able to project the near future by soaking in the nation's mythic past and current popular culture impulses. Draper weaves fabricated dreamscapes and worldviews. His creativity fuels his success and provides him with enough power to break the rules that others are forced to obey. There are no chains that can hold him. He runs away or simply vanishes, often because the disconnect between the freedom he desires and society's expectations creates a situation that leaves him helpless, living inside his own head, and unable to envision the right path, or possibly any path, for that matter. As audience members, we sense something good in Don and that enables us to root for him, even in his worst moments of drunker despair or wanton anger.

Viewers, on the other hand, also know that "Don Draper" is a farce. Impersonating another man is a kind of permanent mask that carries a burden Dick Whitman cannot abide. From one perspective, Draper is simply a fake, a deception, a ruse carried out by an extraordinary con artist. Renowned television critic Tim Goodman astutely sums up the essence of the character, explaining: "So much about Don's past actions, from relationships to actual marriages to friendships and job contracts, are predicated on his reluctance *to buy in*—he never wanted to be trapped, to commit" (2015).

The audience is in on the scam and must come to terms with how to process the competing aspects of Don/Dick and his relationship to the rest of the world. But Dick also becomes Draper: the ideas, vision, and power of his work cannot be detached from the man he becomes. In moments of weakness—like drunken revelry—he tells strangers his secret, much to the audience's surprise.

When traveling back to the beginning of *Mad Men*, when its fate still hung in the balance, Episode 1.1 ("Smoke Gets in Your Eyes"), Draper is a mystery. Initially, viewers do not know his name, but see the drink and the stiff-collared men and fancily dressed women around the bar in the background. The audience really has no idea why this mystery man sits alone in a crowded nightclub, despite the mayhem and general ruckus taking place all around him—puffs of smoke swirl around his head as he downs whiskey.

The fact that he fiddles with a scratch pad is the only indication that he might be there for a reason. His brief conversation with Sam the waiter, an older, uniform-clad African American bar back, is filled with purpose, rather than just what the audience might consider idle small talk. The air of mystery is intensified by the overt racism of the bartender, who appears tableside to ask the man if Sam is being too "chatty."

Although we have yet to formally meet antihero Draper, the drink, the bar itself, the way the patrons are dressed, and even the overt racism and focus on smoking connects the viewer to a familiar era. It may not be the era one grew up in or experienced firsthand as an adult, but it is one that people grasp from a lifetime of 1960s-infused popular culture. Thus, from the opening moments, Weiner puts a stake in the ground related to how the audience will view the show. Barbara Lippert explains, "The rich cinematography, evocative lighting and fantastic devotion to period furnishings and wardrobe could make a mid-century fetishist out of anyone watching. The fact that Draper looks perfectly appointed and dashingly handsome in the midst of all his inner turmoil is part of the appeal" (2009).

History matters, as does scene. With *Mad Men*, the pilot also had to live up to the marketing efforts, which focused so much on the authenticity of the 1960s as represented on the show. What one might not remember is just how large the stakes were for Weiner and cable station AMC. The showrunner/creator had been attempting to get the pilot created for about a decade, while the network invested substantial money and marketing energy on its newfound stab at serial television programming. Making matters more difficult, Weiner and the marketers wanted to entice viewers, but they also did not want to give away too much of the story. Authenticity and vice were the key themes used to rev up the corporate sponsors and the upwardly mobile viewers the show hoped to attract.

Mad Men intentionally introduced the paradox of life as lived in the 1960s as represented on one hand by Camelot-style grandeur and the day-to-day messy grind on the other. The suave stranger that the viewer interprets as the lead in the new show is juxtaposed against the elderly black bellhop, positioned as clearly inferior in a racially charged moment. "I was interested in writing something about American men and their complexity, some of which is ugly," Weiner explains. "There are two conflicting drives: one, to be an ideal father on the PTA . . . and, two, to get drunk, laid and smoke as much as possible" (qtd. in Klaassen and Sanders 2006). From this earliest moment, viewers realize that they are in for a story set around this dashing figure, straight out of leading man casting 101. From a marketing perspective, the show has also nailed the sensationalist aspects in a cloud of cigarette smoke and a tidal wave of alcohol.

The simple fact of the matter is that the Draper character transformed from this early hesitant impression into a popular culture icon. It seems as if Weiner and his team had this goal in mind from the start, particularly given the intrigue and drama produced by the show's opening credits alone. If you want a figure to be an exemplar, then it helps to portray the character in iconic narrative and imagery. Certainly many viewers were won over by the now-famous silhouette alone, as the riff hauntingly provides *Mad Men* with a sound that matches the vision.

GOOD DON

Don's essentially existential worldview is tinged with the horrors he experienced as a youth—his prostitute mother died in childbirth, leaving him to be raised by an angry, poor farmer and indifferent (at best) stepmother. As a youngster, he later sees his drunken father die after being kicked in the head by a horse spooked during a thunderstorm. Destitute, he and his pregnant stepmother are forced to live in a whorehouse where she may or may not be forced to have sex with "Uncle Mac" and others to earn their keep. Her religious views contrast with the severity of the beatings she gives young Dick for spending time among the prostitutes. His only friend, it seems, is a prostitute who treats him well while he is sick, takes his virginity, and asks the boy to rob "johns" while she has sex with them. This is definitely not *Leave It to Beaver* or *Father Knows Best*.

What young Dick Whitman and older Don Draper understands is what Carl Sagan would point out to American television viewers a decade or so after the *Mad Men* time frame: "The universe seems neither benign nor hostile, merely indifferent to the concerns of such puny creatures as we" (1980, 205). The difference between the scientist and the ad man, however, is that the former seemed more attuned to the notion of the beauty and chaos that existed simultaneously. Sagan seemed to find solace in the vision, explaining that "universal order and beauty" both existed and contrasted with "chaotic violence" that "destroys galaxies and stars and worlds" (205). Draper has a murkier view of humanity. He takes no comfort in the consumer, spiritual, or reaffirming aspects of life that concurrently drive and hearten people around him. He lives the moment-to-moment existence of a psychological and physical outlaw, never able to come fully to terms with who he was or what he did to transform like a phoenix rising from the ashes of an empty life.

How, then, does someone so confused, restless, and full of self-loathing become good? Maybe there is a splash of idealism that propels him. The "good" Don is the one who cares deeply about the future and, as such, wants to know that more lies ahead than simply money and other facets of the consumer capitalist experience. Don/Dick yearns for profound meaning. The journey includes his fascination with both American and foreign films, other ads that he meticulously cuts out of magazines, classic and current books, and contemporary world events. "Don is constant master of the cultural moment or historical contest; he has always done his homework," assert David Strutton and David G. Taylor. "Draper says little; thus the words he offers matter a lot" (2011, 469). When he is on top of his game, Don creates worlds out of these influences, sometimes aping entire stories drawn from contemporary popular culture or people around him to spin tales at least tangentially connected to who he is at that precise moment.

As the years pass and the internal and external pressures on Draper increase geometrically, he seems progressively more unhinged. All the booze and philandering drop the pedal to the metal, so when he scandalizes his daughter, Sally (she catches him in the act with neighbor Sylvia Rosen) and realizes that his loveless marriage to Megan is over, he careens into the guardrails, confessing to Hershey (and his fellow Sterling Cooper partners) that the rosy portrait he painted was a whorehouse fantasy (Episode 6.13, "In Care Of").

Still, there is good in Don. When the partners vote to put him on indefinite suspension, taking away "the work," which he could always turn to, Draper packs up the kids and takes them to the dilapidated whorehouse. While the boys do not understand, the look that he shares with Sally reveals that on some basic level she comprehends something fundamental about her father. Or, along similar lines, Weiner explained in a radio interview on NPR:

> I know that this man doesn't want his name on the building at that point 'cause he's afraid of being revealed. I know that he's not motivated by money. I know that he has a fantasy of the kind of person he wants to be and the life that he wanted. And at the same time, I think that we all live with this ambiguous relationship with our work, where we know on some level that it's not life. (2015)

What Weiner reveals about Draper is at the heart of the complexities surrounding the character. He is attempting to understand his past and the horrors he faced. The psychological baggage provides Dick with a picture of what he should aspire to, but simultaneously keeps Don from enjoying his successes. He is not a man that can feel trapped.

Throughout the series, that internal pressure drives him. Draper feels too much or is overwhelmed by the events and he flees. Don's self-imposed escapes take place so often that Roger makes a joke of his most recent getaway when the new McCann overlords question his whereabouts (which sets the tone for how the series will end).

Despite the fatalism and flights from reality, Draper never loses his thirst for the attempt to find truth. In Episode 7.10 ("The Forecast"), Don takes the one-off task Roger throws at him to write a memo about the future of the agency as an opportunity to really try to figure out what will be on the horizon. In searching for an answer, he asks people around him. But he strikes out with Ted, someone who Don respects and feels is smart, but Ted is living his own existential crisis. In response (and perhaps defeated by what he uncovered), Ted accepts the life of an ad executive. When he approaches Peggy, the outcome is worse. Ever the careerist, she turns the tables and makes Don's questions about *the* future about *her* prospects.

Peggy wants to conduct a formal performance review, but he turns it into a philosophical exercise. Don finally pushes her to own up to her goal, which she says is to "create something of lasting value." Don snaps back, displaying the classic Draper smirk: "In advertising?" This moment reveals his love/hate relationship with the profession, as well as his inability to see or articulate his own future. The quip and look on his face seem to indicate that he wants something big from his protégée, but even he has little hint of what that might be. Angry, Peggy storms from the office, finally realizing that the discussion was a one-sided effort by her boss to come to some cosmic idea.

Good Don, it seems, is characterized by the search for deeper meaning, his place in the world, and love for his children (though he is better with kids as they get older, case in point his evolving relationship with Sally as she becomes a more independent person). He enjoys the thrill of advertising and appreciates it as a kind of game, but it does not seem to feed his soul. If creating campaigns meant more to Don, perhaps he would not leave the business behind so easily on his quests.

Then there are moments—like the look exchanged with Sally when he reveals a part of his past to the children—that almost beg the viewer to see the good in Draper. In those rare glimpses, when we feel the pain in his eyes, it is easier to wash away all the wrongdoing, alcohol, and womanizing. Beneath the power suit, Brylcreem, and furrowed brow is a vulnerable person, the talismans representing masculinity and power stripped away. Good Don is exposed and yearning for love.

BAD DON

Bad Don is really bad. Nevertheless, he is not a murderer or drug dealer or mafia king or avenging serial killer. Draper is simply a messed-up guy with a lot of demons in 1960s corporate America. On the scale of the most evil popular culture icons from contemporary film, books, and television, he would not even make the list of despicable characters. Yet, there are plenty of Draper-inspired cringe-worthy moments.

Maybe these flashes of Bad Don disturb viewers so much because of *Mad Men*'s vaunted realism. Somehow the notion of Grandpa back in his heyday at an after-hours office dinner gets serious when we witness how Bad Don conducts himself. Remember in Episode 2.3 ("The Benefactor") what he did to manager/attempted blackmailer Bobbie Barrett when she tried to shake him down outside the women's restroom? In these instances, Don is a tyrant, a bully, and utterly frightening. He is not Tony Soprano or Dexter Morgan scary, but his suave killer determination brings chills. Fans and critics blasted the episode for its chauvinistic theme overall and especially Don's manhandling (literally) of Bobbie Barrett, which seemed particularly cruel and animalistic.

In an interview with NPR's Terry Gross, Weiner gave a peek inside Draper's head, explaining, "This is about a man having a reckoning with himself" (2015). Throughout the last season, the notion of a potential reckoning left many viewers and critics with the idea that Draper might die. Don, though, has a different feeling about mortality. A thrilling aspect of Bad Don is that he both deeply loves and fears death, thus pushing against life in a way from which others would back away or run screaming. "I feel like Don is like a lot of existential characters: brave in the face of death but more deeply, deeply afraid of it—and trying to find some purpose and some control over it—because he is aware of the sort of meaninglessness of life," Weiner said (2013). If bravado dictates a kind of standing up to the idea of dying, then the haphazard manner in which he negotiates much of his personal life makes sense.

Bad Don, whose existential conflict with death and life determines his conduct, is a product of violence and destruction. His childhood and youth is a cauldron of wickedness and the false hope of spiritual fervor that spills out into cruelty, like when his stepmother savagely beat him for having sex with one of the house women at Uncle Mac's. In many respects, Draper is a representation of the violence that marked the Age of Aquarius, despite its free love stereotype.

If one begins with the bungled Bay of Pigs invasion (an estimated 3,500–4,000 total combatants and others killed) and ends with the Kent State massacre on May 4, 1970, when members of the Ohio National Guard killed four students, then the period that *Mad Men* encompasses was filled with extreme violence. Like the nation, Don kind of blunders recklessly and swings wildly at times, while other actions are based on cold calculation. A list of times when the nation seemed out of control would be long, just as it would with Bad Don.

At his lowest point in Episode 7.14 ("Person to Person"), when suicide or imminent death seems like a possibility, Don seems about to crack. The desperation in his voice is electric as he explains to Peggy, "I broke all my vows, scandalized my child, took another man's name, and made nothing of it." Bad Don transforms into Broken Don. In this moment he is traveling the "dark desert highway" that the Eagles sang about in the band's smash 1976 single "Hotel California."

What pulls him back is Leonard, the group therapy stranger. A true everyman, in the ways the handsome, debonair Draper is not, Leonard explains his life, saying, "You don't even know what it [love] is" when people are trying so hard to give it. This observation sparks something deep inside Don, allowing him the mental and physical space to not only hug the man and cry desperately on his shoulder, but also participate in the healing sessions that lead to the Coke epiphany.

JON HAMM IS DON DRAPER

At the end of a long day at Sterling Cooper and angry with the Samsonite account pitch not coming together, Don lashes into Peggy. They are the last two in the office. Everyone else is off with family and friends or preparing for the historic Sonny Liston–Cassius Clay boxing match. He demands she stay, bellowing: "We're going to do this right now. Do you think elves do this?" Later, when Peggy tells him that it is her birthday and that her boyfriend is waiting, he responds sarcastically, "By the way, you are twenty-something years old. It's time to get over birthdays. Go ahead, I'll do it myself" (Episode 4.7, "The Suitcase").

Relenting, Peggy stays. The night devolves: she loses her boyfriend, gets humiliated by her mother, Don and Peggy fight, Don gets wasted, Don and Peggy reconcile, he throws up on himself, Duck tries to defecate on Roger's couch, Duck beats up Don, and Don passes out on Peggy's lap. The debauchery is a way for Don to avoid placing a call to California: Anna Draper is on her deathbed. Her niece Stephanie leaves him the message, but he avoids returning the call. Don cannot face the pain and retreats into the abyss of heavy drinking.

That night, in an alcoholic stupor, Don wakes to a vision of Anna. She is young and smiling. Dressed in a bright yellow dress, Anna carries a suitcase. The next morning, in a daze, he calls Stephanie. He wonders if Anna wanted to talk to him. She says, "You know, she wasn't really there," not realizing that the phrase could also apply to him seeing Anna's ghostly presence.

Don stares at the phone as his eyes fill with tears. When he looks up, he sees Peggy. He starts to cry. "Somebody very important to me died. The only person in the world who really knew me," he cryptically explains. Peggy puts a hand on his back to soothe him. Later, she falls asleep on her office couch. In what seems like an instant but is actually the next morning, Stan rudely wakes her by blowing a whistle in her face. Don, a complete mess when she last saw him, arrives starched, clean, and in great spirits. Looking at the account plans, Don puts his hand on top of Peggy's. They look at each other for several beats.

"The Suitcase" is intricately plotted. In many instances, comedy is delivered in angry tones, while the pathos hanging in the air is eased by moments of close friendship and confession. The glue, as is often the case, is the complicated relationship between Peggy and Don. Given their embodiment of these particular characters on this specific program, it is easy to forget that the real actors here—Jon Hamm and Elisabeth Moss—are deciphering roles created and carried forth by Weiner, his writing staff, the director, and other producers. For television shows, the ability of the actors to get audiences to believe in the characters and their on-screen lives is critical for success.

As Dick Whitman/Don Draper, Hamm personifies a set of traits that viewers largely associate with 1960s businessmen but also the distinctive aspects of this individual. Draper lives by codes that are not often clear and parts of his split personality spill through the mask he wears in an attempt to keep the two halves separate. Early in "The Suitcase," as Don attempts to process what he knows is happening to Anna, he instead turns to alcohol. This is a pivotal moment that will dictate Don's actions for the rest of the episode. Hamm has a way of deflating during times of crisis, which reveals Draper's anguish. The usually near-beautiful persona, bolstered by unending confidence, becomes pallid and shrinks, as if in pain. He looks at a picture of his younger self with Stephanie, then cringes and pours the drink. That brief recoil captures Hamm's expression of Draper's complexities.

Returning to boss mode, Don uses Peggy as a verbal punching bag, berating her and also forcing her into a difficult personal situation with her boyfriend and family. Here, Hamm is quintessential Draper—his voice is machine-gun-like and punishing, using biting sarcasm to exact razor-blade cuts. At the height of their argument over who deserves credit for an award-winning idea, the actors dip and shift like great dancers. Hamm: "It's your job! I give you money; you give me ideas!" Moss: "And you never say thank you!" Hamm: "That's what the money is for . . . you should be thanking me every morning, along with Jesus, for giving you another day!" (Episode 4.7, "The Suitcase").

Don yells, and the window behind him is full of lights, but nothing outside is as bright as his starched dress shirt, a form of armor that accentuates his power. In another example of Hamm's physicality, he becomes pure evil. As his voice grows louder, though, his face contorts, the dark five o'clock shadow stands out, his neck is red and lips askew. Peggy stands in front of Don, almost at attention. She lowers her face and begins crying. Don responds; immediately his features and body soften. "Ah, c'mon," he says in retreat. She turns and bolts from the office. The setting conveys the action. Don is drunk, having had at least half a bottle of whiskey. The alcohol cart sits on the left side of the scene, while Draper is perched on the couch opposite on the right. The coffee table is strewn with papers and an ashtray. Peggy's coat and hat are in the middle, rumpled, and discarded on the chair. He calls after her, "I'm sorry about your boyfriend, okay?"

After the reconciliation, Don—though drunk—is back to oozing seductive charm. When Peggy sees a mouse scurry under the desk, Draper drops to the floor, asking, "Where'd you go, Mickey?" But then they hear a phone ring, and the color drains from Hamm's face. Then he realizes that it's Olson's phone. Again, the actor is able to hit marks of wry humor, concern, fear, and strength in a matter of moments. These little flashes fuse into the multifaceted model Hamm creates, thus bringing Draper to life.

Draper unspools the rest of the episode, which allows Hamm to magnify the character's demise. After throwing up in a diner bathroom and an altercation with Duck, Draper sits in the dark office, sprawled out on the couch. There is a vomit stain on his shirt and his tie is loose. "Can you get me a drink?" he asks. "I have to make a phone call and I know it's going to be bad." Peggy sits down and he slumps over, placing his head on her lap in a display of trust that negates all the anger from earlier. "Sorry if I embarrassed you," he whispers as he passes out on her lap.

Virtually unknown prior to *Mad Men*, Hamm now personifies the dramatic antihero of television's third golden age, along with a handful of others, such as Bryan Cranston (*Breaking Bad*) and Michael C. Hall (*Dexter*). The actor told *Rolling Stone* that becoming Draper is like channeling his father, "a businessman in the Sixties . . . he had a million suits, and he drank at lunch and smoked too much—he was That Guy" (Maerz 2009). Commentators relentlessly return to Hamm's handsomeness because it is a good hook for stories about the actor, yet examining the body of work, it is the actor's physicality that stands out. Small gestures, like the look of horror when Don wakes up with an unknown stranger after a night on the town, or bigger ones, like chasing Megan through their apartment, tripping and dropping them both to the ground, demonstrate Hamm's underrated skills in making the larger-than-life Draper seem real.

DRAPER UNBOUND

The image is priceless and virtually unbelievable—legs crisscrossed (big toe bending in a seemingly impossible way), a rumpled yet stern Don Draper sits seaside. The Big Sur waves crash behind him. Sitting around the New York City ad man are quintessential hippies: a blond woman in a tan, flowered dress and two blond men, both bearded, one old and one young. The older man's palms are raised and eyes closed. Don's right hand hangs from his knee and touches the ground.

This is a collective search for meaning, among those ruminating on the bluff overlooking the Pacific Ocean, yet despite the meditative feeling of the others, Don is focused. The crease between his eyes is a familiar one to *Mad Men* fans; Draper is considering something new. Soon, the audience will catch their final, original glimpse of Don—a close-up of his face and a reassuring smile. Then the iconic Coca-Cola commercial begins, initiated with a single voice: "I'd like to buy the world a home and furnish it with love . . ." Fourteen seconds into the ad, the viewer sees that the youthful singers are all holding a bottle of Coke.

Originally launched in July 1971, the famous brand, jingle, and commercial that pulls it all together take us into the future beyond the *Mad Men* timeline and keeps Don Draper alive (presumably) for nearly a year beyond the audience's picture of him high above the California surf (it is fall 1970 in the series finale). We believe that Don created the piece because it manipulated the peace and love culture of the 1960s by showing teens and young adults from all over the world and different races together, which is the kind of breakthrough creativity that may have been sparked on Draper's California adventure.

Filmed on a hillside outside Rome, the commercial featured the young people singing about the joys of Coke. Later, under the guidance of advertising agency McCann Erickson, two different pop acts released the song as a single, with one of them making the top 10 and the other entering the top 15. The jingle helped Coke strengthen its standing as a global brand. The song's popularity led it to be played in many different languages and sold as sheet music, further extending its influence (Ryan 2012). The peace and love theme captures one portion of the era, yet overlooked the ravages of the Vietnam War raging in Southeast Asia. These kinds of choices were deliberate and conducted by agencies that did research to identify what messages would stick best with consumers.

Associating Don with the famous commercial allows Weiner to give Draper life beyond the show. Television critic Tim Goodman says that what the *Mad Men* series finale did well is end in an "open-ended" fashion. He explains, "On one level the stories the Mad Men characters live go on, even though we have resolution and closure on another level" (2015).

The key here, as usual, is in the manner Weiner allows us to think about Don and his potential future(s). Goodman rightly points out that the audience is free to imagine the ad man's future, and as a matter of fact, by ending with the Coke commercial, viewers are led to believe that Don scores his masterpiece for McCann. Fans, too, have more than enough ammunition and experience with the character to envision any number of alternative scenarios. "This is what closing a window (for the viewers) on lives that still go on (for the characters) allows," Goodman concludes (2015). Many alternative futures probably center on how one feels about Don and his responsibilities, not typically one of his strong points.

Goodman's assessment of the finale also demonstrates one of *Mad Men*'s most enduring strengths—providing viewers with the content to not only consider the past from the characters' perspectives, but to look at the era (filled with nostalgia) anew. This kind of dual viewpoint—looking at a show set in the well-known past and using it to think about that time period and one's own—really fuels *Mad Men*. As the series ended, one could look back and consider the show as either supporting or destroying the stereotypical view of the 1960s.

In comparison, HBO's series *Deadwood* (created by David Milch) won countless fans and critical praise, but no one alive today actually knows what it felt like to live in the Old West during its gold rush heyday. One might argue that *Deadwood* and other great television programs always compel the viewer to think differently about the past and its application to the contemporary world. The 1960s setting, however, gives *Mad Men* viewers who grew up or lived through the era more to contemplate, analyze, and interrogate. Similar thinking can be applied to the way the show used actual advertising campaigns and Weiner's almost manic efforts to make the set details accurate. Though we have countless examples of the 1960s and the gold rush West across popular culture, no one could ask Grandma about the gunslinger days.

Arthur Schlesinger Jr., the great historian and JFK White House insider, no stranger to studying heroes in American history, once claimed, "Great men live dangerously. They introduce extremes into existence—extremes of good, extremes of evil—and ordinary men after a time flinch from the ultimates and yearn for undemanding security" (2008, 38–39). *Mad Men* viewers can read this quote and, just like the epigraph that begins the chapter, see Draper as representative of the age. Applying Schlesinger's definition, one might be forced to accept Don as one of these mythical "great men."

Yet, our contemporary perspective may not allow us to buy into the historian's claim. Along the way, Don lost everything—marriages, money, health, self-respect, friendships, industry status, and many other points that define people in their lives. Draper runs from security and courts good and evil, but to what end? Unlike history's great men (and women) who fight for causes and principles beyond their own interest, Don is often little more than a con man who manipulates people with his good looks and ability to sell dreams.

Despite his foibles, though, Draper benefits from viewers who are more or less inculcated with hope and the notion that even the worst offenders deserve redemption. We have an almost pathological desire and willingness to dole out second and third chances for people to redeem themselves—to be relentlessly optimistic, even when we might know better. Perhaps it is this word "redemption" that is the essential key in understanding the character and his greatness. The viewer is like the barroom minister in search of souls to salvage (Don punches him out and spends the night in jail) or the preacher Uncle Mac pushes down the front steps of the whorehouse, who covered in sweat exclaims to young Dick: "The only unpardonable sin is to believe that God cannot forgive you," before picking up his Bible and limping away. Draper cannot save himself, even believes that he is unworthy of rescue, but as viewers we can grant him redemption.

The distance between our eyes and the screen enables us to both judge and forgive Don, because—in the end—no matter how much someone loves or appreciates *Mad Men*, it is just a television show. Viewers might not be so kind or lenient if they had a real-life Draper in their midst. Then again, this is the nation of second chances. Don is our poster boy.

2

MAD MEN AND THE AMERICAN DREAM

The organization man is not in the grip of vast social forces about which it is impossible for him to do anything. . . . He must fight The Organization. . . . It is wretched, dispiriting advice to hold before him the dream that ideally there need be no conflict between him and society. There always is; there always must be.—William H. Whyte Jr., *The Organization Man* (1956)

The *New York Times* headline blared: "Advertising: Picture for 1960 Looks Bright." Based on a report by a research firm owned by ad giant McCann Erickson (perpetually *Mad Men*'s version of the evil empire), reporter Carl Spielvogel highlighted the findings, including a projection that the advertising industry would double its billings over the course of the decade, from $10 billion in 1960 to $20 billion in 1970 (about $120 billion in 2015 dollars). Though Spielvogel noted that advertisers faced some challenges, including clients that demanded more work done with greater efficiency, the 1960s promised to be a boom time for American corporations and the nation as a whole (1960).

When assessing the large advertising budget in light of historic comparisons, we see just how strong the ad business stood in the 1960s, as well as its enduring power. By 1979, for example, the total spent jumped to $27.9 billion, almost tripling the earlier amount. In comparison, advertisers spent about $180 billion in 2014, an astronomical amount of money but not that much more than the 1960s and 1970s, particularly when one considers the seemingly infinite number of channels available today versus the mid-century marketplace.

The perfect American family: Don, Betty, Bobby, and Sally. *AMC/Photofest ©AMC*

Given the nation's economic power and how the ad business reflected that strength, *Mad Men* is a remarkable tool for examining the evolving American Dream. Within the confines of Sterling Cooper, the viewer finds a multitude of stories that expound on the tenets of the Dream narrative at every point in its development, from the juxtaposition of "Old New York" money lost (Pete Campbell) to up-from-nowhere Horatio Alger success (Dick Whitman/Don Draper). Another draw for *Mad Men* is the way the series interspersed the tribulations of real corporations and brands, including GM, Jaguar, Vicks, and Dow Chemical. Using actual brand names, the viewer might think about the role of corporations and products across historical eras.

Although the series primarily centers on the fortunes (no pun intended) of WASPs, there are many other characters whose destinies question how the American Dream did or did not work. While some critics and social commentators would have liked the show to go into more depth regarding the lives of blacks, Jews, homosexuals, lesbians, and members of fringe groups from hippies to cultists, *Mad Men* confronted these topics from a cultural and socioeconomic perspective.

Almost universally the audience is forced to interpret the show's characters and the age via a corporate capitalist lens. Often the juxtaposition is between the "haves," like the agency partners and employees, and the "have-nots" or "want-nots" that cruise in and out of their lives. For example, in Episode 7.4 ("The Monolith"), Roger Sterling's daughter Margaret, now going by the laid-back moniker Marigold, runs away to live in a free-love hippie commune in a dilapidated farmhouse. Despite his hesitance to intervene in her life, the agency head and his ex-wife drive out into the countryside to bring her back. After seeming to reconcile, Roger decides that Marigold cannot drop out because she is a mother and has obligations to her only child. But as he attempts to physically force her into an old truck, the only vehicle on the farm that will allow them to escape, both father and daughter fall into a mud hole. Roger's trademark expensive blue suit is covered in grime, which paints a stark contrast to his white hair and angular features. Defeated, the ad man limps away, leaving his daughter behind. From the look on his face as he hobbles, mud-soaked, he also loses more than a little of his soul. The juxtaposition of money versus happiness and responsibility versus freethinking is a by-product of *Mad Men*'s deliberate exploration of the nation's values during the decade.

At the heart of *Mad Men*'s examination of the American Dream, however, is Whitman/Draper. The duality in the character is significant—while Draper is the fulfillment of a successful American life, it is a wholly inauthentic life. Since Dick essentially stole the Don identity from a dead man, it is impossible for him to trumpet his success. His wife Betty only finds out by snooping through his locked desk. Later, in Episode 4.10 ("Hands and Knees"), Don forces Pete to drop a potential Air Force account that demands a security clearance. When the FBI interviews Betty and she then tells Don about the visit, his fear is palpable—almost pure terror as he breaks into a cold sweat—as he contemplates life on the run.

Exploring celebrity culture and fame as it developed in the twentieth century, one finds that the very act of publicizing one's rags-to-riches story seems part of the American Dream narrative, but one that Don/Dick must avoid at all cost. In Episode 4.1 ("Public Relations"), Draper is interviewed by Jack Hammond from *Advertising Age* for a short feature story, but his evasiveness comes across as arrogance. When the story appears, Hammond calls Don "a handsome cipher," then compares him to Dorian Gray, the antihero of Oscar Wilde's *The Picture of Dorian Gray*, saying "One imagines somewhere in an attic there's a painting of him that's rapidly aging." In the novel, Gray is a hedonistic, shallow man, on par with a vapid, lust-filled Prince Charming, willing to sell his soul to stay beautiful. As one might imagine, senior partners Roger and Bert Cooper chastise Don, which the younger man attempts to deflect, saying that the article will line birdcages by the end of the week. To counter the bad publicity (especially given the fragile state of the firm at the time), they get him an interview with a *Wall Street Journal* reporter.

As the episode closes, Draper is regaling the writer with a new version of his story and turning on the charm. Like Jay Gatsby, he spins a tale that delivers the American Dream story in a way that potential readers, clients, and his bosses want to see. Fame culture is on full display. Don cannot tell the truth about his boyhood, which would have made a great story, because of what happened in Korea, but he can still craft a heroic narrative that coincides with his personal success and embodiment of the American Dream.

As viewers we are not completely omniscient, but we do know Dick/Don's secrets long before the people with whom he interacts. The drama unfolds on camera, but how it unfolds is important because viewers get sucked into the "mysterious stranger" plotline. Because we know the real

Don Draper is actually a dead man killed in Korea, the contrast with *Ad Age*'s Hammond is poignant. The reporter lost his leg in the war, which points to what a real hero is willing to sacrifice. Grasping that Don's secret identity could also be his total undoing, we are induced to root for him, despite many other aspects of his personality and behavior that are reprehensible at best. The idea that one can more or less be reborn via some external reinvention is a powerful foundational piece of the American Dream.

CREATING THE DREAM

The Drapers—a handsome advertising executive, his former model wife, and their two children (later three)—symbolize American power and prosperity in the Cold War era. They live in an early 1960s version of a "McMansion" in a New York City commuter town. Dashing out the door, Dad grabs his hat and ventures forth to the train station, while Mom stays at home with the youngsters, filling her day with television, gossipy chats with other stay-at-home moms, and a ubiquitous pack of cigarettes at the ready. They have an African American maid, which sets them apart from their slightly less wealthy suburban neighbors. Her job centers on keeping the children contained. Supper is on the table when Dad gets home, as well as a stiff drink or two . . . or three.

In establishing the Drapers as the prototype post–World War II family, *Mad Men* creates a palette that enables the show to explore ideas at the heart of what it meant to be an American family during the era and the tenets of the postwar, booming-economy American Dream. Don is a successful business executive and his status is reflected in every facet of his life, from Betty's culture and beauty to his virility and manliness as a father of a growing family. The home, television, automobile, suit, and attitude all reveal that Don personifies the American Dream.

Draper is representative of the powerful new national economy and culture at its very best—at least on the surface. Like the soft underbelly of the United States, Draper is not what he appears to be. He has a drinking problem, is often narrow-minded, resorts to violence and intimidation, and protects a secret past. These challenges serve as a kind of mirror for what the nation faced at the same time: racism, sexism, homophobia, violence, murder, and warfare.

As a talented ad man, Don creates words and images that play on the ideas that he also lives. He is both a creator and consumer of culture. His agency gauges its success on the skill that is required to reflect the nation back onto itself via visual and written communication to symbolize an idea that they can then associate with a consumer good. In Episode 3.2 ("Love Among the Ruins"), Draper's mantra about advertising is revealed: "If you don't like what is being said, then change the conversation." Yet, this notion of marketing also goes a long way in explaining the American Dream. The United States might be splintered by seismic events and incidents from assassinations and race riots to antiwar rallies and violent clashes between police officers and activists, but it could still change the conversation to its economic might, global cultural influence, and military prowess.

Managing and manipulating the American Dream narrative dates back to the earliest uses of the term, which exist far back in time. Despite its long history, though, historian James Truslow Adams introduced the term "American Dream" into the nation's lexicon in 1931 at the height of the Great Depression in his book *The Epic of America*. For Adams, the Dream centered on the freedom people had to determine their place in the world. As the decades of the mid-twentieth century unfolded, however, the idea morphed to encompass many related philosophies, most often focusing on wealth and the acquisition of consumer goods, particularly in comparison to what one owned versus other people. As a result, the American Dream soon became entangled with broader notions of what it meant to be successful in a capitalist system (Samuel 2012).

As the United States developed as a consumerist society from the early 1900s, the American Dream evolved as well. We can certainly look back on the way advertising changed in the 1900–1910 period and identify that era as foundational since advertising then emerged as the most pervasive technique for promoting the budding consumer culture (Batchelor 2002). After this early period and over the course of the next several decades, the consumer-based culture solidified and expanded so that by the 1930s, the stranglehold was complete. The Great Depression might have slowed the consumer's ability to purchase goods and services, but the ad industry continued to launch campaigns.

In the post-1945 era the concurrent ideas of the American Dream and the "American Way of Life" merged in a sea of consumerist behavior that linked purchasing power with what it meant to be a productive member of society. These factors also had consequences globally. According to scholar Joel Spring, "After World War II, the 'American Way of Life' became a major theme in the Cold War between the United States and the Soviet Union" (2010, 73–74). Because the two ideas dovetailed, schools took up the cause, essentially training young people to be consumers. Consequently, advertisers responded by increasing efforts at young people, particularly teenage females, just as the industry had done with older female consumers across its history. Raising a nation of happy consumers—at least among white Americans—meant that the nation's economic power would be forever tied to what people bought and how much of their incomes went into consumer goods.

As marketing and advertising grew more ubiquitous, the federal government reasoned that it could use similar techniques in its battle against Communism and for the democratic system. America not only continued to teach its own citizens how to be fervent consumers in the Cold War era, but also the federal government embarked on a series of programs that would demonstrate the power of the consumer-based economy to the rest of the world. President Dwight D. Eisenhower, for example, launched the "People's Capitalism" campaign, one in a series of similar propaganda and advertising programs created after World War II to display the superiority of the American way versus the evils of Communism in the Soviet Union and its satellite nations.

Advertising became a tool in the war between capitalism and socialism. On the home front and abroad, the Eisenhower administration worked with the Advertising Council, a nonprofit organization that coordinated the efforts. Under the leadership of Ted Repplier, the Ad Council ran strategic marketing campaigns at home and globally. "These campaigns," explains historian Dawn Spring, "were designed to create an appearance of consensus, yet they were tightly controlled from the top down and were carefully orchestrated at every level, from grassroots activities to print advertisement" (2011, 4). Repplier's group coordinated the initiatives, essentially using business, government, and media sources to run campaigns on behalf of the United States.

Interestingly, given America's commitment to democratic ideas, many leaders looked aside as government-sponsored groups promoted free enterprise around the world using propaganda. In late 1955, Repplier gave a speech proclaiming the Cold War stood as "the world's largest advertising contest." He saw American efforts in this area as compulsory, given the Soviet Union's own push toward selling its system abroad" (Spring 2011, 145). Large corporations and advertising firms worked with Repplier, the Eisenhower administration, and the Ad Council to push America's messages, from McCann Erickson and Procter & Gamble to General Motors.

From the 1930s through the mid-1970s, groups like the Advertising Council and others, including independent organizations, launched efforts to establish, stabilize, and then cultivate the idea that consumption-based societies were the most fruitful and democratic. Historian Lawrence R. Samuel calls the American Dream the nation's "secret weapon, something that was stronger than any army even though it was just an idea" (2012, 50). The ability to spread the idea of consumerism via the propaganda of the American Dream and American Way of Life enabled the country to stand in stark contrast to the dreary, empty shelves lining the Communist world. The Soviet Union did not have the financial means or coordination to thwart the American advertising industry, especially as the business world teamed with the federal government. As a result, the disparity between abundance and scarcity remained an important ideological weapon throughout the Cold War.

DOING THE WORK

Mad Men's aura of mystery is driven in part by Draper's hidden past. In the Season 6 finale, Episode 6.13 ("In Care Of"), Don exposes that history—first in a client meeting with Hershey, and then later to his children. When the armor falls, the powerful ad man is left vulnerable, which costs him his partnership. The weakness and breakdown taking place during a client meeting force his colleagues to remove him from the agency. For Draper, the loss is not about money or its trappings; he spends the entirety of Season 7 trying to get back to "the work," which is his fulfillment of the American Dream—doing the work that one loves.

Draper's emphasis is always on doing "the work." In Episode 7.7 ("Waterloo"), the finale of part I of the show's final season, Don confronts his colleague Ted Chaough, who is suffering a kind of malaise or existential crisis: "You don't have to work for us, but you have to work. You don't want to see what happens when it's really gone." When Don is at his best—not drunk, philandering, running roughshod over his underlings, or sneaking out of the office to catch midday movies (though this is a form of cultural education)—"work" equals winning and winning the client's business is akin to gaining their love, the distorted vision of love that Draper never quite grasps or achieves.

Don's interaction with the American Dream contrasts with the other characters, who outwardly hold more traditional views, centered on attaining an imagined lifestyle, consumer goods, or wealth. For Pete Campbell and Roger Sterling, in contrast to Draper, the American Dream means living up to a family history of power and wealth. Sterling, for example, does not understand Draper's moodiness, given the lifestyle the younger man has attained via advertising. In Episode 1.4 ("New Amsterdam"), Roger complains that younger men do not know how (or why) to drink, explaining, "Your kind with your gloomy thoughts and your worries . . . you're all too busy licking some imaginary wound."

As a whole, the "New Amsterdam" episode is filled with both wounds and characters interacting with the American Dream. Pete must lower himself to his father and brother in hopes of getting financial support for a New York City apartment, even though the family money is all gone. Then he again buries his manhood when the couple takes the down payment from Trudy's parents, whose wealth comes from hard work, not inheritance. At the same time, Pete attempts to assert himself at Sterling Cooper, which causes Don to fire him. In a complicated and ironic twist, it is only his family name and standing that force Roger and Bert to save the young man. Although now wealthy, Don does not understand the power or prestige of "old New York" money. Sterling Cooper cannot afford (literally) to offend the power base.

Placed within the backdrop of a 1960s advertising agency, the self-created stories and roles the employees play in and out of the workplace expose the real power of image. For example, senior partner Bert Cooper plays the role of eccentric, punctuating important decisions by pruning his bonsai tree and referencing Ayn Rand, rather than raising his voice. Viewers do not see the "real" Cooper, how he got to his powerful position or pieces of his personality that might counteract the image he crafts. However, one does get the sense that things like the Japanese art and asking that people take their shoes off in his office are props in Cooper's self-creation. His American Dream is tightly linked to the ability to project a specific image of leadership and power.

As is often the case in *Mad Men*, Draper's interaction with nostalgia is more complicated. While most of the key figures from the first season reveal some degree of romantic yearning for the past, such as a drunken Roger Sterling regaling Don and Betty with war stories in Episode 1.7 ("Red in the Face"), all of Don's memories are negative. From a narrative perspective, the lead character's anti-nostalgia accomplishes two related tasks. First, as Don's story develops, the viewer recognizes that his adult discretions are derived from a horrific, violent youth, in some ways softening them or providing a bit of justification. Also, exposing Don's past in snippets enables Weiner to give the character an aura of mystery and danger.

The running storyline of Don dealing with his past as Dick keeps viewers off-kilter. In Episode 4.1 ("Public Relations"), he lives in a rundown apartment that is dark and foreboding with none of the trappings that most "typical" newly single, wealthy men would flaunt. When he hires a prostitute, he asks her to slap him harder and harder, which shows viewers the depths of his self-loathing. He might be the creative genius behind the new agency of Sterling Cooper Draper Pryce and interviewed by the *Wall Street Journal*, but inside, he is still little Dick, a young boy dealing with the ramifications of an abusive, gruesome past.

Portraying Draper as a mystery also makes a statement about his quest for the American Dream. Once the viewer finds out that "Don Draper" is actually Dick Whitman and realizes the lengths he journeyed to erase his past life, one might assume that he did so to establish his shot at a normal life, filled with a quest for consumer goods that defined the American Dream in the late 1950s and early 1960s. However, in many instances, Draper is shown to have little care for money or its trappings. The most blatant example comes at the end of Episode 1.8 ("The Hobo Code"). Although Midge Daniels refuses Don's offer to run off with him to Paris, he still leaves behind the $2,500 bonus he earned. While she sleeps, he slips out of the apartment unseen.

Years later, when Don and Megan separate for the final time, he writes her a check for $1 million (Episode 7.9, "New Business"). Megan, bitter and callous, takes the money, though her anger is at a squandered career and the new lows she has reached after Don's junior colleague Harry Crane attempts to seduce her with offers of work. Crane giving Megan the casting couch treatment is straight out of the stories about what actresses in the 1960s had to endure and could be interpreted as his attempt to get back at Megan (whom he's always had a crush on) and Don (who has barely hid his contempt for the younger man for years). Megan's American Dream is instant wealth, but the money cannot hide the internal agony she feels about her career fizzling out.

The contrast between what Don wants and his indifference to wealth is significant—Dick risks everything to become Don, yet avoids the trappings of consumerism that drive his colleagues and competitors. His pursuit is more self-centered, hurtling toward some skewed vision of freedom. In "The Hobo Code," the viewer sees that young Dick learns at the knee of a hobo that stays overnight at his family's farm. From this odd mentor, the displaced youngster—a self-described "whore child," with no strong ties to home—learns that "I had a family once; a wife, a job, a mortgage. I couldn't sleep at night tied to all those things. Then, death came to find me. . . . One morning I freed myself, with the clothes on my back. . . . Good-bye. . . . Now, I sleep like a stone." The message stays with Dick as he transforms to dapper Don. But dapper Don is also dour Don, a man perpetually in fear that he will be unmasked.

At the end of the episode, Don's commitment to his own existential search for meaning, despite how he seems on the surface, surfaces when he engages in a discussion with the beatniks at Midge's apartment in Greenwich Village. They blame him for being part of the establishment ("with them") and working in advertising to "invent the lie." One (in hippie fez, nonetheless) even mocks "the adman" by announcing, "I wipe my ass with the *Wall Street Journal*." Don smirks through most of the exchange and then drops an existential bombshell, declaring, "There is no big lie. There is no system. The universe is indifferent." Defeated, the more vocal beatnik sulks, "Man, why'd you have to say that?"

SPANNING THE SIXTIES

For a decade stamped with terms like "hippie" and "free love" and immortalized in pulse-pounding yet poignant songs such as "Like a Rolling Stone" by Bob Dylan and the Rolling Stones' "Sympathy for the Devil," the 1960s turned out to be a great era for corporate America. For many, particularly families headed by white mid-level-managerial types, the thriving business world provided a way of life that seemed unprecedented at the time, powered by a 50 percent gain in real income over the span.

The extremes provide a stark dichotomy of what "the sixties" meant for those living through the era—on one hand, college students and young people resisted the economic and military system, but in contrast, their parents and elders reaped the rewards of the capitalist system and consumer-driven society it yielded.

The power of the corporate model solidified and expanded during the 1960s. As a result, the New York Stock Exchange took on greater importance and gave those closely watching its every movement a daily scorecard touting the nation's might. In early 1966, for example, the *New York Times* reported that the Dow Jones industrial average "crossed the magic 1,000-mark . . . a historic peak" (Carmical). The industries fueling the move were ones that symbolized the nation's capacity as a technological and manufacturing superpower, including defense, television, oil, automobiles, and steel. Even as Wall Street continued to flirt with the "magic" figure, analysts and other commentators debated what it meant for organizations and the national economy from a psychological perspective. One side in the debate worried that moving past 1,000 meant that the economy needed a contraction, while the other saw the move as a reason to push for continued growth (Vartan 1966).

For workers up and down the corporate ladder, business growth equaled higher wages and increased opportunities. The government released figures revealing that personal income for 1965 jumped to a record $550.5 billion. Certainly, economists and business analysts realized that President Lyndon B. Johnson's domestic stimulus package, dubbed the "Great Society," had much to do with the strength of the economy, as did the increased costs of the war in Vietnam. Other indicators of American power included the many corporate mergers taking place in the 1960s, while closer to home, Congress took measures to raise the national minimum wage and women's pay, which helped countless families and individuals (Carmical 1966).

Mad Men's consideration of the American Dream is particularly thoughtful when looking at how the idea changed from the Kennedy Camelot era to the grittier later decade of Vietnam and antiwar protests. Several of the characters physically change as a visual reminder of the national makeover represented by these vastly different influences. Roger Sterling and Ted Chaough grow sideburns and moustaches. Stan's change, though, could be considered the most dramatic. He transforms from slick-haired frat boy to bead-wearing, bearded leftist. Ironically,

Stan is basically a stoner in either guise, just becoming more obvious as the decade progresses and drugs grow mainstream (touted in several episodes as a means to jumpstart creativity).

Perhaps the most consistent thread across these two halves of the 1960s was the steady commitment to the American economic engine and growing fascination with ideas related to the new term being popularized: "mass consumption." As writers, analysts, and other commentators delved into the topic, they realized that consumer spending drove prosperity. With the Great Depression still fresh in their minds, people were keen to understand the roots of the affluence and whatever it might take to ward off another economic downturn.

Research developed at the University of Michigan's Survey Research Center and published as *The Mass Consumption Society* (1964) by George Katona revealed that some 40 percent of American families earned between $6,000 and $15,000 annually. The people in this group had discretionary income to spend, which Katona thought powered the nation's consumer economy. The findings led a *New York Times* reporter to declare: "What does all this mean? As an individual and en masse, the American consumer has a new importance unrealized even 30 years ago" (Fowler 1964).

Katona's pioneering research also showed that the number of working wives in middle- and upper-class families stood much higher than thought. Although the amount of money these women made is not clear, his survey data showed that 50 percent of wives in families with income between $7,500 and $15,000 worked. The *Times* reporter ironically quoted from the survey in identifying that these wives were "bringing home some bacon" (Fowler 1964).

The ad industry also experienced tremendous change in the era, transforming from a kind of gentleman's club for Ivy graduates to a more egalitarian workforce. Speaking to a student group in early 1966, human resources specialist Edwin B. Stern explained that firms looked to hire individuals based on what they could do, rather than simply where they went to school. The move toward building a professional workforce based on skills, Stern said, "is part of the whole evolution of American society and one more sign of broad-gauge thinking" (qtd. in Sloane 1966).

The influx of young professionals also represented an important cultural change occurring as a result of the Vietnam War—more students going to college, particularly as the baby boom generation started to come of age. The tsunami consisted of the post–World War II baby boom kids and those who hoped to stay in school to keep out of the Vietnam draft. As the opportunities for acquiring education expanded, particularly at the college level, more young people used their budding critical and contextual thinking skills to question American society, particularly the ethical consequences of being a global superpower and the nation's place in Southeast Asia.

While this bulging demographic transformed mass culture with its size and purchasing power, it had a similar effect on higher education. The federal government, furthermore, acted as a catalyst in this regard, urging more young people to college as a means of combating the perceived lead by Soviet students in math and science. As a result, in the United States the number of young people in higher education degree programs more than doubled from about 3.5 million to almost 8 million by decade's end (Rielly 2003, 24). The student growth caused increase demand for faculty and resources.

More students in the nation's higher education classrooms naturally meant that the juggernaut U.S. economy had to make room for them. With their focus on creativity, writing, research, and specialized subdisciplines such as television and media placement, advertising firms and their clients were especially attractive employers. As progressive ideas about ending the war in Southeast Asia and stopping racism at home spread to encompass anti-corporation and anti–big business tenets, advertising agencies were viewed as a place where young people could work without completely "selling out" to "the man." *Mad Men* demonstrates how employees adapted to the times particularly well. Only Don's look and style fundamentally stay the same; the others evolve as activism and protest fashions become mainstream.

The sheer size of the population between fifteen and twenty-four years old in the 1960s had profound effects on just about every aspect of American life. Some people found this growth terrifying and either urged or enacted official and unofficial rules for both institutions and parents to use to keep them under control. An example of the latter from popular culture is the treatment the hikers received at the hands of small-town vigilantes in the 1969 film *Easy Rider*. One might even take this notion a step further by assessing the labels President Richard M. Nixon used to describe the antiwar protesters, a constant thorn in his side. Nixon's derogatory remarks obliquely empowered "mainstream" citizens to look down on progressives and activists.

At the other end of the scale, American businesses viewed the enormous population increase as an opportunity and created new ways for consumer goods to be marketed and advertised to young people. Thus, on *Mad Men*, viewers see both the consequences of the agency filling its ranks with young professionals, as well as the impact of how the agency should sell to that demographic. The notion that young people should develop ideas and campaigns that will reach other young people perplexes Don but increases Peggy's status as someone a generation younger than her mentor and with sound pulse on meeting the new consumer's desires.

Consumer products companies read the tea leaves regarding the growing youth market. In February 1967, ad firm Kenyon & Eckhardt searched for young men and women to serve as models for Beecham Products, the maker of Brylcreem and Macleans toothpaste. The challenge, according to director/producer Joe Fitzgerald, was "to get the good-looking type, the general type, that the kids can relate to." Not that these people were scarce. Instead, ad firms found it increasingly difficult to find those who appealed to the "18-to-22" demographic who were not already appearing in a different brand's commercial, or as reporter Philip H. Dougherty explained: "a target area for so many advertised items these days that it's not easy to get models without product conflicts" (1967).

On Weiner's show, there is a constant tension between generations, not only in the office, where the senior executives make condescending statements to young workers, but also in representations of home life. Sally Draper, despite her youth, is often a voice of reason or maturity that neither of her parents really displays. In the end, the daughter becomes the adult, not only managing her mother's cancer diagnosis, but also her father's reaction to the family crisis. Similar tensions play out between Peggy and both her mother and sister, who cannot comprehend why she insists on working, when she should—in their eyes—be concentrating on finding a spouse.

The most intricate example of generational battles and how they reveal a changing vision of the American Dream is the final scene when a smirking Don chants on the California cliffside and then the big reveal of the famous Coca-Cola "I'd Like to Teach the World to Sing" commercial. The implication is that via finally accepting the tenets of the new generation through his tear-filled interaction with Leonard and meditation, Don has transcended the ages. As a result, he discovers the golden key—a way to market to young people using ideas and symbols that represent them. The images in the commercial, from fresh-faced teenage girls with red ribbons in their hair to African American youth, perfectly encompass the ideas at the heart of a new age: brotherhood, spirituality, acceptance, and love. Draper exploits the emotion to sell brown fizzy water to young people too caught up in an image and the bright red package that advertisers created to know any better.

WHAT ELSE IS THERE?

As *Mad Men* drew to its stunning conclusion, Weiner and the writing team put the show's main characters into situations that asked them to contemplate the meaning of work, life, and their individual futures. These are the kind of reflective instances that people consider as they dream, plot, and live out their lives as part of the larger societal system. Entire industries—from self-help gurus to psychological counseling—have grown from the existential angst surrounding "Who am I?" and "What do I want from life?"

In "The Forecast" (Episode 7.10), for example, a seemingly simple exchange between Don and Peggy about her annual performance review turns into a mini-counseling session. However, whereas Peggy wants to hear about her successes from her mentor, Don is caught up in larger questions. Their desires are so vastly different that no room for commonality exists. She needs to hear specifics, while her boss prods around ideas of what constitutes a meaningful life.

Peggy's goals are tangible, the big career that leads to respect, fame, and maybe even to "create something of lasting value." When Don scoffs at the notion of equating lasting value with advertising, she accuses him of being "in a mood." Finally, in a huff, she exclaims, "Why don't you just write down all of your dreams so I can shit on them?" and storms out of his office. Following her exit with his eyes, Don is left wondering what just happened, but more importantly, with no answers to questions that he deems central. His curiosity is stymied by Peggy's relentless pursuit of things rather than answers.

This scene, one that could be chalked up to yet another in a long line of Don and Peggy not seeing eye to eye, is actually a way for Weiner and crew to poke at the meaning of the American Dream and how people interact with its complicated implications. While these kinds of questions are increasingly difficult to answer, our relentless pursuit is central to what we label the American Dream. Peggy's reaction is visceral exactly because she views Don as questioning her aspirations, which many people view as sacred ground.

The idea of Don defecating on Peggy's dreams draws the viewer into a central query about life's meaning and that sanctity of how people employ this vision in creating a mental worldview. There are no easy answers when it comes to what the American Dream means, but there are pat ways of interpreting that make it seem simplistic. In an interview with Terry Gross on NPR, Weiner explained the concept behind the scene, looking at the hard ground these questions force people to cover, saying, "I think most people, if you really asked them and you pursued that question, it's going to be disturbing. It's not that clear for people" (2015). Yet, Weiner also knows that our goals and aspirations essentially make us human and propel our drives as we navigate through complicated situations.

An essential question that *Mad Men* contemplates is what happened to the American Dream as the elders of the 1960s passed down their legacy to their children and their children's children. There is no short answer because the history of the great American ideal of a better life, homeownership, and well-being is deep and complex. Certainly, however, the 1960s changed how people perceived the American Dream. According to literary critic Morris Dickstein, who grew up in the 1960s (born in 1940, a year after the fictional Peggy Olson), "The cold war, the bomb, the draft, and the Vietnam war gave young people a premature look at the dark side of our national life, at the same time that it galvanized many older people already jaded in their pessimism" (1977, xix).

The darkness that Dickstein stresses grew in magnitude as the violence of Vietnam escalated. For many people, the 1960s ended in the massacre at Kent State University on May 4, 1970, when the Ohio National Guard fired into a crowd of students and antiwar activists on the working-class campus in northeast Ohio. "Four Dead in Ohio" not only became the haunting lyrics of a song by rock singer Neil Young, but the rallying cry for the ultimate disillusion of the era.

The recognition—perhaps consciously and subconsciously—that the spirit of the 1960s was pulverized under the weight of the war, capitalism, and a corrupt government seemed to transform the Baby Boomers from peaceniks and activists into perfect consumer machines. According to Dickstein, "Losing its political bearings in an era of economic strain, the counterculture of the sixties turned into the narcissistic Me Generation of the 1970s and the ambitious, self-involved young professionals of the 1980s" (1977, ix).

Yet Draper and many of the other figures central to *Mad Men* are examples of the American Dream attained. Peggy's climb from secretary to copy chief (and apartment complex owner) is a clear-cut march up America's economic class system. The grand narrative is so firmly embedded in our consciousness that we are prompted to a positive view of Don's achievements. Wrapping him in the warm glow of the Dream, the audience forgives him of many, many vices. Americans have always been willing to accept an inordinate amount of evil if the ultimate outcome is victory.

While some fans and commentators lamented the heavy-handed way Weiner ended the series—with Don's redemption at the hands of one of the most popular and significant television commercials of all time—the open-ended finale allowed viewers to mull over what became of the characters and their trip to and through the American Dream into the 1970s and beyond.

3

MAD MEN, BAD MEN: AMERICAN VICES

Mad Men *is like watching the History Channel, except with people screwing around. They've been great at mimicking the time. I was just getting into the business at the end of that period and smoked three packs of cigarettes a day. People had more fun then.*—Jerry Della Femina, one of the original Mad Men (Juarez 2010)

The good guys don't always win; bad people have reasons for why they do things. If you spend a few hours in the shoes of the bad person, you might do the same thing.—Matthew Weiner, 2014

Much of the early buzz derived from AMC's marketing campaign for launching *Mad Men* focused on the excesses of the 1960s and how the show embraced debauchery as a theme. When reporters followed up by interviewing real-life ad executives from that period (like the Della Femina epigraph), they usually confirmed, denied, or attempted to contextualize to what extent the show portrayed reality. Some of the mad men and mad women played along, talking at length about the shenanigans. Others responded angrily, defending themselves and the profession. Few if any, however, denied that there were not major parts of the program that embodied the era and industry perfectly.

Smoking, nonstop drinking, infidelity, and sex came to define Don Draper, and by extension as its primary star, the series as a whole. Early on, viewers were left scratching their heads: should we like this character or not, because we do not like his actions. Yet, as the show unfolded, *Mad Men* proved to be so much deeper and nuanced then a bunch of randy

Roger. *AMC/Photofest ©AMC*

white people drinking too much and working too hard, releasing stress through decadence and general degeneracy.

Even into the final seventh season, though, the commitment to vice never wavered. A variety of drugs, gallons of booze, and even a threesome involving the Drapers and an actress/friend all took place in the last season. Perhaps audiences were not as shocked after Weiner poured it on across ninety-two episodes, but the action (pun intended) on display certainly either confirmed or countered what viewers knew or thought they knew about the Age of Aquarius. People may not like to consider what Grandma and Grandpa were doing "back in the day," but with *Mad Men* as a guide, we have a reasonable understanding.

Although the early buzz about the drinking and smoking fueled the marketing campaign to launch the show, viewers at the time probably could not have imagined how pervasive the drug use would be as the show portrayed the mid- to late 1960s. As smoking marijuana grew prevalent, the younger staff members at Sterling Cooper brought pot into the workplace. It seems hazy, but attempting to remember a moment when big Stan Rizzo is not either smoking dope or high is a difficult task. Rizzo's quick transformation from clean-cut to embracing a hippie mentality demonstrates the impact the peace movement had on the workplace, particularly in a creative atmosphere like an ad agency.

Weiner's brilliance in creating Draper is giving the handsome, creative superman a troubled, mysterious past that fuels his existential angst—holes in his soul that he tries to fill with women, booze, and dangerous behavior. His feet of clay demonstrate the dichotomy between the United States as the real power in the world and its many challenges, ranging from JFK's assassination to urban decay and violent clashes between the establishment and activists fighting for racial equality or against the war in Vietnam. Don's depravity, in essence, is a barometer for assessing the character as a showpiece on the program and the era he symbolizes.

Roger Sterling, on the other hand, is most often given the comedic role, a zinger of great lines, one after the other. His self-indulgence is played for laughs, so people are not asked to harshly judge him or his actions. The star quality in John Slattery's performance as Roger is to create the stereotype of a wealthy, aristocratic business executive (who realizes that he is living a stereotypical life), but use humor to soften the edges and make him likeable, despite the relentless bad behavior. At times, Roger is reduced to a stumbling, bumbling drunk, but always has a quip at the ready. He seems human and with a good heart (though surviving several heart attacks), despite what audiences actually see on the screen.

Again and again, Weiner asks viewers to interpret *Mad Men* through the lens of our collective and conflicting ideas about history and nostalgia to discover new means of interpreting our own times. The amount of vice during the mad men era of advertising could be passed off as a moment in time when people needed outside stimulants to ease their worried hearts, yet drugs, alcohol, and sex are still prime motivators in today's world. Ask almost anyone who works in modern corporate America for a story about the level of outrageous behavior that takes place today, and then strap yourself in for a wild ride. What you hear may curl your hair.

Mad Men is never just throwaway entertainment. Instead, the program confronts the audience by presenting a mirror for similar struggles, issues, and topics that still have significance in the twenty-first century. These powerful vices—many taken for granted in the 1960s—still exist. By placing vice at the epicenter of what makes the show unique, Weiner demands that we rethink and reassess what it meant for the people who lived through the era (like his own parents) and for viewers now, as we intuitively know that these societal challenges have changed (and in some cases lessened) but still bedevil us. Simultaneously, this critical thinking process obliges people to reimagine the 1960s and its aftermaths as a whole.

FACT AND FICTION COLLIDE

In early 1961, Secretary of Commerce Luther H. Hodges convened a twenty-six-member national Business Ethics Advisory Council (BEAC) to discuss the shady ethical practices exhibited by American corporate leaders. In recent days, the era had experienced widespread price-fixing challenges and other unscrupulous routines. For the first time—certainly since the Great Depression—the general public doubted whether it could count on corporate America to carry its values into the future.

The BEAC targeted the advertising industry as one area of concern. Consumers generally felt that agencies and their clients would do or say anything to get people to buy, regardless of the consequences. Leaders decided that a national code of ethics might help executives make more informed decisions regarding ethical dilemmas. Yet, advertising in many industries more or less necessitated that corporations and their firms toed a line that might be considered unethical (concerns that certainly link the 1960s to vibes in the air in today's marketplace). Technological advances in televisions, programming, and production, as well as the general popularity of watching TV, ratcheted up the oversight regarding advertising as more people grew concerned about mass media's influence over people's lives.

In the early seasons of *Mad Men*, for example, Sterling Cooper's work with Lucky Strike cigarettes consistently trampled truth in the name of sales. Even government regulation could not slow down the advertising push. Don Draper, in a surge of creativity, proposed that the cigarettes could be marketed as "toasted," which distinguished the brand from its competitors at the height of regulation. No one cared that all cigarettes were made by the same toasting process; the genius was in the pitch that created a perceived difference.

Just a year after the ethics council convened, *Time* magazine pointed to the work done by Bates & Co., led by one of the original mad men— the infamous Rosser Reeves. Reeves believed in the influence of television, directing his firm's efforts there in a series of aggressive campaigns, most notably for Anacin and M&Ms, the former centered on relieving "tense, nervous headaches," while the other is the iconic "won't melt in your hands" (Cracknell 2011). The repetitive nature of television commercials and the tagline mentality of consumer product companies seemed a natural fit.

Reeves's brand of advertising meant to hit consumers over the head with the message, then pound it home as many times as possible. When the message seemed second nature in the consumer's mind, then the advertising had succeeded. Reeves explained, "Getting the message into the most people at the lowest possible cost . . . we should subordinate our own creative impulses to that one overall objective. . . . The most people at the lowest possible cost? What else is this business about?" (qtd. in Cracknell 2011). No entertainment value or cutesy writing impressed Reeves; instead he focused on increasing sales for his clients. Sometimes this meant overstating or bending the truth. For example, Anacin's claim about tension headaches was not as simple or straightforward in the medical community as it seemed to its advertisers.

By 1969, the advertising industry itself became part of the general outcry regarding vice and its pernicious influence on American life. Consumers realized that advertising was not going away, but simultaneously, they heard from a parade of social critics, commentators, authors, and filmmakers about the industry's negative consequences. According to researcher H. B. Shaffer at *Congressional Quarterly*, "hucksters" became a common word in the English language, while others began equating advertising and the general cost to the nation's soul when constantly bombarded with buying products and the need to emulate lifestyles that were fabricated or exaggerated. Specifically in the case of cigarette advertising and then more generally, Shaffer contends: "How free should advertising be to operate as a creator and conditioner of human wants, activities which affect both the economic well-being and the social temper of the nation?" (1969).

The need to figure out the real and imagined ills the ad business wrought took on new urgency in the 1960s, particularly as people engaged with the chaos of everyday life. A 1969 study by *Congressional Quarterly* revealed that cigarette companies spent about $200 million annually on advertising. Of course, about 75 percent of that total flowed to TV. Yet, the health hazards were on display and grew into an activist cause. Both Doris Day and Lawrence Welk refused to let these manufacturers sponsor their popular programs (Shaffer 1969).

Advertising agencies were not working in a bubble. Those of us who have toiled in the advertising, public relations, and marketing industries are struck by *Mad Men*'s accurate depiction of the creative and brainstorming process, as well as the pitch meetings with clients. The behind-the-scenes look into the practice demonstrates how advertisers were creating culture. In other words, play a jingle long enough and it will stick in listeners' brains, as will logos, taglines, branding campaigns, and other visuals associated with selling products, goods, and services. There is no guarantee that the consumer pulls out her wallet and buys the latest toothpaste, shoes, or loaf of bread, but the exposure to an ad might make it more likely and certainly over the alternative of no message at all.

In contemporary America we see the outcomes of 1960s-style advertising multiplied geometrically. Whether the product is piped into our brains via the fictional Draper's evocative use of symbols and language or pounded in via Reeves's relentless repetition, there are so many more channels for reaching today's consumers, which means so many more ads across a variety of outlets. Even seemingly innocuous ads meant to educate, like the California Milk Processor Board's "Got Milk" campaign or the Partnership for a Drug-Free America's "This is Your Brain on Drugs" commercials, are played over and over until these messages are automatically part of the lexicon of people across generations.

An interesting question to ponder might be how *Mad Men* will impact the way people have and will continue to interpret the 1960s and advertising. There is no way to calculate the number of impressions the show and its ancillary products have accumulated over its initial lifespan. Once it moves into reruns, that number will skyrocket.

SMOKING

Lee Garner and the Lucky Strike cigarette executives visiting Sterling Cooper's New York City office can barely finish a thought or sentence without lighting up. Discussing his alarm regarding impending governmental regulations of the industry, Garner smoothly cups his hand, the puffs of smoke dotting his ideas. His son, Lee Garner Jr.—the embodiment of the new 1960s executive in a sharp suit, with terse manners and slicked-back hair—interrupts: "We might as well be living in Russia." Blowing a plume of smoke that engulfs the space around him and several of his minions, the older Garner responds, "Damn straight!" This exertion causes the older man to cough, which launches everyone else into fake hacking and clearing throats, a perfectly toady response to the alpha male in the room. In the sycophantic world of early 1960s advertising, the client with the big wallet dictates how everyone else acts.

From a tactical viewpoint in the early days of the show, Sterling Cooper lives and dies via its relationship with Lucky Strike. As a result, when the tobacco company executives come into town, the entire agency jumps to their tune. The secretaries run around the office putting cigarettes out on display, and countless cartons appear in every nook and cranny, presenting the image that the agency is at the client's beck and call. Nothing is off-limits or out-of-bounds.

When Garner, his son, and their cronies fly north for a meeting, the conference room is thick with Lucky Strike smoke. The gathered honchos barely finish one cigarette before another is lit. Like in religious rituals dating back centuries, the smoke symbolizes the marriage between the agency and its biggest client. The elder Garner plays the role of priest—or maybe even deity—emerging from the haze to lead the flock. Both teams willfully ignore the truth—smoking leads to death. They reference the government's reports that reveal the link between cigarettes and poor health, but do not see anything wrong with the product or selling it. The goal is to find a new way to sell Lucky Strike in a way that differentiates it from competitive tobacco manufacturers.

As a single moment in *Mad Men* history, the scene is critical in demonstrating that Pete Campbell is an impetuous striver and Don's opponent. More importantly, though, Don rescues Pete—and by association, the agency—as the cigarette team attempts to storm out of the office after Pete's disastrous "You're going to die anyway, so why not die with us?" pitch. Pete got his direction from the research department, engaging in psychological work, while Draper relies on the brilliant brainstorming moment. Magically arriving at the "toasted" tagline—after sketching out the manufacturing process on a blackboard—reveals the sparkle Don possesses when he is put to the task. In the moment, he feeds off the negative energy in the room, this after struggling to come up with a good idea for weeks leading up to the weighty meeting.

From another view, the scene is an opportunity for the audience to perk up and recognize Draper's budding genius. He is truly special and saves the agency from further embarrassment. Viewers see Don as a hero, and one can almost see his power grow as the men around the room share his vision. Roger supports the notion, telling the assembled executives: "Gentlemen, I don't think I have to tell you what you just witnessed here." When Garner Jr. attempts to assert himself by questioning Roger, Don delivers a soliloquy on advertising's association with "happiness," meaning "you are okay." The older Garner's approval establishes Draper's status as a creative virtuoso.

While the scene in the Sterling Cooper conference room is great drama and may have played out similarly in real-life meetings across the 1960s, from a cultural perspective, the agency's relationship with its cigarette-making client peels back the layers of conundrums long felt in American society—how should a product that kills its users be regulated, advertised, and sold? In other words, do the moral and physical implications of tobacco use necessitate that the government or some other entity intervene in a free society?

Like today, the staggering number of people smoking—despite whole-sale evidence of its devastating health costs—bewildered health author-ities and government officials. In 1967, for example, a Department of Agriculture study revealed that Americans consumed some 551 billion cigarettes annually, about 215 packs per year for every person over eight-een years old in the whole country. More mindboggling is that the total number consumed jumped by some 11 billion over the year before, mean-ing that most people simply refused to either believe that smoking would harm them or care about the long-term consequences. As the number of smokers and cigarettes consumed increased, cancer rates skyrocketed, up 55 percent for males and 46 percent for females (Gimlin 1967).

Given these statistics, which would not be common knowledge for viewers as they watched the show, Betty's cancer seems less a shocking way to portray the character's demise than a realistic struggle based on the willful ignorance of a nation that refused to end a deadly habit. In the final episode (Episode 7.14, "Person to Person"), as her children confront the reality of their mother's looming death, the consequences of Betty's illness point to larger implications. Her middle child, Bobby, attempts to help, but burns something as easy as toast (even for a child to make), exposing the bewilderment the children face as their elders make bad choice after bad choice and they must prepare to pick up the pieces. Sally—mature, but forced to take on a greater maternal load than should be expected of a teenager—cancels her summer trip to Spain and must become caregiver to both her younger brothers and dying mother. In both instances, as the 1960s slide into the early 1970s, the succeeding genera-tion has no choice but to clean up a mess that they did not create.

For the Draper children, the real and psychological damage inflicted on them by their narcissistic parents will carry a deep burden. For exam-ple, Don, always a little off when looking into the future but sometimes seeing through the haze pretty well, tells Sally that her beauty and attitude make her just like her parents, but that it is her responsibility to do more with these traits than they did, to become a better, more compassionate person (Episode 7.10, "The Forecast"). The questions Weiner raises are significant. What responsibility do children have for their parents and how do they balance that idea with their own lives? The nation con-fronted (and continues to face) these problems, whether it is the legacy of Vietnam and overseas military expeditions or ongoing challenges with racial, gender, and economic inequality.

DRINKING

In mid-1969, Senator Harold E. Hughes, a Democrat from Iowa, distinguished himself by leading a nationwide education effort to alert people to the dangers of alcoholism. Hughes not only championed the cause, which included forming a subcommittee on alcoholism and narcotics and public hearings on the subject, but also personally battled alcohol and took great pride in his recovery. At the hearings, various alcoholism experts estimated that about five to six million Americans were alcoholics. A vast gap existed between the tax funds collected by the government based on the sales of alcoholic beverages ($8 billion) and the scant federal money put into battling alcoholism, which totaled about $4 million a year. In comparison, the entire National Institute of Mental Health received less than $35 million annually.

Based on this imbalance, it is no wonder that the real-life Hughes fought so diligently for the cause, while the fictional Draper had to dry out (as much as he could) on his own with little or no external support. Academy Award–winning actress Mercedes McCambridge, who won for Best Supporting Actress for *All the King's Men* (1949), the screen adaptation of Robert Penn Warren's Pulitzer Prize–winning novel, and earned a nomination for the James Dean star vehicle *Giant* (1956), spoke out at the hearings about both family members and doctors hiding one's alcoholism, which attached a stigma to the disease. Another commentator, Marty Mann, the co-founder of the National Council on Alcoholism, explained that the medical stigma remained pervasive, explaining that few doctors were even willing to treat those suffering from alcoholism ("Alcoholism" 1970).

A year later, Freeman H. Quimby authored a report for the Congressional Research Service on alcohol and its consequences. As surprising as it may seem in current times, when alcoholism is common as are reports of treatment centers, support groups, and other means to help those fighting the disease, Quimby's research revealed the basic lack of scientific information the medical community had about alcoholism. According to physician John L. Norris:

> We in medicine are grossly unprepared, technically and philosophically [to treat alcoholism], for we share the ambivalence and active disinterest of the rest of society. . . . We have little idea how much of a present problem is caused by alcohol itself, nor do we have as yet any

physical sign or psychological finding which distinguishes those who can drink safely from those who cannot. (qtd. in Quimby 1970, 2)

Interestingly, if one considers the pioneering work in sex studies done by William Masters and Virginia Johnson, which built on the research of Alfred C. Kinsey, then one can only conclude that the rudimentary misunderstandings most people had about sex and sexuality could only be engulfed by their confusion and lack of education about alcoholism.

Using a generic definition of dependence, Quimby estimated that "more than 8 million Americans" are alcoholics, while another 4 to 5 million suffered from alcohol-related "complications" (6). What viewers see in *Mad Men* is an accurate portrayal of the central role alcohol played in people's lives in the 1960s. The chilling aspect of the depiction is just how frequently people drove while intoxicated. According to Quimby, "Alcohol is a factor in over 50 percent of automobile accidents in which death has occurred," as well as "70 percent of single car fatalities" (21). In Episode 2.5 ("The New Girl"), Weiner tackles drunk driving, with Don and Bobbie Barrett wrecking the car. The escapade complicates problems for them both, Draper forced to ask Peggy to pay his bail and to hide Bobbie until her black eye heals. The statistical odds were against Don and Bobbie, but one cannot really kill off the main character, even if people across the nation were dying at alarming rates due to intoxication while on the road.

Ad man extraordinaire David Ogilvy addressed alcoholism in his famous treatise *Ogilvy on Advertising* (1983), suggesting that 7 percent of the executives in American business and advertising fell into that category. "Your alcoholics may include some of your brightest stars," Ogilvy warns, "protected as they always are by their secretaries and their colleagues." He suggests staging an intervention, then getting them into a treatment center, and then daily Alcoholics Anonymous meetings, which "works in about 60 percent of cases" (chapter 4).

Before jumping to conclusions about Ogilvy's acumen being ahead of its times, notice the copyright date on his classic book. It is a distillation of all that he learned over the years but came out in the 1980s, long after the mad men era he lived through and after the war on drugs and research on alcoholism started to be taken seriously at the federal and state levels. Two decades earlier in the fictional *Mad Men* universe (Episode 2.9, "Six Month Leave"), senior copywriter Freddie Rumsen is put on a leave of absence by Roger and Don, so that he can dry out. His real sin is not being drunk, which would place the noose around nearly everybody in the Sterling Cooper offices. Freddie embarrassed himself in front of a client, by peeing his pants before an important meeting, a real no-no for an ad man, even a copywriter.

In the 1960s, almost all the onus for beating alcoholism fell on the alcoholic's shoulders. Although surprising, when Rumsen later reappears, it turns out that his drying-out period worked. He put his life back together by attending AA meetings, even becoming a sponsor to others in need. Poignantly, it is Freddie that channels Don in Episode 7.1 ("Time Zones"), which begins with the former Sterling Cooper stalwart pitching an idea to Peggy (whom he helped get promoted to copywriter, but also his constant nemesis in his drinking days). Viewers are later let in on the secret—Don is feeding Freddie ideas and basically a script. The roles are reversed; Freddie has the power, while Draper is "on leave" to not only dry out, but to get his life back in order.

Later, as the episode ends, Don takes a long look at his most faithful friend—a bottle of Seagram's Seven whiskey—and puts it back on the coffee table. Rather than get drunk, he wanders out on the apartment balcony, despite the frigid temperature. Though it seems as if he might jump, Draper is inflicting this punishment on himself for a decade of bad behavior and the sense of loss since the center of his world has been forcibly snatched away.

SEX

The quote by Della Femina that begins the discussion of the vice that oozes from every pore of *Mad Men* suggests that the "fun" being had by Madison Avenue's ad employees was widespread and, in many ways, diverged from other American workplaces in the era. The liberation vibe that the real-life ad executive describes certainly exists on the show. Sometimes young people are hopping in and out of bed for the pure joy of being young and free. This is what happens when young professionals come together in the jumbled stew of work, alcohol, and boundless hormones. Della Femina's explanation makes sex about having fun. If one casts a bit of doubt on such a cheery notion, perhaps he is serving up a joyful expression of the time or maybe even a wishful, nostalgic look back on the "free love" era.

One might question Della Femina's assessment, since what we see depicted on the show frequently diverges from this carefree idea. Instead, sex is an indicator or signal to larger impulses. It evolves on *Mad Men*, particularly as a tool different characters use for wielding power. Alternatively, in Don's case, sex and its illicit nature is a means for attempting to understand identity and break away from the chains of conformity.

As is often the case, Weiner uses a theme that viewers might assume that they understand to engage with it in a different way. For example, how do we think or feel about Joan's decision to trade sex for a partnership position at the agency and the male figures that were willing to make the swap despite its immorality?

In Episode 5.11 ("The Other Woman"), Sterling Cooper is desperate to win the Jaguar account, headed by the fatuous Herb Rennet. At dinner with account men Pete and Ken, Rennet implies that the deal could be sewn up if they arrange a sexual liaison with Joan. After a great deal of hand-wringing, Joan complies. Initially, they are just going to pay her off for the service, but Lane Pryce suggests that she up the ante to a 5 percent ownership stake in the firm. While it might be easy for a modern viewer to sit at home and shout down Joan's decision, for the character this is an opportunity to completely overhaul both her life and her son's. The audience is forced to think through the lengths one would or should go to ensure the well-being of one's child, particularly when she cannot count on Roger Sterling (the boy's real father) to provide for them in the future.

The murky historical record of sexuality in the United States during the 1960s—conflicted and misunderstood—reveals just how uneducated and unaware people were about the subject. A person might look back on the 1960s and think "free love" or sex-crazed hippies, but these stereotypes do not quantify the gaps between a nostalgic perspective and what actually took place. Just because "free love" gained footing in the media and then solidified under the subsequent weight of popular culture lore does not mean that it became typical behavior.

The contrast is personified in another hit television show, *Masters of Sex*, which fictionalizes the true tale of sexuality researchers William H. Masters and Virginia E. Johnson, who explored human sexuality via in-depth interviews and analyzing people having sex in a laboratory setting. The big reveal of *Masters of Sex* is just how little people understood about their own bodies or those of their sexual partners. First in the book *Human Sexual Response* (1966) and then later in *Human Sexual Inadequacy* (1970), the researchers showed that people did not understand basic body reactions taking place during sex and that this lack of information led to intense problems that destroyed relationships. The two books, certainly helped by a titillation factor among general readers, sold hundreds of thousands of copies and were translated into dozens of languages (Reinhold 1970).

Masters and Johnson took sex into the lab and used special cameras and recording devices to derive scientific results. Their work built on and extended the studies conducted by Alfred C. Kinsey, a geneticist at Indiana University. Offering a course on marriage, Kinsey soon realized how woefully ignorant his students were when it came to sexuality. He and a research team began collecting data by conducting interviews that asked respondents detailed questions about a range of sexual experiences, which eventually reached about 17,500 by the time Kinsey passed away.

The researchers also observed and participated in sexual acts, obviously highly controversial in that era. In January 1948, Kinsey and colleagues Wardell B. Pomeroy and Clyde E. Martin published *Sexual Behavior in the Human Male*, which is generally credited with launching American sexuality studies. Many mainstream publications reviewed or commented on the book. "Overnight," says historian Daniel J. Boorstin, "Kinsey became a celebrity, his name a popular synonym for 'startling revelations' about the secret places in American life" (1973, 241).

Sexuality on *Mad Men* is always right at the surface, infusing nearly every relationship, and encompasses many perplexing implications. Often, the characters use sex as a means of escape, though many of these instances are washed in darkness, such as Peggy's one-night stand with a college boy. More shocking (Episode 2.13, "Meditations in an Emergency"), Betty trolls a dark, sleazy bar in the middle of the day, leading to sex in a coat closet—a one-moment, rather than one-night stand. Betty's renunciation of everything that a "typical" upper-middle-class wife is supposed to be is a defining experience—if only briefly.

On the opposite end of the spectrum, sex is also a brutal awakening for Peggy, who gets pregnant with Pete's child in the first season and has to live with the psychological burden of giving the child up for adoption. Even more chilling, Sally Draper is exposed to sex by first seeing Roger and Megan's mother, Marie Calvert, in a rather compromising position in

Episode 5.7 ("At the Codfish Ball"). When she catches her father having sex with downstairs neighbor Sylvia Rosen (Episode 6.11, "Favors"), the combination of shock, recognition, and shame is agonizing. The revelation of her dad's immoral behavior solidifies at a time when she is still too young to contextualize it (or him) and immediately destroys their relationship. The ramifications of losing his daughter's love eventually lead to Draper's near career-ending downfall.

ANARCHY

Don Draper stands over his dead body. He is floating facedown in a California pool, the partygoers too stoned or too busy (this is Los Angeles, after all) to save him. Arms spread—as if on a cross—he could be the falling icon from the show's famous opening credits. He faces the light eerily coming up from the pool bottom. In his death throes, Don imagines that Megan is pregnant and a soldier who died in Vietnam comes back, seemingly to escort him to the netherworld.

Moments later, still wearing his tan sports coat and tightly snugged brown striped tie, Don is choking up water as Roger Sterling kneels over him. Draper is perplexed and looks wounded, as if he wanted to remain in the other place. The next morning on the plane back to New York City, Don coughs, still feeling the physical effects of the near-death experience. Roger cautions him to stop talking in the past, as in past tense, when Draper alludes to his possible demise. Ever Sterling's Gold, he then quips: "My shrink says the job of your life is to know yourself. Sooner or later, you'll start to love who you are. . . . I'm a curious child. . . . And you're a terrible swimmer." Even though he has picked up on glimpses of his friend and protégé's past, including the ill-fated Hershey's debacle, Roger still does not see what eats at Don's soul—he will never love himself. Even watching himself die only brings a moment of bewilderment. The pain does not subside.

What sets Don off on his near-drowning is a group hookah session in which the straitlaced (on the outside) ad man hits a group hashish pipe offered to him by a beautiful blonde and a bunch of L.A. hippies. His death visions could be his soul opening up as he faces the end or just hash-induced hallucinations. From this grim taste to Roger's full-blown LSD experiment, drugs take center stage on *Mad Men* across its entire run. While viewers probably possess some idea about the pervasiveness of drugs and the sixties era, it is hard to imagine that many would think that they are as full-blown as on the show.

The perfect real-life embodiment of the ubiquity of drug use in the era may have been the high-powered British rock band the Rolling Stones. Led by magnetic singer Mick Jagger and guitarist Keith Richards, the Stones gained notoriety for embracing the wild side of life, including hedonism, drug use, sex, and violence. What they offered young fans was a counterpunch to the more staid Beatles, particularly in the mid- to late 1960s. The group's music, pulsing, pounding, and sharing a great deal aped from the rhythm and blues music that informed their style, sent kids into a frenzy and their parents over the edge.

Music imitated life for the Stones in 1967 when authorities arrested Jagger, Richards, and guitarist Brian Jones for a variety of drug-related charges. Facing real jail time and highly publicized trials, the Stones seemed doomed, while their fans lapped up the attention and railed against "the man" and police corruption. All three Stones were found guilty, but later either had their convictions overturned or were placed on probation. Surprisingly, the band received help from William Rees-Mogg, an influential conservative editor of London's *The Times*, who publicly criticized the police and the courts, pointing out that Jagger received a harsher sentence because of his fame. As if they needed any help in representing the outlaw faction of the popular music scene in the 1960s, the court victories merely fueled the band's place as rock-n-roll bad boys.

Adults lashed out about a lot worse than drug convictions, though. Music critic Ralph J. Gleason summed up the general reaction to rock music, explaining, "To the eyes of many of the elder generation, its music, its lights, its clothes, are immoral" (1967, 560). The Rolling Stones pointed out the hypocrisy of the establishment, singing about drugs in "Mother's Little Helper" and "Get Off of My Cloud." Gleason writes about a group of young radicals that penned an ode to a Stones appearance in California, which included, "As we tear down the military bases and arm the poor, as we tattoo BURN BABY BURN! on the bellies of the wardens and generals and create a new society from the ashes of our fires . . . ROLLING STONES—THE YOUTH OF CALIFORNIA HEARS YOUR MESSAGE! LIVE THE REVOLUTION!!!" (qtd. in Gleason 562). We get glimpses of this amount of anger in *Mad Men*, but the vision is usually conveyed via actual news clips of violence, like the viciousness of police brutality outside the 1968 Democratic National Convention in Chicago (Episode 6.10, "A Tale of Two Cities") or when characters watch or hear clashes on the television or radio.

The Rolling Stones, in contrast to the majestic poetics of Bob Dylan or the crazed popularity of the Beatles, signified a move away from norms to a more violent aspect of youth revolt. They replicated this idea in album titles, such as *Their Satanic Majesties Request* (1967) and *Let It Bleed* (1969). The controversy surrounding the band never really relented. Troubled band member Brian Jones, who could never find a way to work through superstardom, drowned in his pool in July 1969, about a month after being fired from the band.

Don Draper is not the evil incarnate that the Rolling Stones sing about in their classic tune "Sympathy for the Devil." He is a character cloaked in wickedness. Like the seductive figure in the samba-infused anthem, *Mad Men* spins yarns that expose revulsions, but like Mick Jagger, does so in a pretty package. Listeners are soon beguiled. Draper is devilish, along with an armload of other troubling personality traits, just like the Rolling Stones front man.

In Episode 5.3 ("Tea Leaves"), which is directed by Jon Hamm, the year is 1966 and a Heinz executive who manages the beans business wants Don to get the Rolling Stones to do a commercial for the product. Going to a Stones concert simply to appease the exec, Draper lets Harry Crane attempt to talk to the band's manager. While he is off searching, Don talks to a young female teenager. Expressing his own concern for Sally's future, he tells the girl that his generation is worried about hers and shuts down whatever sexual spark might be there.

In an ironic turn, the Rolling Stones, who are turning everyone on in the 1960s, act as a libido-inhibiter for the ad man. He is content to watch Harry's idea of signing the Stones go up in flames, chain smoking and looking on in wonder as he gets a real handle on the gulf between him and the younger set. Don is a pro at looking back and getting others to buy into his nostalgic pitches. The vision of the Stones is the counter—all forward and stomping into the future. The Rolling Stones are rollicking anarchy disguised as a rock-n-roll band. Draper's secret dream is not revolution; it is escape and peace of mind.

Before *Mad Men* debuted, Weiner and others associated with the fledgling show used a well-worn marketing hook when debuting a television program or movie set in the recent past. They claimed that *Mad Men* would deliver a realistic perspective of Madison Avenue in the 1960s, not only in storylines, but almost more importantly via use of authentic set designs, clothing, hairstyles, and props in general. The excitement about a "real" look into the past fueled great interest in the show, and television critics and other commentators used the info as a centerpiece for countless articles and essays.

As a result, *Mad Men* created a new category for viewers to judge and evaluate the show that other history-based shows (think *All in the Family* or *M*A*S*H*) never really had to address. Viewers relished the commitment to capturing the 1960s in detail, from the cut of Joan's dress to the décor of the Draper or Francis homes. Many early commentators applauded the way Weiner and his team depicted the look and feel of the era.

In a serious way, authenticity developed into a kind of unique character on *Mad Men*, at least in its first several seasons. One might ably argue that the commitment to historical realism served as an additional lead actor, and possibly as significant. Over time, as the show's realism became universally acknowledged, it lost some of its allure. However, *Mad Men* never fully relinquished its authenticity, particularly as the 1960s advanced and the show moved from Kennedy-esque to hippie-infused. There are innumerable stories about Weiner and his prop team searching high and low for exactly the right piece of furniture or clothing and the boss's joy or anger over finding them or being forced to make an exception. Across the length of the series, the setting, props, and even the actors' speech and body movements were calculated to stimulate an audience response.

The authentic representation of vice and debauchery also elicited viewer response. The basic questions people asked about *Mad Men* centered on whether the show mounted a realistic portrait of these people drinking, smoking, and having sex. If so, our parents and grandparents suddenly take on a new image. These were people reveling in the excesses of their age at a time in American history that was simultaneously scary and exhilarating. Wouldn't it be fun to image Pop-Pop or Nanny as a potential Don Draper or Peggy Olson?

More pointedly, by placing so much weight on the depiction of sex, drugs, smoking, and alcohol, Weiner asked the audience to reconsider a period that is routinely assessed via a nostalgic lens (perhaps until one gets to the hippies, which are a polarizing topic). According to writer J. M. Tyree, the program and others that attempt to contextualize the decade work as "revisionist fictions that present distinct . . . counter-mythologies of the 1960s, rueful and scornful ripostes to Baby Boomer self-congratulation" (2010, 39).

Tyree's explanation echoes Weiner's, who often contrasts his parents' experiences as Boomers with his own as a Generation Xer watching their lives unfold. Tyree concludes that Mad Men "debunk[s] a rosy view of pre-'68 Americana, excavating a bedrock of depression and insincerity beneath the rhetoric of change and freedom" (39). As lead archaeologist, Weiner is showing us the warts of a generation and the corporate world that soon leaves behind its drops of idealism for the winner-takes-all mentality that created the true "me" culture of the 1980s.

Part II

Mad Men and Culture

Sterling Cooper Pryce: Joan Harris, Roger Sterling, Lane Pryce (Jared Harris), Pete Campbell, Don Draper, Bertram Cooper (Robert Morse), and Peggy Olson. *AMC/Photofest ©AMC. Photographer: Frank Ockenfels*

4

A *MAD MEN* READING LIST

The characters in *Mad Men* (especially lead protagonist Don Draper) are shown reading or discussing books more frequently than are the characters in perhaps any other commercial series in television history. Who but Draper, for example, would run across a man reading Frank O'Hara's 1957 poetry collection *Meditations in an Emergency* in a bar—and then later actually read the book himself (Episode 2.1, "For Those Who Think Young") before sending it on to someone else (Anna Draper) to read? This phenomenon has stirred much interest among fans, as when several different websites have sprung up detailing the books featured in the series, providing guidance to those, too, who would like to read like a mad man. Even the New York Public Library has established a *"Mad Men"* Reading List site, apparently hoping that the series might spur resurgence in literacy.

To cite a typical example, in Episode 7.13 ("The Milk and Honey Route"), Draper's car breaks down while he is on a cross-country car trip of a kind that might have come from any number of American books, from *Lolita* (1955), to *On the Road* (1957), to Clancy Sigal's left-leaning *Going Away* (1961). That all of these books feature cross-country road trips situated in the 1950s, a crucial formative decade for Draper, may be no accident, suggesting that he has grown up at a time when American men, in particular, were taught by their culture that such trips could be crucial to any attempt to redefine oneself. On the other hand, the direct referent of the episode's title would appear to be the 1931 volume *The Milk and Honey Route: A Manual for Hobos*, by the sociologist Nels

Don Draper. *AMC/Photofest ©AMC*

Anderson (writing as Dean Stiff), suggesting the way in which Draper has, by this time, become a peripatetic wanderer rather than a Madison Avenue ad executive.

In any case, it's now 1970, so Don is able to kill some of the time he spends while holed up in a seedy motel outside the sleepy town where his car is being repaired by catching up on his reading—in this case by reading Mario Puzo's *The Godfather*, which had been published the year before. The town, we know, is Alva, Oklahoma, a piece of information the sharp-eyed can garner from the inscription on the side of the tow truck that gives Draper a ride to the Sharon Motel, where he stays while his car is being repaired. *The Godfather* was a major bestseller, of course, so it comes as no surprise that Draper is reading the book, especially to attentive viewers of the series, who know that Draper is in fact a voracious reader and that his taste in reading material runs to the middle brow, tending to focus on relatively high-quality books that are at the same time relatively popular.

As an advertising man, Draper needs to know what clicks with the American public, so it makes perfect sense that he would try to read currently popular books, just as he tends to try to watch most of the popular movies of the day. *The Godfather*, of course, is a very cinematic novel that would become the basis for one of the most important of all American films only a couple of years after Draper reads it in this episode. The book is displayed only in a single scene and without comment, though viewers also know by this point that the producers tend to choose Draper's reading material quite carefully, having him read books that will not just help him stay plugged into the popular American consciousness, but that will also have further relevance to the series and to Draper's characterization.

The Godfather is relevant to Draper's situation for any number of reasons, and no doubt an entire essay will someday be devoted to those connections. For now, it is sufficient to note that *The Godfather* is centrally concerned with the breakdown of traditional family relations in modern America, including a utopian fantasy of the family connections that still obtain in the Corleone family. Given Draper's own troubled family past, this sort of fantasy would no doubt have great appeal to him, even if it is ironized by the fact that the family connections in *The Godfather* lead directly to murderous criminal activity. And, of course, Draper here could have no idea that, some years later, the first sequel to the film version of *The Godfather* would unmask these family fantasies as rooted in the backward and regressive social practices of an essentially still-feudal Sicily. In any case, the connections between gangsterism and capitalism that underlie the narrative of *The Godfather* (including a suggestion that capitalism ultimately destroys traditional social relations of all kinds) provide ideal thematic support for the interrogation of capitalism that runs through *Mad Men* from beginning to end.

My reading here of *The Godfather* as an expression of a utopian fantasy of collectivity via the traditional family owes much, of course, to Fredric Jameson's similar reading of the film (along with *Jaws*) in his now classic essay "Reification and Utopia in Mass Culture." For my purposes, it is important that Jameson sees the family-based fantasies of gangster films such as *The Godfather* as providing images of utopian fulfillment that play a cultural role similar to the one once played by idyllic small towns. He thus argues that the film "offers a contemporary pretext for a Utopian fantasy which can no longer express itself through such outmoded paradigms and stereotypes as the image of the now extinct American small town" (1992, 33). It is thus important that Draper reads the book in just such a small town—and one that had lost all pretense to innocence when it became the site of a World War II internment camp for German POWs who were considered among the most troublesome and dangerous, a little historical tidbit that becomes especially interesting given Draper's later experience as the victim of violence at the hands of a group of U.S. military veterans in the town. This experience, combined with the town's history as the site of a prison camp, confirms Jameson's suggestion that small towns have lost their utopian sheen in American culture and verifies the suspicion (also confirmed by Draper's experience) that the small town has an ominous side, as such towns often do in American popular culture, especially post–World War II.

Of course, this reference to *The Godfather* in *Mad Men* also almost inevitably evokes a link to that other major masterpiece of the gangster genre in American popular culture, *The Sopranos*, a show on which *Mad Men* creator and showrunner Matthew Weiner served as a key writer and producer. Among other things, *The Sopranos* (whose gangster characters are virtually obsessed with the *Godfather* films, especially the first) makes particularly overt connections between gangsterism and "legitimate" American business of the kind potentially made by Draper's reading of *The Godfather* in *Mad Men*. But a major reason why the *Sopranos* characters are obsessed with *The Godfather* (the main action of which is set in the 1950s) is their sense of a breakdown in the utopian sense of tradition and community that the novel and film associate with the family ties of mobsterism. The constellation of images and connections surrounding Draper's reading of *The Godfather* is thus much richer than might at first be apparent, strongly reinforcing the insistence of *Mad Men* that the 1960s were a turning point in American history.

Meanwhile, in this same episode, Draper strolls out to the motel's rather unimpressive pool, only to find a surprisingly attractive swimsuit-clad woman lounging poolside. The sight of the woman immediately kicks Draper's old womanizer's instincts into gear, though we should probably not underestimate the extent to which he is partly attracted to the woman because she herself turns out to be a reader. She is, in fact, reading a paperback copy of Alberto Moravia's *The Woman of Rome* (originally published in Italian in 1947), a relatively weighty volume exploring, among other things, the theme of prostitution (as a metaphor for bourgeois materialism), a theme that also runs through *Mad Men*. It is not clear, of course, whether Draper has any idea what the book is about, but it is probable that he knows enough to know that Moravia was a writer who explored serious themes with sufficient literary dexterity to gain significant critical attention. Moravia, for a serious novelist, was also relatively popular and had several novels adapted to film, including (most notably) *The Conformist*, a 1951 novel that was prominently adapted to film by Bernardo Bertolucci in the very year in which this episode of *Mad Men* is taking place—and a book that includes a substantial amount of material related to the "Mafia." (*The Woman of Rome* had itself been adapted to film in 1954.)

That Draper seems to find the woman more exotic and sexually alluring because of her reading material might simply suggest that he feels attracted to a fellow reader, though it is also possible that he feels a sense of potential connection to the woman because he has been reading the Italian-oriented *Godfather*, while she is reading an actual Italian novel. More generally, however, it suggests the extent to which books and reading play a special role in Draper's life—and one with considerable erotic investment. Draper, after all, is a brilliant man who has virtually no formal education, an autodidact whose lack of learning is still able occasionally to embarrass him but who has, in fact, been able to accumulate a rather large fund of knowledge on his own. Books have a mysterious, almost fetishistic, power for him. In the Lacanian terms recently popularized by Slavoj Žižek, books for Draper are erotic objects that stand in for the *objet petit a*, the original lost object (usually associated with the mother) that all of us spend the rest of our lives in a futile quest to recover, thus filling the hole that lies at the heart of our identities. Draper's own motherless and underprivileged (both financially and emotionally) childhood means that his urge for such objects is particularly strong, thus the never-ending string of erotic conquests that constitute his romantic adventures in the series, as well as the general sense of longing and lack of satisfaction that seems to inform all of his activities.

As an undereducated man who moves in circles populated by less intelligent and less talented men who nevertheless find it easier to make their ways because of their Ivy League degrees, Draper clearly associates education with exactly the kinds of privilege and connectedness that he has never known. In his mind, the quest for women and the quest for books are very much a part of the same, more general quest for personal validation. Little wonder, then, that the woman by the pool is all the more attractive to him because of the book she is reading, just as it also comes as no surprise that Draper immediately loses interest when the fantasy bubble is burst by the quick revelation that the woman is not a mysterious, vacationing intellectual exploring the hinterlands, but an ordinary wife and mother with a schlumpy husband and noisy kids along with her on the trip.

The double episode (Episode 6.1–2, "The Doorway") that opens the sixth season of *Mad Men* begins as Dr. Arnold Rosen (Brian Markinson) attempts an emergency resuscitation of a fallen patient as a woman's voice (clearly Megan Draper's) exclaims, "Oh my god!" in the background. Rosen is a neighbor who lives in the same building as Megan and husband Don (in addition to being the husband of Don's mistress Sylvia), so this scene is clearly constructed to make viewers at least suspect that Don's high-pressure, hard-drinking, chain-smoking lifestyle has finally caught up with him and that he has perhaps had a heart attack. The screen then goes black as an ambulance is heard approaching. Suddenly we hear Don's voice, just before the scene switches to a shot of Megan's belly as she lies on a beach in what will turn out to be Hawaii. Don is, somewhat ominously given the preceding scene, reading the beginning of Dante's *Inferno*, "Midway in my life's journey, I went astray from the straight road, and woke to find myself alone in a dark wood." This choice of reading material suggests that Don does indeed have an occasional taste for high-brow literature, though in this case the reading material is also particularly appropriate given the growing sense that he is at somewhat of a crossroads in his life. He stops reading and looks at his paperback, seemingly puzzled at the fact that the words seem to describe his own mid-life-crisis situation so well. Viewers, meanwhile, are wondering if this narration of the beginning of a descent into hell is occurring in a flashback that foreshadows Don's own descent into hell after his death in the opening scene.

It is not, of course, surprising at this point in the series to see Don reading because we have seen him and the other characters reading so many times. Moreover, this motif in *Mad Men* is not simply gratuitous or even simply a way of suggesting the cultural tastes of the characters or setting the cultural context of the episodes. The books that are introduced in the series quite consistently function as intertextual glosses that comment upon and significantly enrich the events that are narrated in the series itself. As it turns out, Don is *not* the victim in the first scene (a few minutes later the victim will be revealed to be the doorman in his New York apartment building), and he doesn't get past these first lines in his reading, while the *Inferno* is never mentioned again. But Don's reading of Dante does, in fact, foreshadow a descent into hell of sorts as he gradually unravels through much of the sixth season, leading eventually to a meltdown during one of his patented nostalgia-trip client presentations, this time involving a depiction of Hershey chocolate bars as emblems of happy childhood memories, leading him to openly confess to the Hershey's reps the nature of his own decidedly unhappy childhood. This confession leads to his suspension from the company that he himself helped to found and still partly owns, sending him off into a sort of Purgatory through which he must struggle to get back to his former professional status.

The enigmatic first seconds of this movie-length double episode already contain a wealth of material that indicates the way in which literature itself is often used to enrich the fabric of *Mad Men*, and viewers are clearly invited to think of Dante throughout the episode (or even throughout the season and beyond, given how intricately interlinked the individual episodes of *Mad Men* tend to be). Indeed, this opening is typical of the way *Mad Men* often achieves a richness that can only be described as *literary*. In this same episode, for example, Don will soon encounter a soldier on leave in Hawaii, where he is about to be wed (with Don ultimately giving away the bride at the ceremony). In this encounter, the soldier colorfully expounds on the destructive power of the M2 machine gun that he has seen in action in Vietnam. Then, later, Don gives Dr. Rosen a Leica M2 camera, of which his firm has a supply because they are conducting an ad campaign for the camera company. Interestingly, Don also tells Rosen that he believes the M2 is the "best" Leica camera, even though it was an old model about to go out of production and had already, in December 1967 when this episode is taking place, been supplanted by the M4 as the top Leica model. We are not given this information in the episode, but viewers aware of this fact about the camera model might wonder if Don is expressing a sort of subtle violence against Rosen (as is perhaps indicated by the correspondence between the model of the camera and that of the machine gun). This event is only one of many moments in *Mad Men* that potentially take on a much different meaning (even if that meaning is not entirely clear) if certain intertextual or extratextual information is brought to bear.

Television viewers are not accustomed to being asked to seek out this sort of information, but this same sort of intertextual information is key to the experience of reading certain literary texts, most obviously James Joyce's 1922 modernist classic, *Ulysses*—which turns out also to be the first major literary text whose central protagonist is an advertising man. Jennifer Wicke has noted the ways in which *Ulysses* uses advertising not merely as a source of material but as a discursive model, with Joyce constructing certain elements of his text very much like an advertisement—or very much like numerous other works of popular culture:

> *Ulysses* is indisputably allied to mass cultural narrative roots, to Chaplin films, fancy postcards. . . . The "everyday" is charged, an extraordinary effusion of sentiment and wonder taken from popular culture, above all working class culture. Advertising is here a class diction. (1988, 125)

The same might well be said for *Mad Men*. With its famed colorful set design, its highly productive use of music, and its play upon a variety of narrative clichés, the series itself is constructed very much like an advertisement, and like a film, and so on. It is, in fact, constructed very much like *Ulysses*, with the main difference being that *Mad Men* understands, as Wicke apparently does not, that, while advertising is indeed a "class diction," it is a diction belonging not to the working class but to their middle-class masters (such as the affluent ad men of the series), even if it is designed to manipulate the working class and to ensure their compliance with the capitalist system.

Mad Men, in fact, has far more in common with *Ulysses* than might at first be obvious. In one of the key motifs of the early seasons of *Mad Men*, we learn that Don Draper has a variety of secret items (including cash and artifacts from his secret lost childhood) locked away in a special drawer in his home desk. Wife Betty, after several attempts, finally manages to get into the drawer in Episode 3.10 ("The Color Blue"). Betty's shock at the evidence she finds there that Don has not been honest with her about his past initiates a chain of events that will ultimately end in divorce—though it is not entirely clear whether this shock is due simply to Don's dishonesty or whether it is due to the discovery that he does not have the proper bloodlines and background for a pampered Bryn Mawr girl like herself, sending her running into the arms of blue-blood Henry Francis.

In short, the simple event of the opening of Don's secret drawer, however seemingly clichéd and melodramatic, has multiple potential ramifications of a kind that might best be described as *literary*. The whole motif of the secret drawer, for example, is quite reminiscent of a similar motif in that *most* literary of literary works, James Joyce's *Ulysses*. There, protagonist Leopold Bloom keeps a variety of private items in a secret drawer as well, including his secret correspondence with a woman apparently named Martha Clifford. Indeed, Bloom has an entire clandestine life he thinks his wife, Molly, knows nothing about. As it turns out, however, Molly does know most of Leopold's secrets, partly because she has already broken into and searched his secret drawer, which might be one of the things that have driven her into the arms of the oafish Blazes Boylan, though the text does not say so.

To link Don's secret drawer in *Mad Men* with Bloom's secret drawer in *Ulysses* might seem a stretch if *Mad Men* were not otherwise so consistently literary. *Mad Men*, in fact, is reminiscent of *Ulysses* in a number of ways. Joyce's monumental novel, after all, is (like *Mad Men*) a vastly complex work that addresses a wide variety of issues in its contemporary world by way of a plot that might have been derived from a soap opera. Formally, both *Mad Men* and *Ulysses* are intricately interwoven works, individual parts of which take on added power and significance from their resonances with other parts of the same work. In terms of content, there is an obvious connection between *Ulysses* and *Mad Men* in that the central character of *Ulysses*, Leopold Bloom, is himself an ad man, engaged both in the selling and in the creation of ads, combining (in that simpler era for the advertising industry) the "accounts" and "creative" jobs of *Mad Men*.

Ulysses, of course, is famed for its extensive engagement with other literary texts by predecessors such as Homer, Dante, and Shakespeare, a phenomenon I have discussed extensively in my book *Joyce, Bakhtin, and the Literary Tradition*. But *Mad Men*, especially for a television series, is also an unusually allusive work whose intertextual tentacles reach out to a number of other cultural artifacts. Both *Ulysses* and *Mad Men*, in fact, explicitly thematize their own intertextuality by including a number of scenes in which various characters consume other cultural products, including books. For example, early in *Ulysses*, when we first meet the Blooms, we see Leopold's wife, Molly, asking her husband to bring her some new reading material. We also learn that Molly has somewhat questionable taste in reading material, preferring titillating titles such as *Sweets of Sin* or *Ruby, Pride of the Ring* or even authors with titillating names, such as Paul de Kock—though the latter was actually a quite respectable author and a favorite of Karl Marx because of his ability to represent the lives of ordinary working-class people (Lafargue 1947, 139). Bloom, meanwhile, fancies himself as having a bit more literary sophistication and hopes that he can perhaps improve his wife's mind (and her taste in reading materials) through the power of suggestion—perhaps the same power that drives the advertisements that he helps to compose.

Don Draper, like Leopold Bloom, is something of an autodidact with little formal education, though he might have more reason than Bloom to think of himself as a sophisticated thinker and reader. He might also have reason to question the reading material of at least his first wife, Betty (though she certainly has more formal education than he). Thus, in Episode 1.6 ("Babylon"), Don settles into bed to find that Betty has been reading Rona Jaffe's 1958 novel *The Best of Everything*, a rather trashy account of the lives of several New York publishing house secretaries. Don flips through the book as he waits for Betty to join him in bed; he is clearly amused by what he finds inside, commenting sardonically on the fact that the book seems to be "dirtier" than its film adaptation.

Betty does occasionally show better (if not entirely different) taste in her reading material. In Episode 3.10 ("The Color Blue"), for example, she is shown reading Mary McCarthy's then-recent 1963 novel *The Group* in the bath tub. On the other hand, while *The Group* is by almost any standard a better novel than *The Best of Everything*, it was, at the time, also a somewhat sensational bestseller that explores the lives of a group of young women, including the treatment of such controversial topics as sex and sexism.

Meanwhile, Don's second wife, Megan (the daughter of a Marxist professor), turns the tables by occasionally flaunting the fact that she is more educated than is her husband. For example, she gets in at least one shot at what she seems to perceive as Don's questionable reading material. In Episode 5.7 ("At the Codfish Ball"), Megan's French Canadian parents pay a visit to the Drapers. During the visit, we see Don in bed reading Bernard Malamud's 1966 novel *The Fixer*, which Megan suggests he is doing just to impress her father, Raymond, a leftist intellectual. "My father won't care," she teases him, "if he finds out you read James Bond." Don, indicating *The Fixer*: "You know what? This is a good book. You should read it." And a good book it is, having won the National Book Award for Fiction and the Pulitzer Prize for Fiction. Based on a real-world story of the persecution of a Jew in tsarist Russia, it also addresses the engagement with Judaism that runs throughout *Mad Men*— and, for that matter, *Ulysses*.

Don, in fact, reads Jewish American literature at several points in *Mad Men*. For example, in Episode 1.6 ("Babylon"), Israeli representatives come to SC seeking aid in promoting Israeli tourism. To help with the process, they produce a copy of Leon Uris's wildly popular bestseller *Exodus*, which is apparently supposed to help Don and his WASPish colleagues understand what Israel and Judaism are all about. Don, of course, actually reads the book. Meanwhile, in Episode 7.4 ("The Monolith"), he is briefly shown reading Philip Roth's *Portnoy's Complaint*, the relevance of which to the action of the episode is not really clear, though it is now 1969 and *Portnoy's Complaint* was, in fact, the literary sensation of that year. It would seem that Don tends to read fashionable books, perhaps suggesting that he reads books at least partly for one of the main reasons he watches so many movies—to make sure he knows what is on the minds of the American people and thereby to garner potential advertising ideas.

Don's reading of such books is, of course, part of an engagement with Judaism that runs throughout the series, beginning with the very first episode. A similar engagement runs through *Ulysses*, in which Bloom is regarded by his fellow Dubliners as Jewish, even though he has been baptized a Christian multiple times, hasn't been circumcised, and is the son of an Irish Catholic mother (Jewishness being matrilineal). Bloom's "Jewishness" in the highly anti-Semitic environment of 1904 Dublin makes him very much an outsider, just as Don's debased childhood growing up as an impoverished orphan in a whorehouse in Pennsylvania makes it difficult for him genuinely to fit in among his affluent friends and colleagues in Manhattan.

Such parallels between *Ulysses* and *Mad Men* are surprisingly easy to find, perhaps because both are encyclopedic works that seemingly contain everything *including* the kitchen sink, drawing a great deal of energy from an extensive engagement with and vivid representation of their cultural and historical contexts. For example, in Episode 2.4 ("Three Sundays"), set during Easter season of 1962, Peggy has what might be described as an odd flirtation with the young priest Father Gill, who enlists her to help with one of his sermons and then later seeks her help in other advertising and marketing campaigns for his church as well. Though reluctant (and though her work is not entirely appreciated by the church ladies), she turns out to be quite helpful, suggesting a strong affinity between the kind of marketing she does and the kind of marketing in which priests such as Father Gill are engaged every day. Of course, Leopold Bloom had understood this affinity as early as 1904; he is a great admirer of the marketing expertise of the Catholic Church (as when he notes that the ritual of the Eucharist can be used to help convert cannibals in Africa), and at one point he even compares this expertise directly to that which reigns in his field of advertising. Overhearing a mass in a nearby chapel, Bloom notes the repetitive nature of the service. He then ruminates on the effectiveness of repetition in religious ceremonies: "Good idea the repetition. Same thing with ads" (13.1122–24).

Joyce is not, in fact, the only major modernist author whose work is relevant to *Mad Men*. Other works, in fact, appear more directly. In Episode 2.11 ("The Jet Set"), Don has an encounter in California (land of the young) with an unconventional twenty-one-year-old named Joy, who reads William Faulkner's *The Sound and the Fury* in bed after making love with Don. Don, still looking a bit dazed from his recent exertions, asks her about it and is informed that she "took a survey of American literature" by way of explanation for why she is reading Faulkner. She then tells him that their sex was good but that "the book is just okay." Don is apparently not all that impressed, either. Thus, still later, he arranges a mysterious meeting (we eventually learn that he is going to see Anna Draper, the widow of the original Don Draper), jotting down the details for the meeting on the last page of the book, which he then rips out to take with him, tossing the book itself aside on a table. There is no real indication that the gesture is meant as an expression of contempt for Faulkner's work, though the moment is rather reminiscent of the scene early in *Ulysses* in which Bloom visits the "jakes," then wipes himself using the paper from a story he has been reading there.

D. H. Lawrence also gets relatively little respect in *Mad Men*. His notorious *Lady Chatterley's Lover* makes an appearance in Episode 1.3 when Joan Holloway returns a copy that she borrowed from another member of the secretarial pool at Sterling Cooper, leading to some giggly commentary about the racy content of the book. That content, of course, had led the novel (first privately printed in Italy in 1928) to be banned in the United States until 1959, when a U.S. appellate court judge ordered that it and similar works could be published under First Amendment protections on the basis of their "redeeming social or literary value." The book was thus still quite new to most Americans in 1960, when the events of this episode took place, and it was definitely one of the books on the minds of American readers in that year—though much of its prominence in America came out of curiosity about its supposedly racy content rather than any perception of its literary value.

Numerous other books have found their way into *Mad Men* as well. Moving, for example, from the sublime of *Ulysses* to the truly ridiculous, we are told multiple times in the series that Bert Cooper, the firm's seemingly avuncular senior partner, is a great fan of Ayn Rand and particularly of her then fairly recent 1957 novel, *Atlas Shrugged*. This novel, which promotes Rand's notorious belief in unfettered *laissez-faire* capitalism and unrestrained individualist selfishness and greed, suggests that Cooper is not nearly as cuddly as he sometimes seems to be and that he might have gotten to where he is at least partly by sheer ruthlessness. Cooper is seen recommending the book to Don and other employees as early as the first season of the series (set in 1960), so he must have gotten to it fairly early in its career and fairly late in his, but it is easy to imagine that the book attracts him because it endorses certain attitudes that helped him get to the top of his profession decades earlier.

Atlas Shrugged thus directly supplements the critique of capitalism that runs through *Mad Men*, however vaguely. In other cases, books are simply props that help to create atmosphere, but do not seem to have any great thematic significance. In Episode 6.8 ("The Crash"), Don's kids are left alone in his Manhattan apartment at night while both Don and Megan are away pursuing their professions. With her younger brothers already in bed, daughter Sally (now fourteen) settles into bed as well, reading Ira Levin's 1967 novel *Rosemary's Baby* (the episode is set in 1968, so, again, the novel is quite new at this point). This now-classic tale of supernatural horror lurking in a New York apartment building is, of course, somewhat problematic as reading material for a young girl who is home alone in a New York apartment at night. To make matters worse, Sally does indeed hear something go bump in the night as she reads, only to discover an actual (if unconventional) intruder in the apartment. Her reading of *Rosemary's Baby* thus helps to set a tone of foreboding (both for Sally and for the viewing audience) as she encounters the burglar, a black woman who claims to be Sally's grandmother Ida.

This sequence is indeed quite scary, though not in a supernatural way—and it is debatable whether it is really made scarier by the presence of the book, which in this case is almost too clever to be truly effective. On the other hand, Sally's reading of the book suggests just how popular the book was at the time and prefigures the role that would be played in the series by the 1968 film adaptation when Peggy Olson conceives the idea of using it as the basis for a baby aspirin ad in an arc that begins just a few episodes later in Episode 6.12 ("The Quality of Mercy"). This sort of "seeding," in which a seemingly insignificant motif is planted in the text only to take on greater significance later, is a classic literary motif—and again one that is epitomized by *Ulysses*.

All in all, the many scenes in which Draper or other characters in *Mad Men* are shown reading books constitute an important part of the rich engagement with other cultural texts (and with historical contexts) that is so crucial to the series. Indeed, in this case text and context overlap: one implication of the prominence of books in *Mad Men* is that books represented a more important part of the cultural context of the 1960s than they do today. The effectiveness of the references to books is enhanced by the fact that the choice of books to feature in the series so often enriches the episodes in which the books appear. Finally, that the series itself is so literary makes these references to books and reading especially appropriate, while the reading motif that runs through the text is also used as a technique of characterization, particularly in the case of Don Draper.

5

THE MUSIC OF *MAD MEN*: SATISFACTION NOT GUARANTEED

When television burst on the scene as a major part of the texture of daily life in America, it was quickly established that music was a key ingredient in effective programming—just as it had long been in film and radio, the two media to which television can most directly trace its lineage. Similarly, especially in the age of television, music can be a crucial component in a successful advertising campaign.

Not surprising, then, music is also a crucial ingredient in *Mad Men*, which so richly combines the resources of conventional television programming with those of advertising in order to achieve its objectives of both entertainment and social commentary. In addition, *Mad Men* engages in an extensive dialogue with the context of the American 1960s—and especially with the popular culture of that period. Music was one of the most distinctive elements of that culture, providing a soundtrack to the revolutionary changes in American culture that saw young people rise to the fore as a political force—and as a key new market demographic for a rapidly expanding consumer culture that needed new customers in order to sustain the explosive growth that had begun in the postwar years. Historian Howard Brick may be correct when he concludes that our understanding of the role of music in the sixties counterculture is still "sketchy," but it is clear that this role was a major one, whatever the details (2000, 114).

Many scholars have attempted to elaborate the role of music in the culture of the 1960s, as when Michael J. Kramer (2013) provides a good

The Rolling Stones, 1965. Shown from left: Bill Wyman, Brian Jones, Charlie Watts, Mick Jagger, and Keith Richards. *Photofest*

overview of the issue that makes clear the importance of new forms of popular music in the historico-cultural phenomenon we know as the "sixties." Among other things, the rise of rock music as a pop cultural phenomenon is among the many narratives that *Mad Men* tells as part of its effort to establish the 1960s as a pivotal decade in American history. For example, as Tim Anderson demonstrates, one of the ways in which *Mad Men* uses music is to demonstrate that American pop culture (like American culture in general) was not as simple and innocent in the pre–Kennedy assassination years as it has sometimes been portrayed to be, allowing us instead "to hear the despair and discontent that percolated through the period" (2011, 83).

The importance of music as part of the texture of the 1960s, of course, is one of the key reasons that music takes on such importance in *Mad*

Men. Indeed, most of the most memorable music from *Mad Men* involves well-remembered popular songs from the 1960s, though the series also occasionally employs more recent music, as in the case of its well-known opening theme music, "A Beautiful Mine," which was taken from the instrumental portions of the 2006 album *Magnificent City*, by the rapper Aceyalone in collaboration with the hip-hop producer RJD2, who also included an instrumental version of the song in his 2006 album *Magnificent City Instrumentals*. Finally, the most conventional use of music in *Mad Men* occurs when its use of popular tunes is supplemented by original scores by David Carbonara, used to help provide atmosphere for various scenes, as is the case with most film and television music.

The role of music as a key element in *Mad Men* is clearly reflected in the strong role played by music amid the highly visible online presence that the series established over the course of its eight-year run. One of the key elements in the show's fandom, for example, involves the online availability of a variety of playlists that allow fans of the show to relive, in a convenient way, the music they had encountered in the series. The online music service Spotify, for example, includes an "Ultimate *Mad Men* Playlist" that includes original recordings of more than one hundred songs that played a role in the series, either directly (as with the weekly closing songs that became a much-anticipated part of the show) or indirectly (as when they are simply related to or illuminate events or motifs in the series). YouTube, meanwhile, contains a "Complete *Mad Men* Music Playlist" that includes more than two hundred videos of songs that made an appearance in one way or another in the series, including Carbonara's original scores. In fact, *Mad Men* playlists are so popular online that the site 8tracks Internet Radio includes a meta-list of 196 different *Mad Men* playlists that are available online.

The popularity of such playlists can be taken as a testament to the quality of the music selected for use in the series, which makes that music stand up quite well on its own. On the other hand, the music employed in *Mad Men* is quite carefully integrated with the series itself, so that it is impossible to appreciate the significance of the show's music when that music is heard in isolation from the show itself. For example, Episode 4.8 ("The Summer Man") features the Rolling Stones classic "(I Can't Get No) Satisfaction," one of the iconic songs of the 1960s. The song is not mere background music, but emanates diegetically from a small portable radio on a beach near Don Draper, who clearly hears it.

One irony of this scene, of course, is that Draper does not exactly have his finger on the pulse of contemporary rock music, however good he otherwise is at gauging what might interest American audiences. Nevertheless, the choice of this music is brilliantly appropriate. The song shifts into a nondiegetic mode that fills the background of the scene that proceeds from this beginning, the clever timing of cuts at which *Mad Men* is so good syncing up the song's references to cigarettes (and cigarette advertising) with Don lighting one, while aligning a line about shirts (and shirt advertising) to a shot of Don's signature nicely starched ultra-white dress shirt. This cleverness aside, the song (like so many of the show's references to popular culture) serves the obvious function of helping to locate the episode in time.

Released in the United States on June 6, 1965, the song was an immediate hit, placing on Billboard's Hot 100 chart that same week and reaching No. 1 on the chart by July 10, staying on the charts into September. It was the first No. 1 hit in the United States for the Stones and thus has special importance in the history of rock music. It is the perfect accompaniment to an episode set in the summer of 1965, helping to establish the historical context as a moment when American popular culture was in the early stages of a revolution that would change it forever. Even the fact that the song is playing on a transistor radio on the beach contributes to this contextualization—such radios first appeared only in 1954 and exploded in popularity in the 1960s, consonant with the rise of precisely the kind of rock music of which "Satisfaction" is a key example.

The song would also seem thematically appropriate as a sort of anthem for Draper, given his well-established wandering eye and seeming inability ever to be satisfied with what he has, sexually or otherwise. However, despite the fact that "Satisfaction" has often been seen as an anthem about the insatiability of youthful lust (or, more idealistically, about the never-ending demand of youth that we should constantly strive to build a better world), the song is actually about advertising and consumerism, which makes it about as appropriate a musical companion to *Mad Men* as one could possibly imagine. Thus, the line in the song that "rhymes" with the shot of Don's sparkling white shirt actually refers to a television commercial in which an announcer comes on to tell the singer "how white my shirts can be." It is, in short, a reference to an ad for laundry detergent. Similarly, the line that immediately follows (accompanied by a cut to Draper lighting up still another cigarette) is a reference to cigarette branding by association with manliness ("He can't be a man 'cause he doesn't smoke the same cigarettes as me"). Given Draper's extensive smoking habit—as well as his professional adventures with (and against) cigarette advertising—the reference is particularly rich.

Given these overt references to advertising, it seems fairly obvious that "Satisfaction" is, first and foremost, a commentary on consumerism—and one that is conducted from the point of view of a youthful rebellion against materialist values of the kind that are Draper's lifeblood. Little wonder, then, that the song focuses on the inability to attain satisfaction, on the unquenchability of desire. After all, the desire upon which consumer capitalism is built is, of necessity, a desire that can never be satisfied. Consumers are urged (by people like Draper and his fellow mad men) to believe that purchasing certain products will solve all their problems, but of course this promise is and must be a false one. If purchasing any product could solve all of one's problems, then one would need to make no further purchases after that one, bringing to a halt the cycle of consumption while at the same time bringing the capitalist system to its knees. Consumerism, by definition, must create a desire that cannot be fulfilled, so that consumers must continue to buy in an ongoing attempt to fill, through participation in the capitalist economy, a void that this economy works hard both to produce and to perpetuate.

Of course, from a Lacanian perspective, the desire that drives consumerism (unfulfillable by definition) is structurally quite similar to sexual desire, which is similarly driven by a doomed quest for fulfillment and completion, by a never-ending and hopeless search for the lost *objet petit a*, for the original sense of wholeness and satisfaction that fill the world of the infant. To a large extent, a recognition of this parallel has driven the entire career of Slavoj Žižek, whose combination of the seemingly incommensurate theoretical worlds of Marxism and Lacanian psychoanalysis is centrally informed by an understanding of the way in which a never-ending quest for romantic/sexual satisfaction so closely resembles consumerist desire.

The recognition of the connection between eroticism and consumerism is neither unique nor new to recent theorists such as Žižek. It is crucial to Flaubert's *Madame Bovary* (1856), in which the title character so desperately (and hopelessly) seeks escape from emptiness and boredom through the twin expedients of adultery and shopping. But this parallel is also crucial to *Mad Men*, where it is clear that Draper's crippled childhood endows him with a particularly strong sense of incompleteness and loss that both drives his quest for sexual fulfillment and fuels his ability to tap into and stimulate consumer desire for the products he hawks as a mad man. He, of all people, understands all too well just what it feels like to want something and to keep wanting, no matter how much you seem to get what you want.

From this point of view, "Satisfaction" lies at the very heart of *Mad Men*'s main narrative and thematic projects and is thus the perfect tune to accompany the series. It also raises some key issues in the interpretation of the series and especially of its treatment of the counterculture of the 1960s, especially in relation to consumer capitalism. However anti-consumerist it might be, for example, "Satisfaction" was itself a huge hit and a major consumerist success. As Thomas Frank has outlined, rock music in general was a boon to advertisers in the 1960s, and many of the hip new stars in the field established their hipness by demonstrating a familiarity with the new music (1998, 113). But then, for Frank, the counterculture as a whole was more a product of consumerist expansion than of resistance to that expansion. Four decades later, *Mad Men* would emerge with many of these same issues intact, and the exact status of the series as an endorsement or critique of consumerism is clearly debatable.

Given the close connection between the issues raised by "Satisfaction" and those addressed by *Mad Men*, perhaps it is not surprising that the series associates the Rolling Stones with marketing in other ways as well. In Episode 5.3 ("Tea Leaves"), which takes place early the following summer (1966), Don and Harry Crane try to sign the Stones to record a jingle for Heinz beans, having been asked to do so by Raymond Geiger (John Sloman), the Heinz beans rep, whose daughter is a big Stones fan. Aware of the song "Time Is on My Side," Geiger loves the idea of having the Stones record a new jingly version called "Heinz Is on My Side." (Unfortunately, "Jumpin' Jack Flash," which might make a hilarious beans anthem, was not released until 1968.) Draper is repeatedly portrayed in the series as being clueless about the landscape of 1960s rock music, so it is not surprising that he has no idea that the Rolling Stones are a really big deal—probably far too big at this point to record a jingle for beans. Both Don and Harry seem to feel that the Stones are some sort of teenage bumpkins who will probably be thrilled at the chance to appear in a real TV ad. In reality, though, the two ad men (the latter of whom should really know better, being the SCDP media consultant) don't even manage to get to meet with the Stones, who have far better things to do.

On the other hand, Draper in this episode might not be quite as out of it as he seems because he himself points out that there is a precedent, the Stones having two years earlier recorded a jingle for cereal back in Britain. And he's right, the Stones actually did record a spot for Rice Krispies that plays on the notion that this particularly noisy cereal (advertised for years in the United States on the basis of its signature "snap, crackle, pop" sound) is so loud that some in the older generation might find it unpleasant—much in the same way that they react to the music of groups like the Stones as extremely annoying sonic pollution.

Of course, the landscape of popular music was changing rapidly in the mid-1960s, and the Rolling Stones were a huge phenomenon in 1966 (when Draper tried to sign them to hawk beans), as opposed to 1964 (when they were just releasing their first studio album and were still hungry enough to be willing to pitch cereal). In addition, neither Don nor Harry appears to have any idea what the Stones really represented to their legions of new, young countercultural fans in 1966, for whom the raw, brash, blues-inflected sound of the original bad boys of rock 'n' roll seemed both a challenge to and a repudiation of the very establishment values that are embodied by Don and Harry as they awkwardly make their way backstage to try to sign the band. In short, signing to do a beans commercial in 1966 would have no doubt made the Stones seem like sellouts to their fans, the result being that signing them to try to help sell such a lowly commercial product would have probably resulted in significantly reduced sales for their music, which of course was their *main* commercial product. Effective marketing required that the Stones not be perceived as participating in marketing.

As an interesting side note to this episode, it might be pointed out that this segment of *Mad Men*, which serves so well to help establish Draper's estranged relationship with both contemporary music and the counterculture, might also be a reference to a real event in rock history. The Who, only one tier below the Beatles and the Stones in the hierarchy of British rock royalty, themselves recorded a number of commercial jingles in the mid-1960s (obviously the advertising industry was quick to realize that *something* potentially marketable was going on in the new world of rock music), but then attempted to distance themselves from that practice through self-parody in their 1967 album *The Who Sell Out*, which is filled with mock advertisements, including (oddly enough) a song entitled "Heinz Baked Beans." It is in fact featured in the album's title art, which shows Roger Daltrey (no Mick Jagger but a major figure in 1960s music nevertheless) sitting in a tub of Heinz baked beans while holding up a giant can of the gooey legumes. This brief parodic jingle (written and sung by John Entwhistle, it runs for exactly one minute, like many TV ads of the time) features a British mum who decides to serve Heinz baked beans for tea, thus theoretically opening up a whole new market for this quintessentially American product.

The prominent role played by the Rolling Stones in *Mad Men* is just one example of the way in which most of the major players who made 1960s popular music such a special phenomenon make an appearance in one way or another in the series. For example, Bob Dylan's classic break-up anthem "Don't Think Twice, It's All Right" plays over the closing scene of the first season, in which it is becoming clear that Draper's first marriage is spiraling downward into doom. Meanwhile, the Beatles probably play an even more important symbolic role in the series than do the Stones, their music factoring in via a string of episodes that help to establish both the changing face of American culture in the 1960s and the inability of Draper (very much a man of the 1950s in many ways) to keep up with it. For example, just two weeks after the "Satisfaction" episode, in Episode 4.10 ("Hands and Knees"), Draper's new secretary Megan Calvet wins some points with him by delivering tickets to the upcoming (and now legendary) concert of the Beatles that was held before a record crowd at New York's Shea Stadium on August 15, 1965. Draper himself hopes to win some points with daughter Sally by taking her to the concert, though he is only half kidding when he threatens to wear earplugs through the whole thing. We don't actually know, incidentally, if he carries through with the threat, because we never see Draper and daughter attend the actual concert, which seems to have been forgotten by the next episode. It's one of those perplexing moments of failure to follow through that often happens in *Mad Men*, another of which, interesting enough, also involves Shea Stadium (then home of the New York Mets baseball team). In Episode 7.4 ("The Monolith") Draper finds an abandoned Mets pennant in an episode set in 1969, appearing to set up the ascent to baseball legend of that year's "Miracle Mets," who went from ninth place (out of ten) the year before to win the National League pennant in a stunning late-season drive, then won the World Series against the heavily favored Baltimore Orioles (considered one of the greatest teams of all time) in one of the great upsets in Series history. Mike Bertha has presented a spirited argument for the metaphorical importance of this pennant as a sign of Draper's own arc in the series, but the fact is that—while Draper does attend a Mets game with Freddie Rumsen—the Mets are largely forgotten after this episode and their stunning world championship victory is never mentioned in the series. Shea Stadium is apparently the place in *Mad Men* where motifs go to die.

Nearly one season later in the evolution of the series after the Beatles concert episode, a client requests music that sounds like the Beatles for use in his firm's ads. Draper seems puzzled by the request, still having failed to grasp the marketing potential (or overall cultural import) of the rock revolution of the decade. Seeming, in fact, surprisingly out of step with the times, he consults new wife Megan (presumably because she is much younger and thus might be more in touch with contemporary music) about the phenomenon. "When did music become so important?" asks Draper, suddenly feeling old.

Trying to help out (and to remedy Don's cluelessness), Megan responds in the very next episode (Episode 5.8, "Lady Lazarus") by giving her husband a copy of *Revolver*, perhaps the greatest of Beatles albums. *Revolver*, incidentally, was released on August 5, 1966, so it was still new at the time of the action of this episode, as a radio broadcast embedded in the episode (one of the time markers that appear so frequently in *Mad Men*) identifies it as set in October 1966. Megan especially recommends the album's acclaimed closing track "Tomorrow Never Knows," which Draper subsequently plays, alone, after she leaves. A song filled with references to death, it seems an ominous choice, especially for someone as seemingly self-destructive as Draper. On the other hand, the song (whose lyrics were inspired by an adaptation of *The Tibetan Book of the Dead* co-authored by none other than drug guru Timothy Leary) is actually about the death of the ego during the experience of meditation under the influence of LSD, so that the references to death in the lyrics are metaphorical and not nearly as dark as they might first sound.

This Eastern-inspired erasure of the ego (somewhat analogous to the nihilation of the self in Sartrean existentialism) is, in fact, meant to be a positive experience. It is also a quintessentially countercultural product (in terms of the music, as well as the lyrics), and "Tomorrow Never Knows"—one of numerous Beatles songs inspired by their experiences with drugs and/or their encounter with Eastern (especially Indian) mysticism—can be taken as a rejection of precisely the same Protestant-work-ethic, materialist striving that has driven Draper throughout his adult life. This striving has gained him a certain amount of professional recognition, two beautiful wives, and a boatload of money, but it hasn't made him happy. He is not, however, quite ready for the anti-materialist message of the Beatles song, and it is not surprising that he isn't impressed. It could be argued that this moment sets up the ultimate end of the series, when Draper possibly finds a sort of enlightenment at a California hippie-esque New Age institute, but at this moment he simply dismisses the song and turns it off before it has played through.

In addition to the role played by popular music by major artists such as the Beatles and the Rolling Stones within episodes of *Mad Men* to help place them within the context of the 1960s, the show also gets considerable mileage from the well-chosen ending music that plays over the closing credits each week. Indeed, this ending music became one of the most anticipated features of the show as audiences eagerly waited to see which of their favorite songs from the 1960s might show up as a kind of coda to the action that had gone before. In this (and in many other ways), *Mad Men* follows in the footsteps of predecessors such as *The Sopranos*, though the technique is especially effective in *Mad Men* because the music is typically taken from the same time period as the action of the show, thus enhancing the impact of the episode that had just gone before. A good example occurs at the end of Episode 6.10 ("A Tale of Two Cities"), which is filled with psychedelic sixties imagery and even ends with the square accounts man Pete Campbell sparking up a doobie. It is thus highly appropriate that the ending music to this episode is the Big Brother and the Holding Company recording of "Piece of My Heart," not only because of the psychedelic tenor of the entire episode, but because this song appeared in the album *Cheap Thrills* and was released in August of 1968, the month of the action of this episode itself. It was also the group's last album with Janis Joplin on vocals, as she left the group almost immediately afterward, thus reinforcing the things-fall-apart tenor of the entire sixth season of *Mad Men*. At the time, though, *Cheap Thrills* was a success, launching Joplin into a short period of major stardom that made her an icon of the sixties counterculture, though she would die of a drug overdose only two years later—in October of 1970.

Joplin would thus die just a month, as it turns out, before the action of the final episode of *Mad Men*, though her death does not factor in the series. Still, including her in the ending music of the "A Tale of Two Cities" episode contributes to a network of images of death that gave the entire sixth season undertones so ominous that numerous fans were assuming the series would eventually conclude with Draper's own death. Indeed, Draper himself smokes hashish at a pool party in this episode and then very nearly drowns in the pool. It would, however, be Don's first wife, Betty, who would be done in by smoking, consigned to death by cancer at the end of *Mad Men*, thanks (no doubt) to the cigarettes she had puffed so assiduously throughout the series; she was thus killed by her own kind of drug overdose.

The use of music to create ominous imagery in *Mad Men* was also effectively employed in the final season's Episode 7.3 ("Field Trip"), which used ending music from the other sixties icon of towering talent, soaring success, and early death: Jimi Hendrix, who died of a drug overdose the month before Joplin did the same. This episode closes with Hendrix's raw and bluesy recording of "If 6 Was 9," which appeared on the 1967 Jimi Hendrix Experience album *Axis: Bold as Love*, but is also well remembered for its appearance on the soundtrack of the 1969 countercultural film *Easy Rider*. Among other things, the song includes an in-your-face challenge to a "white collared conservative . . . businessman," whose values Hendrix defiantly rejects in the song. This businessman, of course, could easily be Draper, though (given the ending of the series) the song could also be taken as an anticipation of either Draper's own ultimate rejection of the materialist values that had driven his advertising career or of Draper's response to Hendrix via his ultimate realization that the imagery and ideas of the counterculture could be conscripted for use in big bucks marketing campaigns.

"Field Trip," incidentally, has some fine moments and includes major turning points in *Mad Men*, including Megan's announcement to Don that their marriage is over and Don's return to SC&P after a period of exile. This return, of course, is extremely problematic and seems to take place on terms that are designed to humiliate Draper and teach him, with his low-class background, not to be so arrogant and uppity at work. These terms, in fact, might be taken as the beginning of an arc that will lead to Draper's sudden bolting from a business meeting, followed by his cross-country drive to California in apparent search of the kind of spiritual enlightenment that his career in capitalism can never bring him.

Hendrix's "If 6 Was 9" clearly reinforces this motif, while its title imagery reinforces the "world-turned-upside-down" tenor of the entire episode. Of course, the song is also an anthem to sixties-style individualist authenticity, with Hendrix essentially declaring his determination to be his true self whatever pressures the society might bring to bear upon him to conform to narratives imposed by others. The song thus ironically addresses Draper's key existential dilemma involving the inauthenticity of his own identity: the one thing he has never done is remain true to himself despite such pressures. He has, in fact, continually remade his identity on the fly, as it were, seeking (in good ad man style) to do and say whatever works and whatever helps him to get what he thinks he wants.

By this point in the series, though, what Draper wants is a mystery, even to him, though it is clear that he is fed up with the inauthenticity of his previous tell-them-what-they-want-to-hear style. The Hendrix song is extremely effective at providing a focus on this aspect of Draper's character, while at the same time placing his individual existential dilemma within the larger historical dilemma of American society in the 1960s, also struggling to define itself and to find an identity based on something more meaningful than capitalist greed. The song is thus central to one of the key themes of the entire series and to the central strategy by which *Mad Men* carefully interweaves the private stories of individual characters with larger public narratives, giving all of the characters something of an allegorical quality.

Draper, of course, is the *Mad Man* character who is most directly involved in a struggle to find a viable identity for himself, and by this time in the series he has become an almost textbook example of Sartrean existentialism. Having broken free of the facticity of his original existence as Dick Whitman and gone through the nihilation of that self, Draper finds himself trapped in a new facticity associated with his new identity as an ad man. He seems, in this segment of the series, to be approaching a new nihilation as he struggles to break free of the cutthroat world of Madison Avenue advertising in order to move toward the newer, more authentic existence that Sartre calls the Being-for-itself.

This motif of the search for one's true identity—or of "finding oneself"—was, of course, a favorite avocation of Americans in the 1960s, and we should remember that existentialism was still a very current mode of thought at the time. Indeed, Sartre was himself still around, working against the Cold War grain by attempting to reconcile his youthful existentialism with his newly adopted Marxism. Little wonder, then, that many characters in *Mad Men* are involved in such identity searches, including women characters such as Joan Holloway Harris or Peggy Olson, who struggle to find viable identities for themselves in a context in which the roles available to women were under significant revision.

Other than Draper, however, the character who seems most overtly to be in search of an identity for himself is Roger Sterling, who seems to have an odd connection with Draper throughout the series, despite the dramatic differences in their backgrounds. Unlike Draper, Sterling grew up with every advantage. The son of one of the founders of the Sterling Cooper ad agency (the "Sterling" refers to his father, not to Roger), he has inherited considerable wealth and everything has pretty much been handed to him on the silver platter to which his name might be taken as a reference. Sterling is something of a lovable rogue; capable of highly selfish and irresponsible conduct, he nevertheless has a number of charming qualities.

The unpleasant side of Sterling's character is summed up in one of occasional moments in *Mad Men* when the characters themselves perform music, adding still another element to the importance of music in the series. For one thing, their performances are usually quite good, highlighted, perhaps, by Megan's sexy rendition of "Zou Bisou Bisou" in Episode 5.1–2 ("A Little Kiss")—a performance that leaves an uncomfortable Don squirming in his seat at his wife's display of sexiness in front of all his friends and colleagues in a way that perhaps presages the coming end of the relatively short marriage. Megan, of course, is a show-business professional, so perhaps her performing talents should come as no surprise. Not so for others in the show, though, including those who appear in Episode 3.3 ("My Old Kentucky Home"), which includes not one, but three counterpointed musical performances that turn out to be key moments in the episode.

The first of these performances occurs at a posh (but somewhat outré) country-club garden party being held on the occasion of the 1963 Kentucky Derby. The event is being hosted by Sterling and new wife Jane, the dazzling young secretary he has recently married in an apparent attempt to stave off aging, at the same time ending a long-term marriage that was punctuated by an ongoing affair with Joan Holloway, another of his secretaries. Many of the principals from Sterling Cooper (including Don and Betty Draper) attend, but the party (something of a throwback to earlier, more genteel days for rich folks) is attended mostly by pretentious rich snobs. The musical highlight of the party is Sterling's own stirring, banjo-playing rendition of the Stephen Foster classic "My Old Kentucky Home" (official song of the Kentucky Derby) in full blackface, with a giggling Jane by his side, already well on her way to being falling-down drunk, the show wife become spectacle. Sterling seems to have no clue that his performance might be racially offensive, and there are no black guests anywhere in sight. But even in 1963, this performance is problematic enough that it causes Draper to retreat from the garden party to seek refuge (and a drink) inside the club.

Intercut with scenes from this upper-class Derby Day party are scenes of a much more modest middle-class dinner party hosted by that same Joan Holloway (now Harris) and her husband, Greg, for some of his doctor buddies and their wives. At this party, Joan delivers her own musical performance, which serves as a sort of counterpoint to Sterling's. Among other things, the talk at this party reveals to us the news that Greg has recently had a mishap (previously unbeknownst to Joan) that calls his skills as a surgeon into question. Joan, meanwhile, regales the guests (at Greg's insistence) with a nicely sung rendition of "C'est Magnifique" while accompanying herself on the accordion. This song was written (in French) by American songwriter Cole Porter for the musical *Can-Can* in 1953 and had, by 1963, become a standard, though it was not a hit when first released as a single ten years earlier.

"C'est Magnifique" is a rather light-hearted number, and the attendees at the party receive Joan's performance of it as a mere entertainment. Nevertheless, the lyrics of the song, suggesting an on-again-off-again love affair, can be taken as a commentary on Joan's former relationship with Sterling—which in fact will briefly flair up again in Season 4, leading to Joan's pregnancy with a child she will pass off as Greg's. Interestingly, "C'est Magnifique" is all about the sweetness of the renewal of a former love, when in fact, Joan conceives her child in a moment of rather rough sex fueled by the adrenaline rush experienced by Joan and Roger after they are mugged on a New York street. The song thus anticipates the brief resurgence of the affair between Joan and Roger but in a highly ironic way. Meanwhile, its suggestion of a long-suffering woman who

continually (and gladly) welcomes back her straying lover oddly anticipates the use, three years later, of "Piece of My Heart" in the ending
music, indicating the way in which the music used in *Mad Men* participates in an ongoing and developing dialogue of the kind seen in other
elements of the series as well.

In addition, if Sterling's blackface performance indicates the cluelessness of his class, Joan's faux-French performance can be taken as a
suggestion of the (somewhat halfhearted, middle-brow) pretentions of the
middle class to culture. Meanwhile, as the two parallel parties in this
episode proceed, another group of characters is engaged in a sort of
working-class counterpart to the upper- and middle-class parties. In particular, a group of "creative" characters is back at the office working
through the weekend to develop new ideas for an advertising campaign
for Bacardi Rum. Embittered at having to work while their rich bosses
play, they spend much of the time smoking marijuana and don't really get
a lot of work done. After all, they are not truly working class, but in fact
envision themselves as "artists." They do, meanwhile, get in a musical
performance of their own, this time performed by copywriter Paul Kinsey, who himself once had a fling with Joan, though apparently a brief
one. Goaded by a former Princeton classmate (who is now a drug dealer)
into demonstrating his singing talents, Kinsey breaks out (in an homage
to his days as a member of the a cappella singing group the "Tigertones"
in college) into a performance of "Hello! Ma Baby," an 1899 Tin Pan
Alley song that resonates with Sterling's performance in that it was initially marketed as a "coon song," complete with racist lyrics and racist
caricatures as illustrations for the sheet music.

The overtly racist lyrics are missing from the portion of the song
performed by Kinsey (and from the part of the song that is still a well-
known artifact of American popular culture), but the implication seems
clear: racism has long been a part of the fabric of American society and
continues to be well into the 1960s, especially among the very rich and on
the hallowed campuses of the Ivy League. Meanwhile, Kinsey's participation in the singing group seems to have been part of a concerted effort
to fit in at Princeton, despite the fact that he was a young man from a
modest background who was able to go there only because he had a
scholarship—a fact he himself appears to find embarrassing because it
undermines his pretentions to social status.

Sterling's sudden blackface performance of a mid-nineteenth-century minstrel song is pretty startling, but perhaps the most surprising musical moment in *Mad Men* occurs at the end of Episode 7.7 ("Waterloo"). This episode, which ended the first half of the final season (leading into a break of nearly a year between episodes), features the death of longtime Sterling Cooper patriarch Bertram Cooper. Yet it ends, oddly enough, with a sterling soft-shoe musical number featuring a seemingly resurrected Cooper as he performs Irving Berlin's "Let's Have Another Cup of Coffee" (from the 1932 musical comedy *Face the Music*), accompanied by a bevy of dancing mini-skirted secretaries.

The strangeness of the performance seems to invite viewers to try to interpret its significance, and significant it may well be. The song seems to express values that are diametrically opposed to the Ayn Rand–inspired cutthroat capitalist values that had driven Cooper while alive. Meanwhile, the performance suggests the variety of ways music is used in *Mad Men*, from seamless integration of songs such as "Satisfaction," to the jarring intrusion of Roger Sterling's blackface, to the perplexing, estranging weirdness of Bert Cooper's soft shoe. But this diverse and innovative use of music is but one aspect of the way in which *Mad Men* uses the resources of American culture in diverse and innovative ways throughout. Draper might cannibalize the broader culture in building his ads, but Matt Weiner and the other makers of *Mad Men* avowedly do the same in constructing their series.

6

MAD MEN AND THE MOVIES

One of the things that makes *Mad Men* special is the meticulous effort that it makes to remain engaged with its cultural context throughout the series, from its beginnings in the first season (set during the Kennedy-Nixon presidential campaign of 1960) through its end. One of the most important ways in which *Mad Men* effects this engagement is by incorporating specific works of contemporary culture, including movies, which are often introduced in episodes of the series that take place within days or weeks of the premieres of the films that are involved. Characters in the series often punctuate their conversations with passing references to films—as do people in real life. But movies figure in the series in more prominent ways as well, and we often see characters (especially central character Don Draper) actually in theaters watching movies, sometimes as research in an attempt to get ideas for their work in advertising.

Of course, *Mad Men* itself is overtly cinematic, and virtually anyone who has watched the series extensively must surely have experienced those moments in the show when the action suddenly seems like something from a movie—even if one cannot always tell *which* movie. For example, in Episode 3.13 ("Shut the Door. Have a Seat"), when Mssrs. Sterling, Cooper, Draper, and Pryce decide to bolt their old advertising firm to form a new firm of their own, there is an entire sequence in which they make off with as many resources from the old company as they can in order to help start the new one. That sequence, which takes place over a weekend in which the original Sterling Cooper offices are otherwise deserted, reads like some sort of heist film, as they daringly steal whatev-

**Ann-Margret in *Bye Bye Birdie* (1963). *Columbia Pictures/Photofest* © *Columbia Pic-*
*tures***

er they think they can use, in the meantime threatening to lock up witnesses in a closet until the weekend has passed.

In other cases, situations in *Mad Men* are reminiscent of more specific films, even though those films are not referred to directly. The title of Episode 1.10 ("Long Weekend") might sound like a reference to the Billy

Wilder classic *The Lost Weekend* (1955), but in fact the episode revolves around the motif of men being left behind in the city while their families flee to escape the summer heat. This motif, of course, lies at the center of another Wilder classic from the same year, the Marilyn Monroe vehicle *The Seven Year Itch*.

Mad Men engages with film in much more specific and concrete ways as well. Thus, however enigmatic he might be in so many ways, one of the things we know about Don Draper is that he is a frequent watcher of movies. In Episode 3.2 ("Love Among the Ruins"), Sterling Cooper hopes to land the account for "Patio," a new diet soda from Pepsi, which hopes to compete with Diet Coke via the product. Their idea for a Patio TV spot is essentially a re-creation of Ann-Margret's career-boosting musical performance that both opens and closes the then-new *Bye Bye Birdie* (released in New York on April 4, 1963). However, when Peggy shares the idea with Don, he notes that he hasn't seen the film. Peggy is taken aback: "You see everything," she says with surprise, indicating her realization of his status as a frequent moviegoer.

It is certainly the case that movies, for Don, are grist for the advertising mill, just like pretty much everything else. But Don also watches movies because he likes movies. They often play a part in his casual conversation, as in Episode 1.6, which begins at bedtime on Mother's Day in the Draper house. Settling into bed, Don is somewhat amused to find that Betty has been reading Rona Jaffe's 1958 novel *The Best of Everything*, a rather trashy account of the adventures of several New York publishing house employees that was adapted to film (starring Joan Crawford) in 1959. Flipping through the book, Don sarcastically declares it "fascinating," to which Betty responds that "it's better than the Hollywood version." "It's certainly dirtier," says Don with a smile, at which point the conversation devolves into Betty's critique of Crawford's prominent eyebrows and Don's counter that "some men like eyebrows, and all men like Joan Crawford."

Bye Bye Birdie might not be to Don's taste in movie fare, but it is a perfect choice as a model for an ad campaign that derives its energies from contemporary popular culture, because the film itself is a light-hearted satire of that culture. Adapted from a 1960 stage play of the same title, the film is a musical comedy that derives its central plot from Elvis Presley's famed drafting into the U.S. army in 1958. In particular, it explores the drafting of young rock star Conrad Birdie (whose name is derived from that of Conway Twitty, in the late 1950s himself a budding rock idol, though he would ultimately make his name mostly in the field of country music). The texture of the film, meanwhile, is very much like the texture of a television commercial, filled with bright colors, jingly music, and general silliness.

Don, of course, sees "everything" partly as research for his job, at which he actually works hard, despite seeming to come up with brilliant ideas effortlessly. For Don, watching movies is a way to take the pulse of contemporary American culture so that he can immediately know the kinds of things that American audiences respond to in the here and now. It is, of course, part of his genius to be able to recognize such things and to distill them to their very essence, which, among other things, means that his use of film as a source of advertising ideas tends to go beyond pastiche of specific films, instead drawing upon general motifs or even whole genres, as when his award-winning Glo-Coat ad from Season 4 draws upon recognizable iconography from the Western.

Don's ability to get to the root of the way ads work on consumers can clearly be seen when Peggy expresses her doubt about the efficacy of the Ann-Margret figure as an attraction for Patio's intended female audience. Ann-Margret works as a lure for both men and women, Don tells Peggy, because, while men might want Ann-Margret, women want to *be* Ann-Margret. Peggy realizes that he is right and then spends much of the rest of the episode trying to be like Ann-Margret herself, including one scene in which she re-creates the *Bye Bye Birdie* title song in front of her mirror at home.

Movies (and related entertainment of various kinds) often provide useful fodder for advertising in *Mad Men*. In Episode 5.3 ("Tea Leaves"), Michael Ginsberg (Ben Feldman) secures a job as a copywriter at SCDP thanks to his portfolio of sample ad ideas, one of which (described by Don as "provocative") he admits was inspired by his watching of a Times Square peep show. In Episode 1.6 ("Babylon"), Israeli representatives come to SC seeking aid in promoting Israeli tourism. To help with the process, they produce a copy of Leon Uris's wildly popular bestseller *Exodus* and note that it "is soon to be a major motion picture starring Paul Newman," as if that fact automatically means that the book must contain ideas that will appeal to American consumers, suggesting a strong correlation between the work done in Hollywood and the work done on Madison Avenue.

In perhaps the most extended engagement in the series with a particular film as a source of advertising ideas, Peggy, once again following Don's lead, also uses film as a sort of inspiration for her advertising ideas. In Episode 6.12 ("The Quality of Mercy"), she is charged with coming up with a campaign for St. Joseph's Aspirin. Despite the Shakespearean title (and the fact that the episode was first broadcast on Bloomsday), the principal cultural referent for this project is a film, the 1968 Roman Polanski horror classic *Rosemary's Baby*, still new in theaters (and making a sensation) as the events of this episode are taking place. In fact, the film is such a hit that Peggy decides to use it as the basis for the aspirin ad. Early in the episode, Don and Megan go to a late afternoon showing of the film and are visibly shaken by it. Preparing to exit the theater, they run into Peggy and Ted Chaough, who are seeing the film together (and who are in the early stages of a soon-to-be-aborted affair). Embarrassed to be caught together, Peggy and Ted quickly explain that they had to catch the film again as research for the TV spot they are doing based on the film. The ad is to be shot from the point of view of the ailing baby, who is offered various cures by the Satan worshippers from the film, only to have his mother step in and say, "You don't need anyone's help but St. Joseph's." It's a great ad, but far more complex and costly than the aspirin manufacturer originally bargained for. At the pitch, Don steps in when the client balks and gins up an explanation that Ted is so devoted to the idea because it was the last one proposed by Frank Gleason, Ted's recently deceased partner.

The implications of the ad are, incidentally, also more complex and ironic than might be indicated by a casual viewing. *Mad Men* in its earlier seasons had already addressed the question of the advertising of cigarettes and other tobacco products in the light of growing evidence of the health risks associated with such products. What the episode involving the *Rosemary's Baby* aspirin ad does not indicate (as Peggy and others in 1968 would not know) is that there are serious health risks associated with administering aspirin to babies. In particular, evidence of a link between aspirin and the onset of the potentially deadly Reye's syndrome in infants began to mount in the early 1980s, leading the U.S. Food and Drug Administration to demand warning labels on aspirin in 1986 that caution against its use with infants. As a result, Peggy and her colleagues, by working to encourage parents to give aspirin to their babies, are acting to promulgate a serious health risk, just as the advertising industry had earlier made a significant contribution to the spread of lung cancer and other health risks associated with tobacco use. The implied criticism of capitalism (and especially of the tobacco and pharmaceutical industries) as a system fueled by greed and willing to do untold harm to its customers in the quest for greater profits is quite clear.

From this point of view, *Rosemary's Baby* serves as an effective gloss on *Mad Men*'s critique of capitalism because its presence in the episode suggests that there is something downright Satanic about capitalist greed—though of course it also suggests that this greed, and not Satan, is a principal source of true evil in the world. In a similar way, *Rosemary's Baby* is a terrifying film not because it involves a conspiracy against a vulnerable young woman that is led by Satan, but because this conspiracy involves virtually all of the seemingly ordinary people who surround Rosemary, including her own husband, who has essentially sacrificed his wife in the interest of his own greed and professional ambitions, which Satan has promised to further. Rosemary, in short, is in many ways very much in the same position as the one in which Peggy (who is also surrounded by more powerful men, though she herself gradually gains more power as the series proceeds) continually finds herself in *Mad Men*, which helps to explain why Peggy might have found the film inspirational in the first place.

Incidentally, *Rosemary's Baby* had already figured in *Mad Men* a few episodes earlier—in Episode 6.8 ("The Crash")—when Don's daughter, Sally, was shown reading the Ira Levin novel on which the film was based. This double appearance suggests the importance of *Rosemary's Baby* as a marker of American culture, circa 1968; it also indicates that the story might be particularly important as a gloss on *Mad Men*. Within the context of "The Quality of Mercy," reading *Rosemary's Baby* in this way would clearly cast Peggy in the role of Rosemary, and it is certainly the case that she and Rosemary Woodhouse have much in common, including the fact that both come from relatively unsophisticated backgrounds but now live in crumbling apartment buildings in Manhattan where they are exposed to considerable dangers. They are also both surrounded by powerful men who often try to use them to further their own agendas. One must, of course, avoid being overly literal in making such connections, as the allegorical resonances of *Mad Men*, like the allegorical resonances in contemporary culture in general, are far more subtle and complex than a simple "table of one-to-one correspondences." Draper himself, for example, has many things in common with Rosemary Wood-house, as he almost must given the careful way in which the series has constructed its representation of Peggy as a sort of female Don following in the footsteps of her male mentor and role model. Meanwhile, both Peggy and Don might sometimes be seen as Satanic in their efforts to advance the interests of their soulless corporate clients.

In addition to using *Rosemary's Baby* as the source of the most promi-nent ad campaign she constructs in the series, Peggy also shares Don's love of the movies in their own right. In Episode 5.6 ("Far Away Places"), for example, she turns down boyfriend Abe Drexler's invitation to go see *The Naked Prey* (1965) because she is too preoccupied with work on Heinz beans. Even Abe's claim that the film sounds dirty and that it might give her a chance to see a naked Cornel Wilde wrestling a boa constrictor cannot stay her from her appointed rounds. Later, though, following a run-in with the Heinz beans rep in which she excoriates the man very much in the style of the old Don, a frustrated Peggy goes to see the film alone in the afternoon. In the near-empty theater, she accepts a toke from a stranger and then ends up giving him a handjob in return for the favor.

Finally, in Episode 5.4 ("Mystery Date"), Peggy shares a moment with Don's new African American secretary, Dawn, noting that she herself was once a secretary but was then "discovered" as a copywriting talent, comparing herself with Esther Blodgett, the rising star of *A Star Is Born* (played by Judy Garland in the 1954 version, which is probably the one of which Peggy is thinking). In fact, Peggy, modeling herself on Don here as in so many other ways, seems to become more and more immersed in film as *Mad Men* proceeds, while film in general becomes more impor-tant as a backdrop as the series goes on—even as the series also makes clear the advancing shift of cultural power from movies to television as the 1960s proceed.

Often, the series combines Don's attendance at movies with the use of movies to provide commentary on the historical context of the 1960s. For example, Episode 6.5 ("The Flood") is dominated by the assassination of Martin Luther King Jr., which occurred on April 4, 1968. Much of the episode deals with the awkward attempts of the white characters to cope with the news, though it ends with an attempt by Don to bond with son Bobby by taking him to the movies, though Don here of course is also seeking a way to cope with the shock of King's death. Among other things, this motif suggests the way in which the shared experience of watching movies can facilitate such bonding. What is particularly significant, however, is their choice of viewing fare, which in this case is the original *Planet of the Apes*, which had opened in the United States one day earlier. The outing is a success for the two Drapers, and father and son decide to remain in the theater to see it a second time. Between the showings, Bobby sums up one of the important functions of film in American culture when he says to the African American usher who is cleaning up in the aisle, presumably as a way of offering condolences for the death of Dr. King, "Everybody likes to go to the movies when they're sad."

The choice of this particular film is a good one for *Mad Men* as well because it so nicely illustrates the way in which Don is in fact correct in his perception that the movies often have a striking ability to reflect what is going on in American society at the time. *Planet of the Apes* is, most obviously, a science-fiction film that serves as a cautionary Cold War tale about the dangers of the nuclear arms race, which certainly makes it relevant to the political climate of the 1960s. However, it is also an allegory about the damaging social impact of racial intolerance, which makes it the perfect accompaniment to this particular episode—and which makes the timing of its release one day before the King assassination especially striking.

What is also striking about this timing is that Stanley Kubrick's *2001: A Space Odyssey*, one of the landmark films in science-fiction history, premiered in New York on exactly that same April 3, making it perhaps the most important single date in the history of the genre. That film also becomes a particularly important intertextual referent later in *Mad Men*, especially in the way that film's crucial use of the HAL-9000 intelligent computer serves as a commentary on the introduction of a new IBM-360 computer into the advertising firm's offices in Season 7. Episode 7.4 ("The Monolith") takes its title from one of the central images of *2001* and includes many other visual references as well, calling attention to the thematic relevance of this film to what is going on in the series at the time.

Interestingly, despite such thematic use of films (and despite the acknowledgment of a correlation between films and advertising as cultural phenomena), *Mad Men* makes relatively little use of the obvious expedient of referring to movies that are explicitly about advertising or business or in other ways directly relevant to the series. Perhaps the most obvious film in this category is the 1956 entry *The Man in the Gray Flannel Suit*, based on the 1955 novel by Sloan Wilson, one of the signature books of the decade. In the film, ad man Tom Rath (also a man with a secret in his past) is played by Gregory Peck, probably (along with Gary Cooper) the major movie star of whom Jon Hamm's turn as Don Draper is most reminiscent. But Rath comes from an earlier era, his conformist manner of dress indicating the banal conservatism of the marketing and advertising strategies of the 1950s. Granted, Don is something of a throwback, somewhat old-fashioned in many ways. And he often doesn't "get" the sixties, but he does get the need for more diverse and innovative advertising of a kind that would have been out of place in the stodgy world of Tom Rath. He is also a stylish if conservative dresser, his business suits always somehow looking a bit better than those of the other suit-clad businessmen who surround him, so it is no real surprise that the 1956 film is seldom evoked as a precedent in the series. In fact, it is mentioned only once, in Episode 2.9 ("Six Month Leave"), when Don's old nemesis, shock comedian Jimmy Barrett, greets him in an illegal gambling establishment by exclaiming, "Well, if it isn't the man in the gray flannel suit!" Don lets us know what he thinks of Barrett (and the allusion) when he answers with a punch to the face.

Even more subtle is the allusive casting of an aging Robert Morse as old Bert Cooper, Sterling Cooper's patriarch and senior partner, forty years earlier an inspired young go-getter but now just a touch out of it. For many viewers, this casting is itself allusive and cannot fail to evoke the 1967 musical comedy *How to Succeed in Business Without Really Trying*, which featured a young Morse in what was surely his best-known role—as an inspired young go-getter who rises to become chairman of the board of his firm—exactly forty years before the premiere of *Mad Men*. In the film, Morse's Ponty Finch uses rather unscrupulous (though charming) methods to rise to the top, and one can imagine that the Ayn Rand–loving Cooper has used some pretty ruthless methods in his day as well, even though he now seems a rather avuncular old coot.

In addition to their use as a source of advertising ideas, movies often impact the world of *Mad Men* in other ways, as they do the real world. In Episode 3.11 ("The Gypsy and the Hobo"), for example, Annabelle Mathis, a long-ago flame of Roger Sterling, hires Sterling Cooper to help rescue her struggling dog-food company, whose sales have plummeted in the wake of the recent film (starring Clark Gable and Marilyn Monroe) *The Misfits* (1961), which cast a bad light on the dog-food industry. Meanwhile, *The Misfits* itself plays a special role in American film culture, as it was the final film for both Gable and Monroe, two of the biggest stars in film history. "We're all dying, aren't we?" says Monroe's Roslyn Tabor early in *The Misfits* , and she couldn't have been more right. Within months after the film wrapped, both she and costar Clark Gable would be dead.

Monroe, possibly the Hollywood star whose image had the most impact beyond film of any star in history, casts a long shadow over the early seasons of *Mad Men*. In Episode 2.6 ("Maidenform"), Paul Kinsey comes up with perhaps his best advertising idea of the entire series when he suggests (in a campaign for Playtex bras) that American womanhood is embodied in the two opposed (but complementary) figures of Monroe and Jackie Kennedy. The campaign doesn't fly (due to Playtex's conservatism), a fact that comes as a great relief to Sterling Cooper soon afterward in Episode 2.9 ("Six Month Leave") when Marilyn dies of an apparent suicide, an event that casts a pall over the entire episode—and that would no doubt have torpedoed the proposed Playtex campaign.

Marilyn Monroe, of course, was one of the most recognizable stars in Hollywood history, and all of the characters in *Mad Men* seem quite familiar with her. Importantly, though, Don Draper's awareness of film goes well beyond a simple knowledge of the best-known films and stars. In Episode 2.5 ("The New Girl"), Don's lover Bobbie Barrett invites him to her beach house in Stony Brook (Long Island), having learned that he likes the ocean. On the drive out, she also learns that he likes bridges and asks what else he likes. "Movies," he immediately responds, with a thoughtful smile. She agrees that movies are appealing, citing Stanley Kubrick's 1960 film *Spartacus* as an example, then notes that foreign films are especially appealing because they are "so sexy." Don nods knowingly and simply says, "*La notte,*" citing the 1961 Italian film directed by Michelangelo Antonioni, which deals with the infidelity that is part of a deteriorating marriage. The film thus might have special relevance to Don's own life, but his familiarity with it suggests that his engagement with film goes beyond the American hits that might be expected to be most valuable as advertising material.

As Robert Rushing has pointed out, *La notte* is not merely sexy: it is an intellectually challenging film that "stresses interpersonal, socioeconomic, and existential forms of alienation" (2013, 193). Moreover, Rushing notes that Antonioni is a prominent presence in *Mad Men*, which is entirely appropriate given both Don's love of film and the extent to which Italian films were popular in the United States in the early 1960s (192–93). Rushing goes on to suggest that *Mad Men* shares three basic concerns with the films of Antonioni in general: "(1) the impenetrable surface of things, especially other people; (2) the fragility and fluidity of identity . . . and (3) a dedication to watching things—especially people— disappear" (194). In short, Rushing sees *Mad Men* as a complex work of art that explores fundamental issues in a manner reminiscent of the best and most complex of films.

As in the case of *La notte*, the specific films referenced in *Mad Men* are often chosen quite carefully for their thematic relevance, though it sometimes takes some digging to determine just what that relevance is. At the beginning of Episode 7.3 ("Field Trip"), Don is once again at the movies in a New York theater, this time watching *Model Shop* (1969), an English-language French-American coproduction directed by French director Jacques Demy—in a mode that is, in fact, reminiscent of Antonioni. We see a brief moment from the film in the episode, though not enough to reveal the full relevance of it to the situation of the episode, which deals with Don's problematic relationship with his actress wife, who is now living in Los Angeles to pursue her career. *Model Shop* does have a plot (featuring a problematic relationship between an American man and a French woman) that vaguely speaks to Don relationship with his French-Canadian wife. But the strength of the film is its ultra-colorful cinematography, which provides a vivid and fascinated portrait of late 1960s Los Angeles, which seems (for the European Demy) to serve as a sort of mysterious and exotic locale, much as Los Angeles tends to feature in *Mad Men* in general.

Demy, incidentally, was at the time still riding a wave of international prominence from his earlier film *The Umbrellas of Cherbourg* (1964), which itself garnered a passing mention in Episode 4.3 ("The Good News"), when a lonely Don hangs out on New Year's Eve with an equally lonely Lane Pryce (who has just learned that he is seemingly about to join Don in the ranks of the divorced) in the offices of the still-new Sterling Cooper Draper Pryce. They decide to pass the evening (as is Don's wont) by going to the movies, and one of the films they consider seeing is none other than *The Umbrellas of Cherbourg*, a prospect that brightens Don's visage for a moment when he recalls that it stars Catherine Deneuve. In the event, however, they simply get drunk and attend a screening of *Godzilla* in a seedy theater before going on to spend the rest of the night at dinner and with prostitutes.

As Deanna K. Kreisel (2014) usefully points out, George, the protagonist of *Model Shop*, is a rather typical cool-but-aimless-and-troubled French New Wave male hero, as such serving as something of a role model for Don himself. Meanwhile, the scene that Don watches features George driving in an antique auto that is surrounded by more contemporary autos, potentially suggesting the situation in which Don (who is at least in certain modes an old-fashioned guy) often finds himself. Kreisel also notes that this episode of *Mad Men* includes a scene in which another character, the ultra-mediocre Lou Avery (Allan Havey) explicitly, though fleetingly, compares Don with Longfellow Deeds, the protagonist of Frank Capra's *Mr. Deeds Goes to Town* (1936). The comparison is apt, as Deeds (like Don, a country bumpkin who becomes a rich New Yorker) serves as another clear cinematic analog for Don's identity, even if on distinctly different terms. Of course, the cool *nouvelle vague* hero and the hardy Deeds are about as far apart as two movie characters can be. That both of them clearly echo parts of Don's personality demonstrate just how strained and fragmented and contradictory that personality can be.

That Don's personality can be so multifarious should come as no surprise. The "Don Draper" featured in the series is a self-made man who has literally manufactured his own identity, and it is clear that his self-fashioning has included a liberal contribution from his viewing of films, somewhat in the same way (as convincingly demonstrated by Michael Rogin) the identity of Ronald Reagan was carefully crafted from materials that were largely derived from the movies. For Rogin, Reagan "found how who he was through the roles he played on film," ultimately merging his real-life identity with those of the characters he played in movies (1988, 3). Of course, Don has essentially abandoned his real-life identity (though it still haunts him); he is always playing a role, always performing the identity of someone else, though it is also the case that this someone else is not the "real" Don Draper who died in Korea, but simply a fictional version invented by the substitute Don Draper, who is thus a sort of walking simulacrum, a copy of a man who never existed in the first place. Dick Whitman, in becoming "Don Draper," merely assumes the name of the dead man, not his identity. That identity itself remains an empty container, a blank slate ready to be written on and loaded with content, but also subject to constant erasure and re-emptying, to ongoing change and revision.

The movies are, for Don, a prime source of this constantly evolving content, so it should come as no surprise that he also turns to cinema when he is in need of content for the advertising campaigns that he is so noted for creating. Indeed, his creation of his identity and his creation of advertising are very much part of the same process. He is a builder of images, whether they be the images used to market products to potential consumers or the images of himself that he presents to the world, which is also, of course, a matter of marketing as well. His own identity, in fact, is very much like the ads he creates. Don lives in a hyperreal world of images that is essentially devoid of any contact with concrete reality; this fact, combined with the fact that his identity is so fragmented and tenuous, his temporal bandwidth so narrow, suggests that Don is the prototype of the postmodern subject, as described by Fredric Jameson.

One can, in fact, describe the overall project of *Mad Men* as the narration of the emergence of postmodernism (which, per Jameson, is also the story of the emergence of late capitalism) as a cultural dominant in America. Then again, *Mad Men* can also be seen as the narrative of the rise of technology as the most important force determining the texture of daily life in America—or as the story of the rise of the media (especially television) as a force saturating and penetrating every aspect of life in America. Most fundamentally, the series can be seen as the narrative of the death of the American Dream. It is, in fact, a series that lends itself especially well to characterization via such capsule summaries, very much in the mode of the advertising slogans Don and Peggy and their colleagues are so good at creating. *Mad Men* operates, in fact, very much like an extended advertisement; but it is also a highly cinematic series that acts very much like a movie. Indeed, one of the things the series demonstrates most clearly is just how similar movies and advertisements really are, as they should be in the world of an emerging postmodernism in which all such cultural artifacts are in the process of being reduced to commodities, all commodities being interchangeable with all others.

7

THE SCIENCE FICTION OF *MAD MEN*

In Episode 7.10 ("The Forecast"), Roger Sterling, now president of a Sterling Cooper that has been reconstituted as a subsidiary of the much larger McCann Erickson, assigns Don Draper the corporate-bullshit task of producing a "Gettysburg Address–type statement" outlining the firm's vision for its future. "Just reasonable hopes and dreams. It doesn't have to be science fiction," Sterling explains. But *Mad Men*, we know, *is* in a very real sense science fiction. At the inception of the series, creator Matt Weiner (a self-professed fan of science fiction) famously declared his view that the series was a form of science fiction that was intended to address issues in the here and now (such as racism and sexism) by presenting those same issues through the defamiliarizing lens of a shift to a different time. Thus, the series employs a strategy similar to that of conventional science fiction, except that the normal science-fiction leap into the future is replaced by a leap into the past. In addition, one of the key ways in which *Mad Men* situates itself in the historical context of the 1960s is through a careful tracing of a variety of cutting-edge developments in contemporary technology, from space-age rockets to disposable diapers. In addition, *Mad Men* situates itself in the culture of the 1960s through references to a variety of contemporary works, many of which are themselves science fiction. Finally, *Mad Men* often relies for its effects on surprising, even shocking moments that produce cognitive estrangement in viewers of a kind that theorists of science fiction have long associated with the genre.

2001: A Space Odyssey (1968). ©MGM

Sometimes, the defamiliarizing perspective of the 1960s is used for largely comic effect, but even then the reminders of how clunky certain technologies were in the 1960s serves as an important reminder of just how far we have come. For example, in Episode 7.2 ("A Day's Work"), the newly bicoastal Sterling Cooper & Partners attempts to hold a partners' meeting via conference call, two of the partners (Ted Chaough and Pete Campbell) now being located on the West Coast. Communication turns out to be comically difficult, as everyone stumbles over themselves trying to determine if the partners on the other end can actually hear them, with most participants yelling at the top of their lungs in an effort to be heard, while others worry about the astronomical cost of the long-distance call. This scene, however amusing, provides a stark reminder of just how far the technology of business has come since 1969 (when this episode is set), while also reminding us that it was indeed for the convenience of capitalist enterprise that the vast increases in communications technology (so vast, in fact, that they have the texture of science fiction) since that time were primarily made.

Of course, science fiction itself is not always set in the future and has sometimes achieved cognitive estrangement through settings in the past, as in the cases of alternate histories and steampunk. In addition, as Fredric Jameson has noted, science fiction set in the future often plays a role in today's culture similar to that played by the historical novel in the past, but with a focus on the future rather than the past. Noting Lukács's identification in *The Historical Novel* of the work of Flaubert as a marker of the collapse of the conventional historical novel in the late nineteenth century, Jameson suggests that it is no coincidence that this same historical moment also saw the rise of science fiction in the work of Jules Verne. For Jameson,

> We are therefore entitled to complete Lukács account of the historical novel with the counter-panel of its opposite number, the emergence of the new genre of SF as a form which now registers some nascent sense of the future, and does so on the space on which a sense of the past had once been inscribed. (2005, 285–86)

For Jameson, the historical novel and science fiction are twinned genres that can be viewed as performing similar functions because past, present, and future are all part of the same historical process. If the historical novel reminds us of the pastness of the past, science fiction conventionally reminds us of the futurity of the future. In both cases, we are urged to recall that the present in which we live is not eternal but part of an ever-evolving process that can work fundamental changes in the way we live.

This suggestion that thinking historically works both forward and backward in time resonates in an interesting way with the advertising strategies typically employed by Sterling Cooper and its various successors in *Mad Men*. Many of the firm's younger creative personalities (such as Paul Kinsey) tend to favor what might be called science-fictional advertising strategies, touting the futuristic properties of the products they are attempting to sell. Thus, very early in the series (Episode 1.2, "Ladies Room"), the firm is charged with coming up with an ad campaign for

Gillette's new Right Guard deodorant in a spray can. Kinsey responds with an approach that emphasizes the high-tech nature of the product, building upon the physical resemblance of the can itself to a rocket. This campaign points toward the important role that will be played by the space race throughout the series, at least up until Episode 7.7 ("Waterloo"), which features the Apollo 11 moon landing. On the other hand, Kinsey's high-flying idea is immediately shot down by Don Draper, who is in a bad mood from budding domestic problems at home. But, bad mood or not, Draper's dismissal of Kinsey's idea is rather predictable given Don's consistent preference for the sentimental and nostalgic campaigns, often attempting to hawk new products by linking them in the imaginations of consumers to good times in their own pasts.

Kinsey, in fact, is often shot down by Draper in the series, as in Episode 2.11 ("The Jet Set"), in which Kinsey (representing "creative") and Pete Campbell (representing "accounts") are set to travel to Los Angeles to attend a "Rocket Fair," hoping to round up new business from the high-tech aerospace firms that will be attending the convention. At the last minute, Draper decides to displace Kinsey and go to the convention himself, leaving Kinsey (something of a would-be science-fiction writer) stewing because he will now be unable to visit the land in which Edgar Rice Burroughs had established his Tarzana Ranch nearly half a century earlier. It eventually becomes clear that Kinsey had other motivations for wanting to go to California, as the trip would give him an excuse to escape his commitment to his new black girlfriend to accompany her on a Freedom Ride into the Deep South, a trip about which Kinsey (not the bravest of souls) is experiencing severe trepidations. This motif is presented in the episode without comment, though anyone with a knowledge of the background of Tarzana will appreciate the delicious irony of the fact that the Tarzana community had initially been established by Burroughs as a segregated white enclave, complete with a panoply of racist discourse derived from the history of the British Empire.

A little knowledge might be a dangerous thing, but it can sometimes go a long way in helping one to appreciate such moments in *Mad Men*. Of course, in line with the notion that *Mad Men* is science fiction set in the past, even Don sometimes turns to the language of science fiction in constructing his past-oriented pitches. Season 1 of the series ends, for example, with Episode 1.13 ("The Wheel"), in which Don delivers what is perhaps his greatest pitch of the entire series. Here, Don describes his campaign for the new Kodak carousel slide projector, which, because of its shape and innovative technology, was envisioned as a flying saucer analog. Don, though, argues that the carousel is not a spaceship, but a nostalgia-fueled time machine that takes its users back to the fondest times of their past lives. The pitch is, of course, a success, and Sterling Cooper gets the Kodak account. In fact, it is such a success that even Don is overtaken by a fit of family-oriented nostalgia, given the fact that his own childhood family history was so grim. Having already arranged to send the wife and kids off packing to visit Betty's family for the upcoming Thanksgiving holiday, Don rushes home after the pitch so he can join them after all. Of course, when he arrives home, he finds that they have already left, leaving him in his customary lone state as the episode and the first season of the series come to an end. Families may function perfectly in Don's carefully tailored advertising visions, but they don't work very well in real life as depicted in *Mad Men*, suggesting the extent to which idyllic images of family bliss are merely fiction, part of the mythology of an American life that is becoming increasingly manufactured and commodified as the 1960s roll forward.

The action of *Mad Men* spans the entire decade of the 1960s, a decade during much of which science fiction in both film and television was in something of a lull. Still, 1966 saw the emergence of what would go on to be arguably the most influential work in the history of the genre, television's original *Star Trek* series, which debuted on NBC on September 8, 1966, and lasted for three seasons, despite consistently low ratings. Predictably, *Star Trek* makes an appearance in *Mad Men*, in Episode 5.10 ("Christmas Waltz"), which takes place during Christmas season of 1966. Here, Kinsey (having disappeared from the series amid the various reshufflings of its central advertising firm) resurfaces, now having become (in good 1960s fashion) a Hare Krishna. But he has also continued to pursue his dream of being a science-fiction writer, which we learn when he approaches Harry Crane (who has become the firm's central liaison with the television industry) hoping that Crane can use his business contacts with NBC to help Kinsey market the new script he has just written for an episode of *Star Trek*.

Kinsey seems, by this time, to have fallen pretty much off the deep end, so it comes as no surprise that the script is not a good one. In fact, from what we hear about it, it reads more like a parody of *Star Trek* than an actual episode, though it is in fact a work of heavy-handed racial allegory, on which *Trek* episodes such as "Let That Be Your Last Battle-field" (January 10, 1969) fundamentally relied. Kinsey's script is also a virtual parody of the science-fictional strategy of cognitive estrangement, presenting a world that is recognizably similar to our own history but with several key parameters reversed. In particular, it features a planet populated by a white race and a black race that employs slavery as a key element of its economic structure. The kicker is that the whites are the slaves and the blacks are the masters—and to make matters even more "surprising," the "Negrons" of the title are actually the white race, rather than the black.

If Crane's reaction is any indication, the clumsiness of this allegory is matched by the clumsiness of the writing in general. It's so bad, in fact, that Crane elects not to risk his reputation by even attempting to hawk the script, though he tries to placate Kinsey by telling him that the *Star Trek* people loved the script but just aren't currently in the market for unsolic-ited manuscripts. He then gives Kinsey money and urges him to head for California to try to make a new start there as a science-fiction writer, a suggestion that echoes Kinsey's own earlier identification of California as a locus of science-fiction writing in "The Jet Set."

Even when *Mad Men* refers to specific works of science fiction, it often does so in extremely complex ways the significance of which re-quires considerable unpacking. A good case in point is Episode 6.5 ("The Flood"), which centers on the assassination of Dr. Martin Luther King. With practically everyone in the episode feeling sad and distraught (and awkward, as when they feel they must offer personal condolences to Dawn, Don's black secretary) over the assassination, Don decides to take his son Bobby to the movies to see *Planet of the Apes*, which, in fact, had opened in New York on April 3, 1968, just one day before Dr. King's shooting.

In addition to the coincidence of dates, *Planet of the Apes* provides a perfect gloss on this *Mad Men* episode, which focuses on race, racism, and the clumsiness with which Americans deal with both. *Planet of the Apes* was also a landmark in the evolution of science-fiction films. For example, the film is an impressive technical achievement in many ways, including its now-famous Oscar-winning ape makeup. However, most of the considerable serious critical attention given the film and its sequels has focused not on their technical achievements but on their political implications and their serious treatment of issues such as the possibility of nuclear holocaust. This particular issue is, in fact, the most obvious one in the original film, but the most important political commentary of that film (and, especially, its sequels) probably resides in the way the depiction of relations between apes and humans can be read as allegorizations of the relations between different human races in our own world, especially in the United States. As Eric Greene has argued, these racial allegories and other political aspects of the film are what make it truly important as a cultural artifact. For Greene, "the makers of the *Apes* films created fictional spaces whose social tensions resembled those then dominating the United States. They inserted characters into those spaces whose ideologies, passions, and fears duplicated the ideologies, passions, and fears of generations of Americans. And they placed those characters in conflicts that replicated crucial conflicts from the United States; past and present" (1998, 9).

Interestingly, Draper's viewing of *Planet of the Apes* is quickly duplicated in Episode 6.9 ("The Better Half"), when Roger Sterling attempts to follow Don's example of parental bonding by taking his four-year-old grandson to see the same film. Apparently, however, the cognitive estrangement in this film is a bit much for the underage boy, who is subsequently so traumatized that his mother fears they will have to get rid of the family dog because her son is now so "afraid of fur."

Planet of the Apes was not the only major science-fiction film released that spring. While much of the 1960s was a relatively fallow period for the production of science-fiction film, that same April 3, 1968, also saw the New York premiere of Stanley Kubrick's *2001: A Space Odyssey*, meaning that two of the most important films in all of science-fiction history were released on the same day, at least in terms of their official New York premieres. Not surprisingly, *2001* also figures prominently in *Mad Men*, more prominently, in fact, than does *Planet of the Apes* . Indeed, while Don Draper also attends *2001* in the course of the sixth season of the series, that film becomes particularly important in the seventh and last season when it becomes a crucial gloss of some of the most important themes of the series.

One example is Episode 7.4 ("The Monolith"), the title of which (accompanied by specific visual cues) is a clear reference to the large monoliths that periodically appear to announce the onset of a new leap forward in human evolution. The presence of the film in *Mad Men* thus helps to support the contention of the series that the decade of the 1960s was a major turning point in American history in a number of ways, including the importance and function of technology. One of the great achievements of *2001* is its ability to present technology as beautiful and graceful, almost more a form of art than of machinery. But it also suggests a sinister side to this technology, which can become so advanced as to outstrip its human makers, making them unable to control their own creations.

"The Monolith," meanwhile, is built around the somewhat science-fictional theme of the introduction of a massive new computer into the offices of SC&P in 1969, a theme that had already been anticipated in Harry Crane's complaints in the previous episode that the firm was losing a potential competitive edge by not having a computer.

Commenting on that previous episode (7.3, "Field Trip"), Donna Kreisel has noted that the role of the (then nonexistent) computer is clear, setting up an opposition between the work of talented humans like Draper and the soulless, number-crunching otherness of the computer: "The face-off is made explicit: an 'old-fashioned' and romanticized vision of humanistic (and human) inspiration and creativity versus a future-oriented, mechanistic brute intelligence that threatens to render human agency obsolete." This opposition, of course, goes well beyond the offices of this specific advertising firm and was, in fact, a central reality of the trajectory of the 1960s, so that the events of the series, as always, are placed firmly within that trajectory.

The significance of the new computer, an IBM 360, can best be understood by looking back to the key year of 1964, when that hugely successful line was introduced, for the first time making available an entire range of computers of different sizes with extensive compatibility and expandability, including interchangeability of a number of components and allowing smaller versions to be expanded to larger ones at any time. The introduction of the IBM 360, which turned the previously exotic (and science-fictional) device of the computer into a genuine commodity, brought about an unprecedented penetration of computers into various aspects of American life, so that, by the end of the 1960s, computers were being extensively used in a variety of American businesses and institutions, whereas before they had been largely limited to research facilities and large corporations.

It is thus appropriate that a key event in the final season of *Mad Men* involved the 1969 installation of an IBM 360 in the offices of the relatively small advertising agency featured in the series, an installation that requires considerable reshuffling of the limited space in the offices, making the computer the dominant feature—as opposed to the previous setup, in which the centerpiece of the offices had been a "creative lounge," where various creative types interact and explore ideas. The symbolism of introducing this computer in an episode that overtly refers to *2001: A Space Odyssey* is quite clear: the computer marks the beginning of a new stage in the development of the agency (and American advertising industry and American society as a whole), just as the famous monoliths of *2001* marked the beginnings of new epochs in the evolution of the human species.

2001: A Space Odyssey, through the figure of its HAL 9000 computer, which attempts (murderously) to wrest control of the central space mission in that film from the human crew, also deals centrally with the threat posed to human hegemony by ultra-advanced computers. Similarly, there is a certain implication in *Mad Men* that the introduction of the IBM 360 into the advertising agency's offices represents a sort of spiritual death for the firm, signaling the end of the era when advertising was dominated by genuine human creativity, with artist figures such as Draper soon to be supplanted by bureaucrats and management types. The computer thus announces the beginning of a new machine-dominated age when advertising itself would become as commodified as the products it attempts to sell.

The brilliant, groundbreaking *2001* brought new cultural respectability to the whole genre of science-fiction film, demonstrating that such films could be genuine works of art. Indeed, even the technological devices featured in the film are often works of art, and one of the most striking aspects of this extremely striking film is the sheer beauty of the technology represented in the film. *2001* is, however, anything but an unmitigated celebration of technology. In particular, the film's most remembered image is probably the intelligent HAL 9000 that goes off the rails and murders most of the human crew of the space expedition that provides the central plot arc of the film. As a major cultural event in its own right, *2001* firmly established the notion of artificially intelligent computers as potential dangers to humans, at the same time introducing a new wrinkle into the fear of intellectuals that pervades much of American cultural history. The ultra-logical HAL 9000 is a new sort of movie character. But in some ways he is a quintessential pop-cultural intellectual: devoid of human feeling, he is so caught up in logical thought that he loses touch with common sense, despite his vast processing power.

HAL was the first major example of a threatening artificial intelligence in American film. It is thus a key marker of the film's achievement that he remains the most prominent example of this important motif nearly a half-century later. It was, in fact, the influence of *2001* that helped to establish artificial intelligences as key "villains" in science-fiction film. That the IBM 360 in *Mad Men* is also to be seen as villainous is marked in the series in all sorts of ways, including the fact that its introduction finally drives Michael Ginsberg (already a high-strung creative type) off the deep end into full-on paranoia.

A key sign of this paranoia, incidentally, occurs in the next episode (7.5, "The Runaways"), when Ginsberg observes Lou Avery (the firm's new, highly uncreative head of creative in the wake of Draper's exile) conferring with Jim Cutler (the new, less-charming counterpart to Roger Sterling, acquired in the recent merger of SCDP and CGC) inside the sealed glass room that contains the new computer, computers at that time requiring highly controlled environments in order to operate efficiently. Unable to hear because of the enclosed room, Ginsberg can nevertheless see the lips of the two men moving, and he attempts to read their lips very much in the way HAL attempts to read the lips of two astronauts who are plotting against him in *2001*. Eventually, the perceived threat posed by the computer will drive Ginsberg into insanity and self-mutilation, though this odd moment of lip-reading complicates the reference to *2001* by placing the computer-phobic human Ginsberg in the position of the film's human-phobic computer.

Ginsberg's reaction to the computer, which involves a belief that the computer plans to turn them all into "homos" and ultimately involves cutting off his own nipple (to open the "valve") and presenting it to Peggy in a gift box, seems a bit extreme. But Ginsberg, born in a concentration camp and then orphaned (though at one point in the series he claims to be from Mars), has had an extreme life and perhaps has good reason to be paranoid. And there have been signs of this paranoia before, as when, in Episode 6.10 ("A Tale of Two Cities"), he becomes upset with Cutler and calls him a fascist. Following the Freudian-Lacanian view that artistic types can ward off insanity by sublimating their unconscious energies into their creative endeavors, one might speculate that Ginsberg has now lost that remedy due to his feeling that the computer is making his work as a "creative" obsolete. Following a more historical arc, meanwhile, one could argue that Ginsberg's mental illness is a sign of the general sickness of modern society, a sickness that at least partly emanates from having never properly dealt with the twin phenomena of Nazism and the Holocaust.

Ultimately, the claim that *Mad Men* can be viewed as a kind of science fiction probably rests less firmly on the series' frequent references to science fiction and frequent use of the iconography of science fiction than on its use of the central aesthetic/affective strategy of science fiction: cognitive estrangement. One of the most striking overall characteristics of *Mad Men* is its ongoing ability to surprise even its most loyal viewers with sudden moments of jarring strangeness (such as Ginsberg's surprising nipple-ectomy), very much in the mode of the best science fiction—as famously noted long ago by Darko Suvin. For Suvin, cognitive estrangement is the central strategy of science fiction as a genre, which for him is distinguished by its ability to unsettle audiences from their customary habits of thought by projecting them into strange, new worlds that are different from their own. Moreover, they are different in ways that encourage audiences to think about these differences and to wonder what has caused them—triggering a process of interrogation that presumably helps to open the audiences for science fiction to new ways of thinking about the world. Cognitive estrangement in science fiction (like the "estrangement effect" in the epic theater of Bertolt Brecht, from which Suvin in fact took the basic idea) can thus potentially serve a strongly utopian function by helping audiences to realize that the world could be different than what it is.

Mad Men's moments of strangeness often perform a similarly positive political function. A classic case occurs in Episode 3.3 ("My Old Kentucky Home"). Here, Roger Sterling and new wife Jane host a Derby Day garden party (placing this episode in the first weekend of May 1963, when the Kentucky Derby was won by Chateaugay) attended mostly by pretentious rich snobs, though a number of the less-rich principals from Sterling Cooper (including Don and Betty) attend as well. The setting itself is no doubt estranging to most of today's viewers, who will never circulate in such an environment of genteel wealth and privilege, itself something of a throwback, even in 1963, to earlier times. Indeed, hearing of the party, Smitty immediately responds, "Going back in time?"

As it turns out, the party does indeed reach back into the past when it is highlighted (or perhaps lowlighted) by Roger's stirring rendition of "My Old Kentucky Home" in full blackface, with a giggling Jane by his side, already well on her way to the full-on inebriation that will later in the party become something of an embarrassment. Roger, the charming rogue who has lived his life in a cocoon of privilege that often makes him indifferent to the problems of others, is clearly clueless concerning the racist implications of his song. But even in 1963, this performance is problematic enough that it drives Don (who has enjoyed no such cocoon until very recently in his life) from the gathering to seek sanctuary elsewhere. For viewers in 2009, meanwhile, the scene cannot help but serve as a jarring reminder of the extent to which racist attitudes could be publicly (and proudly) performed less than fifty years earlier. The rich, in 2009, were of course still rather indifferent to the sufferings of the less fortunate, but the scene serves as a reminder that some things have at least changed between 1963 and 2009; moreover, if some things change, other things can change as well. The scene thus serves both as a stern reminder of how deeply ingrained racism is in American society and as a suggestion that even such fundamental attitudes can indeed change over time. It thus contains a potentially powerful utopian reminder of the possibility of change, as does the best science fiction, per Suvin. Meanwhile, this episode's representation of the party, which also features a rousing performance of the Charleston by Pet and Trudy, suggests the general way in which the rich are still rooted in the past, oblivious to the sweeping changes that are on the horizon in American society.

The sudden intrusions of shocking events that punctuate *Mad Men* often carry with them a similar political charge. In Episode 2.3 ("The Benefactor"), for example, as the principals at Sterling Cooper try to repair the damage done to their relations with the Utz potato chip company by the barbs of insult comedian Jimmy Barrett, Don pulls Barrett's wife, Bobbie, aside for a consultation. That Bobbie clearly serves essentially as the manager of the out-of-control Jimmy makes this consultation perfectly understandable, even though the male-dominated world of the series makes Bobbie's status stand out. What shocks us, though, is that Don turns vicious when he gets Bobbie alone: not only does he threaten Bobbie in no uncertain terms, suddenly dropping his smooth visage, but he violently grabs her by the crotch to emphasize his threat. Granted, it soon becomes clear that Don and Bobbie are involved in an affair (one that nearly wrecks the Draper marriage after Betty finds out about it), which makes this rather intimate threat a bit less out of the blue. Nevertheless, the revelation of this gangsterish/sadistic side of Don, already clearly the protagonist of the series, surely came as quite a shock to viewers conditioned to expect that such protagonists would be virtuous and heroic good guys. Moreover, the particular sexual violence with which this threat is issued was unprecedented on American commercial television—and really in American culture in general, where such crotch-grabbing threats had only been seen when directed at men. The implication is clear: if Bobbie wants to wear the pants in the family, she is going to have to face up to that responsibility like a man. The swirl of gender-based implications surrounding this moment is very rich—and made richer by the shocking nature of the scene as well as the disorienting reversal of genders that it involves.

Don's sometimes erratic behavior is often the source of defamiliarizing moments in *Mad Men*, as when his rough treatment of Bobbie Barrett is to some extent echoed in "The Monolith" when he suddenly confronts Lloyd Hawley, the man responsible for installing the IBM 360 in the firm's offices, with whom he had earlier had a perfectly friendly conversation about the possibility of creating an advertising campaign for Hawley's computer firm. Out of the blue, Don warns Hawley that "you talk like a friend, but you're not." "I know your name," he tells him, in a rather threatening manner. "No, you go by many names, but I know who you *are*. You don't need a campaign. You've got the best campaign since the dawn of time." Don's hostility might be understandable given the structural opposition in this episode between the kind of humanistic tradition represented by Don and his typical advertising strategies and the runaway posthumanist modernization represented by the computer. Still, it seems a bit over the top, especially in the suggestive way Don describes Hawley almost as a kind of vaguely inhuman (perhaps Satanic, perhaps capitalistic) villain, his words echoing both *2001: A Space Odyssey* and things such as the Rolling Stones classic "Sympathy for the Devil," which had first appeared on the December 1968 album *Beggars Banquet* and which was still quite current at the time of this episode.

Draper also experiences several moments in which he undergoes what appear to be hallucinations or visions, though these can often be recuperated realistically as either simple flashbacks or the effects of alcohol or drugs. At other times, Draper's "visions" are not so easy to explain away.

Sometimes, as when he sees a clear vision of his father in Episode 3.7 ("Seven Twenty Three"), the event can fairly easily be attributed to the effects of mind-altering substances such as alcohol or drugs. In other cases, the source of the vision is harder to locate, as in the stunning moment at the end of the first half of Season 7, when Draper suddenly experiences a vision of the recently deceased Bertram Cooper performing a soft shoe and singing "The Best Things in Life Are Free," accompanied by a group of scantily clad dancing secretaries and creating a scene that looks like something out of Dennis Potter. This moment is strange for a number of reasons, even beyond the obvious one that Cooper has recently died. In particular, the song itself is a sort of anti-materialist, even anti-capitalist anthem, and the irony of the fact that Cooper (a follower of Ayn Rand) chooses this particular song for his "comeback" is especially telling. One could, of course, argue that death has changed his perspective or that such a change was wrought by his last (somewhat science-fictional) experience in life—watching the Apollo 11 moon landing on July 20, 1969. After all, a key line in "The Best Things in Life Are Free" declares that "the moon belongs to everyone," suggesting the moon as an image of the fact that there are bigger things than the tawdry capitalist scramble for profits.

Of course, one could argue that the choice is actually Draper's and that it functions as part of his ongoing questioning of the ethos of business, which has driven his career to the brink of ruin even as he seeks to return to the real roots of his success in his love for the art of advertising, rather than its commercial aspects, which have gradually taken over his life and work. In short, as in the very best science fiction, Cooper's posthumous soft-shoe routine raises questions that demand cognitive responses—and responses that might have strong political connotations, while suggesting that the world might be very different than it is. How are we to interpret this scene, for example? Self-referential, nonrealist postmodern shenanigans that mirror the workings of advertisements, while commenting on the fundamentally dishonest nature of those workings? A sign of Draper's own cognitive dissonance due either to his impending psychic collapse or to his estrangement from the dog-eat-dog ethos of modern capitalism? A simple nod to the song-and-dance talents of Robert Morse—though one that possibly isn't so simple, because it evokes a link to Morse's best-known role in the 1967 musical comedy *How to Succeed in Business*

Without Really Trying, which itself satirizes corporate ethics (or the lack thereof)?

Such questions clearly align *Mad Men* with the best science fiction. Given this alignment, the periodic allusions in the series to specific works of science fiction, the continual engagement with questions of technological transformation, and the occasional references to iconic science-fictional images (such as time machines or spaceships) all take on added significance. Together, all of these aspects of the series work to confirm Matt Weiner's original characterization of *Mad Men* as a work of science fiction, though of course this complex series participates in a number of other genres as well.

Part III

Mad Men and History

8

MAD MEN AND NOSTALGIA

Every great ad tells a story.—Don Draper, Episode 7.7 ("Waterloo")

Mad Men itself is a kind of powerful advertisement for American life in the 1960s. The difference between the show and a real ad, though, is that advertisements usually focus on positive images and content based on a product, good, or service. In contrast, *Mad Men* reveals a warts-and-all perspective of its era that may surprise some viewers. No one on the series is isolated from the turbulence of the age, from racism and misogyny to adultery and violence.

Maybe, then, the show is also the anti-advertisement. Would anyone really want to go back to that era? It seemed pretty awful for a whole lot of people. Yet, countless viewers reveled in the decadence the *Mad Men* characters depicted, even to the point that the drugs, drinking, smoking, and sex were used as major tenets of the early marketing campaign to sell the show in its first couple of years. For every person who looked on in disgust, several more must have retained their nostalgic views of the 1960s.

Obviously, Weiner and his team—from writers and directors to the actors and production crew—understood the power of nostalgia when dealing with a period so steeped in folklore. They knew that people would bring their preconceived notions with them when viewing the show. From a creative perspective, the idea that people "know" the sixties gave *Mad Men* a framework that enabled Weiner to build on its foundations and, simultaneously, take entirely new leaps into revealing "real life" as it may have been lived by this group of characters. Juxtaposing the lead and

Betty and Sally (January Jones and Kiernan Shipka). *ABC/Photofest ©AMC*

ancillary characters versus the age also provided a method for commenting on related issues and concepts from the chaotic era.

As a result, nostalgia as an outlook or philosophy is never straightforward on *Mad Men*. Historian Jerome de Groot sees the program's use of nostalgia more cynically, explaining that it "plays fast and loose with nostalgia, quite deliberately invoking it to explode it . . . revisionist in its approach to the past, disrupting the historical imaginary by undermining the sheen of nostalgia" (2011, 279). Even when Don Draper seems to be explicitly discussing nostalgia, as in Episode 1.13 ("The Wheel"), his vision of the concept darts in and around its meaning, thus creating new notions of the power contained in this idea. Draper, as the series protagonist, is an example of how convoluted the past, present, history, and nostalgia become under Weiner's master hand. According to de Groot, "Draper's cynicism enables him to be a brilliant advertising 'creative,' because he has a vision unencumbered by the everyday" (280).

All the characters on the show change and transform with the times, even someone who seems to have timeless beauty, like Joan Holloway. Over the years, her look becomes softer and more professional, which mirrors her rise from head secretary to agency partner. Externally, though, Draper changes little. He is a throwback to the 1950s and its button-down culture. Don's casual look—whether at home on weekends or on an excursion into the California desert—is shocking, since the suit is part of his armor. On the outside, the serious Draper would seem a cardboard cutout of the American businessman in the 1960s, but the viewer learns what only slowly dawns on the other characters—Don has a deep interior world. As an audience, Weiner grants us a limited omniscient perspective, which provides insight into Draper and the others that they do not have in the imaginary *Mad Men* universe. The viewpoint is not dictatorial, though. Weiner provides a lot of room for the observer to range across the age, fusing what one "knows" of the controversial era with what is presented on the show.

For seven seasons, *Mad Men* asked viewers to reflect on America's contemporary history and culture and make hard choices about how this era might be interpreted. To make the decision making more difficult, Weiner made many of the characters amorphous or malleable—easy to love or despise, some actually transforming from minute to minute. The love and hate characteristics displayed by Draper or Roger Sterling actually make the series more realistic by making them seem human. We know people have good and bad sides and those opposites sometimes fight for control on a minute-by-minute basis.

Based on the era being represented, it is no accident that Jon Hamm, cast as series lead Draper, is Kennedy-esque in his masculinity and handsomeness. Not too pretty, the way some modern actors can be, Hamm is a rugged figure, able to simultaneously exude rough-hewn virility and a kind of old Hollywood manliness that informs the character and the show. He immediately draws viewers back to the heyday of Camelot, a fabled time in American history that one might argue stood mainly as a creation of the master marketers who built and refined JFK's legacy after the president was murdered in Dallas. Hamm also possesses an uncanny ability to almost distort or contort his face and accompany this feat with exaggerated body and hand movements. As a result, Draper's internal strife is reflected in his external appearance. The audience readily views Don's pain, anxiety, anger, and confusion because Hamm masterfully morphs into these guises.

The idea of nostalgia wraps inward and twists into knots on *Mad Men*. One cannot be on safe footing without really thinking through ideas of history, past, and nostalgia, as well as how these influences have consequences today. "Draper," explains de Groot:

> is using nostalgic feelings to force his feeling but unthinking audience to consume the product in the present that seems to allow them entry to the past. . . . America can wake from the nightmare of the present, taking refuge in a fantasy of pastness constructed mainly out of capitalist desire and quite literal renderings of false consciousness. (2011, 282)

While the series obliges viewers to look back, it also provides a means of filtering modern trials and tribulations, which are not the same as they were fifty years ago, but certainly echo the past.

In some senses, Weiner is a master historian, able to re-create a portrait of the past that adds to the historical record by focusing on authenticity as a foundation for many visual and storytelling aspects of the series. However, he also creates new narratives and interpretations that rival the best historical fiction. Weaving back and forth and intermixing history and fiction creates *Mad Men*'s ambiance, a masterful patchwork in which nostalgia emerges as a leading character. Examining the show's universe, one sees that nostalgia plays a critical role, from Weiner, who often discusses how he lived through the early years of this era and how his parents were then, to the characters, who interpret their lives via a nostalgic lens.

Moreover, the audience both holds nostalgic memories of the 1960s and then is asked to engage and evaluate those interpretations as they watch *Mad Men*. It is as if Weiner is saying: "I know you think you understand the 1960s, but I am going to blow them up by providing my own analysis, as well as have the characters also contemplating the historical consequences within the overall narrative." The result is a fascinating and complex use of history and nostalgia at the heart of a show that demands viewers think about interpretation, interrogation, and nuance.

NOSTALGIA AND HISTORY

Matthew Weiner understands that *Mad Men* is built on the dueling foundations of nostalgia and historic re-creation. In 2014, as Season 7 set to launch, he told a writer that he experienced these forces himself, admitting that the characters brought out the "meta- experience, if you go back and watch the first season, of nostalgia" (Rosin 2014). His deep love for the characters (and the actors who played them) is evident on the audio commentaries included on the season DVDs. Listening to the joy in Weiner's voice when he talks with Jon Hamm as they talk over an episode reveals their intense bond. We even hear, along with insider details about the making of particular episodes, a tinge of nostalgia in Weiner's tone.

Mad Men is a nearly flawless example of a show based on nostalgia from a viewer's perspective that then employs the tactic internally as a plot device to propel the narrative. Since nostalgia is built into the audience's interpretive mindsets, they are consistently referencing and referring back to days when life seemed better, a vague designation, but within the wheelhouse of both the characters and those watching. Viewers use nostalgic judgment to assess *Mad Men* while at the same time watching the characters do the same, easily interpreting the actions of the characters based on the same techniques they use to establish identity, place, and worldviews.

Ironic, given the care he utilizes in showing modern audiences an accurate interpretation of the 1960s, Weiner is no fan of the decade.

Many times he has mentioned how the decade's idealism faded in the harsh light of sociopolitical and military power. According to writer Hanna Rosin, Weiner sees the death of 1960s-style idealism leading directly to the greedy 1980s when the flower children sold out. He tells Rosin that in his own youth, he watched "the world being run by a bunch of hypocrites . . . repressive, selfish, racist, money-grubbing" (2014). Regardless of these strong feelings, though, Weiner does not beat the characters up in a way that might expose his resentment (though Betty's slim number of devoted fans might have a bone to pick over Weiner's imagined or real mommy issues).

Nostalgia is central to mass communications and the way people think. It is not a stretch to label it the heartbeat of popular culture. The list of mass media that employ nostalgia as a central theme would fill countless shelves, since many creative pieces hinge on looking back, whether with pride, agony, anxiety, or joy. Every era is filled with nostalgia-based programming.

Viewers across the ages have indicated that they also want to watch certain shows and films over and over again for the personal nostalgia that is derived. For example, all of television reruns programming is built around reliving shows that take people back to days they remember fondly. As a result, even mediocre TV shows like *The Brady Bunch* and *Three's Company* have aired for decades after their debuts, thereby exuding some modicum of influence over generations of viewers and their beliefs. Films play a similar role, such as the urge people get to watch *It's a Wonderful Life* every Christmas season or the many Rankin/Bass stop-motion Claymation holiday specials. Even though these programs have been viewed dozens or hundreds of times, or more, there is still a yearning associated that plops viewers down in front of the television once again, particularly if it involves passing the shows onto children who represent the next generation of nostalgia consumers.

An interesting aspect of nostalgia generally (perhaps like the adage that all stereotypes have some truth contained within) is that some of the "good ol' days" notions synch with reality. In 1958, for example, the noted historian Arthur Schlesinger Jr. wrote about the way life changed for many people, explaining:

> The bureaucratization of American life, the decline of the working
> class, the growth of the white-collar class, the rise of suburbia—all this

has meant the increasing homogeneity of American society. Though we continue to speak of ourselves as rugged individualists, our actual life has grown more and more collective and anonymous. (2008, 40–41)

For many people across the United States, the historian's analysis nimbly appraised their lives (particularly for upwardly mobile, educated whites). Furthermore, this assessment is largely in harmony with the way many people would portray the late 1950s.

Weiner, then, can use these nostalgia-based stereotypes in a variety of thought-provoking ways. First, he can counter the general impressions by revealing that something different could or should exist, such as the way blacks were discriminated against or the way women held secondary roles in the workplace, even when smarter or more hardworking than their male counterparts.

Simultaneously, there is the opportunity to use common stereotypes to propel plots or action. In the later seasons, for example, characters are shown in what today's viewers would interpret as "hippie" clothing and smoking marijuana, which is a kind of shortcut to saying something larger about the disconnect between the corporate world and the youth movement. In Episode 6.10 ("A Tale of Two Cities"), for example, before his unfortunate mental breakdown later in the series, Michael Ginsberg (possible Martian and actual Holocaust survivor) gets into a heated verbal fight with Jim Cutler, one of the partners in the newly merged Sterling Cooper & Partners. Ginsberg rails to Cutler that he stuck his "fascist boot on my neck," then later calls him a "Nazi." The elegant, quick Cutler points out the hypocrisy of "hippies who cash checks from Dow Chemical and General Motors."

In both instances, the audience is given identifiable markers of the corporate versus hippie spat. Cutler, sporting a sharp blue suit and stately manner, is recognizable, as is Ginsberg, spouting anti-establishment ideas about racism, fascism, and anti-Semitism. The examples are so overt that Weiner does not have to expend much on building the visual cues or what each party might say to the other in this kind of clash.

Nostalgic ideas and impressions really give a tremendous amount of interpretive leeway to audiences. What viewers know for sure, however, is that the use of nostalgia is deliberate. Weiner talked about it at length in interviews during marketing campaigns to promote the program, but more important, he had Don and the others perpetually using the idea as a frame of reference for what they did creatively and how they thought as individuals.

THE WEINER TOUCH: AMERICA'S HISTORIAN AND THERAPIST

Weiner demonstrates a keen understanding of the difference between "the past" and "history" that historian Keith Jenkins famously outlined in *Rethinking History*: "The past has occurred. It has gone and can only be brought back again by historians in very different media . . . not as actual events." Explaining the intricacy, he notes, "The past has gone and history is what historians make of it when they go to work" (2003, 8). Weiner's work in refashioning the 1960s is built on authenticity, his meticulous desire to get details correct, in terms of props and scenes. Yet, he knows (and the audience too) that this is active interpretation, not actually revisiting the past.

As a historian, Weiner relies on the past to provide a narrative of exterior events. Then he builds the internal story with genuine props and scenery to provide a sense of authenticity that lends credibility to his vision of history. Yet, the entire program is also a re-creation of famous events interwoven with fiction. Jenkins explains:

> How the historian tries to know the past, is crucial in determining the possibilities of what history is and can be, not least because it is history's claim to knowledge (rather than belief or assertion) that makes it the discourse it is (I mean, historians do not usually see themselves as writers of fiction, although inadvertently they may be). (2003, 12)

What one discerns in Jenkins's explanation is that even those who consider themselves professional historians (trained, advanced degrees, etc.) debate what history is or should be. The larger issue at stake is the significance of these historical interpretations on readers, listeners, viewers, and others that engage with the material. Over ninety-two episodes, countless repeats, DVD sales, and digital downloads, more people will have engaged with *Mad Men* as history than any single text or lifetime of books ever written by a professional historian. As viewers, we get "lost" in the content because of the writing, the visual interpretation, and the impressive acting, but when we emerge, we are in our own time and realize that the show is just a series of fabrications (even if well-conceived).

In Episode 7.1 ("Time Zones"), Ken Cosgrove, now head of accounts because Pete Campbell has sauntered off to Sterling Cooper West in Los Angeles, is so busy that he exclaims to Joan: "I don't have time to take a crap!" Instead of meeting with Wayne Barnes, the new marketing director at longtime client Butler Footwear, Ken asks Joan to make the meeting go away. Always on the lookout to prove that she is more than a former secretary, Joan stealthily meets with young Barnes, seemingly fresh from an MBA program, which he boasts about. She lies and says that Ken got pulled away, and then learns that Barnes wants to take all the company's advertising in-house to cut costs, thus firing SC&P.

In response, Joan takes a Saturday morning trip to Columbia University (and gets ogled by two undergrads in this pre-Cougar age) to find a counterargument for the MBA-holding Barnes, who claims that his education enables him to see marketing as a somewhat scientific endeavor. After some initial sexist allusions ("the company looks interesting"), Professor Podolsky explains that the shoe company would be better off diversifying its shoe line or opening foreign offices. Joan asks for the recommendation in writing, so the professor wonders if she has "anything to trade." Based on the earlier comments, she thinks he wants to barter for sex, but being the good academic, Podolsky simply wants insider information about the ad business for his research. Realizing her mistake, Joan gives him what he wants, even though he talks down to her in the process.

Joan saves the day with Butler Footwear, convincing Barnes to reverse his decision. More importantly, though, the exchange provides insight into Weiner's thoughts about history and re-creating the past. The storyline (one could argue, a minor arc in the larger narrative) receives the Weiner touch, not only making a point about the rise of trained leaders with MBAs in the late 1960s, but also the power of "scientific" management in the era. "The MBAs are coming into the business," Weiner explains in the episode's audio commentary, indicating that "marketing" was not even really used in the early 1960s when the series time frame begins (2014).

The Weiner touch then moves from story to scene. Walking on campus, Joan rounds the bend and slips on some ice. The *Mad Men* creator explains that the editing staff in piecing together the sequences liked to uncover "anything that smacks of a blunder or a flub" because "it [the action] becomes real." Wiener's view of authentic moments when the "actors get caught off-guard" contrasted to the specific way he orchestrated the series, "especially in a show that is choreographed and controlled as this" (2014).

Here, and perhaps with the show in general, the audience assumes it knows something about the 1960s as the era actually unfolded. The Weiner touch is the process of using moments from the past and transforming them into history. There is no way for a fictional character to have slipped on ice in the real-world past, but the experience can re-create the time and make it seem genuine. We are slipping between memory, present, and created history to "see" what takes place on the screen.

Even more to the point of how Weiner adds authentic moments to the show, he actually sent a person to Columbia to take a photograph of what would have been the view out of Professor Podolsky's window in the late 1960s, even though it is from the old business school, not the business school's current location. To Weiner, the detail is significant because "it feels like college" (2014). In other words, he did not settle for the real feeling created by the authentic-looking office, clothing, bookshelves, or other accouterments. Weiner had to have the "real" view out the window. America's historian is giving viewers his best restoration.

Weiner understands that he has a responsibility in the past/history interplay. He explained to writer Hanna Rosin as the last season began:

> The weirdest thing about all of this is that I do have something to say and I say it in the show, but I really try very deeply to not judge people that I am writing about. And that means characters don't help each other through scenes. Everybody has a point of view. And the show captures a lot of private moments. That behavior, it's real. (March 19, 2014)

Essentially, Weiner plucks moments from the past to create a history-infused series using authentic props, scenery, and actors who seem reminiscent of the era or real-life figures. The commitment to authenticity enables viewers to interpret the show from a number of different positions, including nostalgia. At the same time, the latter is a tool employed by characters on the show as they negotiate their onscreen lives. Weiner then infuses the program with scenarios that ask (perhaps compel) the audience to not only rethink what they believe they know about the 1960s, but also to reassess their own lives and modern times.

DRAPER'S WORLDVIEW

A ragged hotel, Don and Peggy sit close together on the bed, their shoulders touch, his hands are only inches from her short skirt . . . this moment sounds like the dream or nightmare of every *Mad Men* fan. Are Don and Peggy taking their odd relationship to a new place?

No! The reason they sit—completely enthralled—drinking two beers Peggy has pilfered from somewhere in the dry town is more momentous than mere sex . . . it is the 1969 Neil Armstrong moon landing. They stare intently—enraptured—probably not even realizing that they are so close.

A man on the moon! The whole nation watches in gleeful happiness but also with an air of anxiety. Potential "what ifs" cause passionate speculations. For the Burger Chef team on the road for the client pitch the next day, there is tense rubber-meets-the-road anxiety. If there is some kind of devastation, there is no way the pitch will take place. However, this is secondary. Don and the crew are aware of the epic moment taking place. They give it the reverence it deserves.

Across the country, in the Francises' Rye, New York, enclave, the extended family and their overnight guests also gather around the television set for this historic moment. But there is discord. The generations are arguing over the cost of the program—the parents taking the patriotic stance, while the teens argue that the money could have been spent on social justice causes at home. The generational clash over the cost of space exploration symbolizes the growing schism between adults and their children, particularly as Vietnam, civil rights, and antiwar demonstrations sweep the nation.

Finally, the only member of *Mad Men* who represents an even older generation and the only one born before the new century turned—Bert Cooper—sits alone on his oversized couch, the TV picture illuminating his face and the room. He calls to his maid to come witness the world-changing event. It will be the last moments of his long, distinguished life.

Later in Episode 7.7 ("Waterloo"), Bert will be resurrected as a vision, sending a not-so-subtle message to Draper. The old man dances and sings through the Broadway classic "The Best Things in Life Are Free," a point that on the surface seems antithetical to the fast-paced world of Madison Avenue firms.

Don, though, is the person who might comprehend its significance. His deep historical thinking, mixing nostalgia, personal experience, and a keen ability to contextualize history thematically, provides a means of looking beyond his profession to consider existential challenges. According to scholars David Strutton and David G. Taylor, "The examination of history allows one to acquire experience by proxy; that is, learning from the harsh or redemptive experiences of others. . . . Mythology is less reliable than history as narrative of actual experience; yet, it may hold more power than history" (2011, 468). Don, professional interpreter of contemporary history and culture, grasps the correlation between myth and history. Bert's song and dance alerts Draper to what the moon landing demonstrated—history's great moments are free and should lead to deeper reflection regarding our place and time.

Focusing on the moon shot and its consequences (both on a personal and macro level), "Waterloo" is an example of the way *Mad Men* asks viewers to think and reinterpret their ideas about historical moments or themes, many of which the audience actually experienced in real life. There are multiple ways of viewing history here: an event "happening" to the characters, something they are interpreting, a depiction that viewers are interpreting, a portrayal that viewers experienced in real time or as a piece of history, and a program purposely based on history that asks viewers to assess that representation.

Concentrating a television show on history is a risky proposition. On one hand, history-based programming is a staple in popular culture—just imagine the innumerable movies and TV shows running the gamut from *Forrest Gump* to *All in the Family*. The spotlight on history, though, also threatens to seem boring or antiquated to audiences that have countless entertainment options. The challenge, then, is presenting history in a manner that is new and different but building on familiar ground viewers and critics understand. What so many of these vehicles have in common is the use of ideas that spark immediate recognition while drawing on themes one might deem timeless, like Neil Armstrong walking on the moon or the assassination of JFK or Martin Luther King Jr.

A television series like *Mad Men* that uses nostalgia and historical memory as a central feature necessarily sprints into uncharted territory. Just as the idea of nostalgia is contested on the show, the notion of history (and exactly who can be considered a historian) is as well. In the broader culture, "history" has a general meaning that orbits around foundational ideas such as truth, objectivity, chronology, and facts.

However, history is also reworking the past. In that revision, one finds the historian slipping into the portrait. Alun Munslow explains, "It is the historian's narrative acts—emplotment process, arguments, ideological and moral positions and all the other epistemic choices and preferences—that ultimately invest the past with meaning" (2002, 20). This decision-making process on Weiner's part accounts for why *Mad Men* is a drama versus musical or comedy or even film versus television program. This discussion of history as a conscious, creative act on the part of the creator is fundamental to understanding *Mad Men* and what it asks of its viewers.

DRAPER'S NOSTALGIC MOMENT

"Nostalgia . . . it's delicate . . . but potent," Draper explains, launching into a highly personal, dramatic pitch to win Kodak's account for its new wheel slide projector. In that two-minute span, his dazzling monologue leaves one staffer running from the room in tears. The Kodak executives are spellbound, despite their desire to feature it as a technological innovation. "It's not called 'The Wheel'; it's called 'The Carousel,'" Draper proclaims, his voice quivering. "It lets us travel the way a child travels, 'round and around, and back home again . . . to a place where we know we are loved." The images that shuffle by feature Don with his wife and children, zigzagging back and forth through time. On the surface, they appear to be the perfect family (Episode 1.13, "The Wheel").

Despite Draper's claim of delicacy, though, little about nostalgia on *Mad Men* is subtle. As part of the show's narrative arc, the carousel speech solidifies Draper's creative genius, a breathtaking moment that shows him standing atop Madison Avenue, regardless of his personal failings and mysterious past. For the *Mad Men* franchise, the carousel scene symbolizes the zenith of powerful writing, direction, style, and setting, culminating in overt audience outreach by appealing to viewers' nostalgic notions of the Camelot era.

The key to this multilayered interpretation within the storyline and on the part of the audience is that each accepts nostalgia's "potent" place in the way people live and as a way of synthesizing their stories into the broader culture. Ending the first season of *Mad Men* by clobbering the characters and audience over the head with nostalgia as a part of the plot, it is as if Weiner and his production team are asking viewers to reexamine what they think they know about work, relationships, family, and history as it unfolded over the first season.

Michael Janover explains that "nostalgia is the pain of homesickness." Expanding on the notion, though, he offers a new term, "nostalgias," defined as "the pangs of longing for another time, another place, another self . . . almost certainly romantic in seed and, potentially, corrosively decadent in growth" (2000, 115). This view contrasts with Draper's "ache," which causes psychological pain but has a positive outcome by returning one to a better place—"where we know we are loved." In the carousel speech, nostalgia is heart wrenching but with a happy ending. Ironically, Draper's understanding of nostalgia as a tool to win an account is crystal clear, yet the concept is neglected in his own life.

For *Mad Men* viewers, nostalgia may also provide the tools for comparing and contrasting today's world with the fictional vision of 1960s America. According to Jason P. Leboe and Tamara L. Ansons, "Nostalgic experiences represent a distortion of both the past and the present. The 'good old days' may not have been as good as they seem in retrospect. In turn, the present is only as bad as it seems when compared against an unrealistic ideal" (2006, 596). Given *Mad Men*'s focus on booze, cigarettes, sexism, and other decadent behaviors, today's audience may thump its chest in superiority in comparison or at least sense that modern ills are no worse than back in the supposed good old days.

However, this is not the only way to watch *Mad Men*. Viewers have options as they watch and decode the show. The same viewer who prides herself on condemning the era's harsh sexism and other shortcomings can simultaneously get wrapped up in the romantic or glamorous visions the show renders. *Mad Men* is unflinching in portraying life's dark side, but the power of the representation appeals to the audience. Thus, what could be considered pretty dour or perhaps even depressing programming is elevated to hit status.

Rather than simply make the heroes heroic and the villains evil, Weiner created a multifaceted series in line with other popular and critically acclaimed contemporary shows, such as *Breaking Bad, Boardwalk Empire*, and *Dexter*. The 1960s proved to be the ideal tool for examining the muddled daily lives of people as they experienced a culture undergoing a series of watershed moments. The leftover aspects of JFK's Camelot, however, also provided insight into the high glamour of the period. Don is a witness and participant in both worlds. His mask may be the trappings of a successful businessman and creative genius, but it hides away the vestiges of an early life mired in the lowest rungs of society. Don's nostalgia is another parlor trick, created by an ad man to sell himself to a world in which he does not fit. Writer Emily Nussbaum explains, "Having spanned so many years, both imaginary and real, 'Mad Men' has become a show that induces nostalgia for itself" (2013).

The outsider/insider nostalgia device loops full circle in Episode 7.7 ("Waterloo"). At a moment when all seems lost for Draper—his marriage has crumbled and he is about to be fired from the agency he created—Don does the right thing by having Peggy Olson deliver the Burger Chef pitch. According to Weiner, Draper's looming downfall made viewers uneasy, especially when discomfort seemed a constant factor in our own times:

> I am always writing about the period we're in, and sometimes I'm telling people things they don't want to hear. Some people have an insatiable need for violent retribution. . . . The economy, the Internet— all these things are isolating us and making us feel defeated. Our national culture feels defeated, our exceptionalism. To see Don lose his confidence was hard for them: They want to be in a world where even if crime doesn't pay, you go down shooting. (Rosin 2014)

The scene begins with Olson in the classic Draper back-of-the-head silhouette made famous in the show's opening credits montage. Rather than a position of power, though, she is vulnerable. The all-male voices in the room are clubby and masculine; the men freely and easily laugh and engage with one another in a stuffy boardroom, the ultimate stronghold of male power in the corporate world. In a kind of dreamy state, Olson turns and coughs loudly, which brings her back to reality and the pressure of the situation. In another nod to *Mad Men*'s internal nostalgia, the first face Olson focuses on is Pete Campbell's as he greases the client sitting by him at the table. Next, though, with a slight nod, Draper masterfully introduces Olson and she launches into the account-winning pitch.

It is not just that Peggy's delivery and performance are reminiscent of Draper's Kodak carousel pitch from Season 1; rather the significance rests in the way Weiner (director and co-author of the episode) frames the scene itself as simultaneously revelatory and self-reverential. He knows that loyal viewers will think back to the carousel scene, their own nostalgia for *Mad Men*'s early days. At the same time, as a scene, the handoff symbolizes the older generation (Don) giving power to the next (Peggy), just as it represents a shift in influence from male to female. Olson explains the breakdown of the American family in relation to the fast-food joint, saying, "Dad likes Sinatra. Son likes the Rolling Stones." Society is being ripped apart by a move away from what we now call family values and the chaos wrought by the Vietnam War. For *Mad Men*, the scene solidifies the connection between the macro and micro perspective—each infusing the other, while fundamentally transforming the whole.

In that one cough that launches the scene, the entire *Mad Men* world is brilliantly revealed—iconic pose (a symbol for the show itself and Draper) and a quick, abrasive cough signaling a watershed moment. Finally, after seven seasons of wondering what will become of Peggy, her moment has arrived and the promise of brilliance is fulfilled. Her triumph demonstrates the newfound power of females in the workplace (outside) and her personal victory (inside), the two parts of the nostalgia narrative forming a whole. Olson's transformation is not in past successes, owning an apartment building, or climbing the agency ladder when history is against her. Rather, it occurs in the small space, surrounded by men, but delivering a short speech that leaves them in awe. Peggy emerges from this trial by fire with a new identity, a fulfillment of the show's narrative arc dating back to its earliest moments.

REALITY AND HISTORY

Selling *Mad Men* to a television network took Weiner a decade. Even after getting the pilot episode made, the show's future hung in the balance. The early promotion centered on portraying the show as a realistic look at the early days of Madison Avenue and its leaders—eventually, as it seems with most campaigns, the show garnered criticism.

Several famous, real-life "mad men" (and women) slammed *Mad Men* for focusing heavily on negative, sensational aspects of agency life in the 1960s. For example, George Lois, who created the legendary Xerox commercials that featured a monkey using the copier to show its simplicity, explained, "It has nothing to do with the creative evolution. It was really obnoxious, the whole thing. I guess the world can watch it and say, 'That's exciting; that's wild.' But I was throwing up watching it. I kept moaning" (qtd. in Steinberg and Hampp 2007).

Cynically, the desire to question the show's authenticity may have merely been an effort of media outlets to sell papers, gain viewers, or knock down something that received nearly universal praise. While *Mad Men* never reached the kind of audience numbers of a major network hit, the show gained credibility for its artistic sensibilities and drew strong numbers for the fledgling AMC network. Then it ran off a string of four straight Emmy Awards for Best Drama.

Despite some criticism from the real ad leaders still alive from the 1960s, the show's style created an atmosphere that triggered the audience's nostalgic feelings about the era, particularly the Camelot days, even if one's memories are fanciful. Leboe and Ansons explain, "Many instances of nostalgic experience represent distorted perception, leading to an appreciation of the past that is more fantasy than reality" (2006, 607). Fantasy, then, is a tool that Weiner wields in telling the story of a fictional ad agency and its employees, while simultaneously using nostalgia to market the show as a financial entity. Leboe and Ansons discuss the outcome of using nostalgia in this manner, claiming that "out of this bias to distort the past in the positive direction emerges a biased characterization of contemporary circumstances" (607).

The commitment to authenticity and its resulting influence on viewers grew critical in creating an atmosphere that allowed the audience to root for often-vile characters. Comparable to motion picture cinematography, every aspect of what would normally be considered background comes alive in *Mad Men*. Barbara Lippert explains that the show's "rich cinematography, evocative lighting and fantastic devotion to period furnishings and wardrobe could make a mid-century fetishist out of anyone watching." While all these factors added to a dynamic that made the series feel authentic, she points to Jon Hamm and his impact, saying, "The fact that Draper looks perfectly appointed and dashingly handsome . . . [despite] all his inner turmoil is part of the appeal" (2009). As such, careful viewers recognized nostalgia's role in creating and propelling the story. Hamm is a throwback to Hollywood's Golden Age, playing a character who thinks about the past nostalgically as a cover to the actual horrors of his childhood. Draper's fantasy is a happy past, perhaps one that most people would call "normal."

Mad Men also capitalizes on the way people kind of naturally deconstruct commercials—similar to the Super Bowl take on advertisements, in which the commercials become part of the spectacle. In its early seasons, its producers sought episode-length sponsorships and other heritage-based commercials to add to the show's authority. For example, BMW served as the exclusive sponsor of the second season premiere. The luxury brand created *Mad Men*–like commercials highlighting its history in the automobile industry, thus drawing a tight link between the fictional show and the real brand. As a result, one of the world's premier luxury brands tacitly elevates the show to its level and provides it with an additional stamp of validity.

Other real-life brands and products become series regulars, such as Lucky Strike cigarettes, Coca-Cola, Jaguar, and even various advertising agencies and individuals, including McCann Erickson, Mary Wells, and David Ogilvy, the latter two receiving passing mention but names that would be recognizable to the multitude of viewers from the ad, public relations, or marketing industries. In these instances, Weiner is asking the audience to rethink the role of history as a way of interpreting the past, as well as reconsider what we think we actually know.

Returning to the carousel speech, one sees many divergent threads merge in a single two-minute span. Foremost, as a way to conclude the first season, the new business pitch solidifies Don's status as creative genius. Poor then-junior staffer Harry Crane flees the room after tearing up during the presentation, which represents Draper's amazing powers. Crane's reaction also doubles as a signal to the audience: pay attention, nostalgia is a powerful topic.

In the climactic scene, Don also embodies the image of a dashing young executive, thus tapping directly into a nostalgic vision of 1960s America. For viewers who grew up in the era, Draper could be a stand-in for the cool uncle they remember (or wanted) as children. For a younger audience, there are touches of Kennedy-esque language and mannerisms that might take them back to nostalgic visions of the decade that they learned about in school or viewed in the countless popular culture episodes featuring JFK.

The speech is also critical because in delivering it, Don experiences a moment of clarity, a brief flash of his life falling apart based on living within a web of lies. Again like JFK, who balanced an admired persona with unsavory private behavior, Don is masterful under pressure. The creative victory lets the audience understand that Draper is also a highly intelligent person, but with the street smarts to maneuver the ramifications of a secret identity and two separate lives. As viewers, we know Don is projecting a series of lies, but he does it with such bravado that it seems heroic in a sense.

In a more overt sense, the nostalgia speech and slides showing Don happy establish nostalgia as a kind of talisman for more deeply interpreting the character and the show. Making it part of Draper's heroic moment, Weiner tugs on the viewer's nostalgic feelings and ideas. We see Don happy, romantic, with a beautiful wife and wonderful children. The scene demands that people place themselves in Don's position: what is real and what is illusion when we look back on the past? Weiner does not provide an answer, but he uses Draper's success to illustrate that nostalgia is essential as people make sense of themselves in relation to their place in the world and society.

9

MAD MEN VS. THE YOUTH
COUNTERCULTURE OF THE 1960S

One of the many stories told by *Mad Men* is the historical narrative of
the evolution of American countercultures from the relatively marginal

Woodstock (1970). Photofest

(and noncommercial) Beat subculture of the 1950s to the much more visible youth-dominated counterculture of the 1960s. This new culture, while politically engaged (and potentially politically powerful), also offered convenient opportunities for corporations (such as the clients of the Sterling Cooper advertising firm in its various incarnations) easily to organize a new grouping of customers for efficient exploitation. *Mad Men* thus centrally addresses one of the key historical questions concerning the significance of the 1960s: whether the youthful counterculture of the period represented a genuine (and potentially revolutionary) attempt to change the world, or whether it simply offered new and better ways for America's youth to be managed as a demographic and incorporated within and exploited by the capitalist system.

Mad Men offers no easy answer to this question, which surely, in fact, has no easy answer. However, it is clear that, whatever the actual nature of the counterculture, it did not entirely succeed in achieving its most radical political goals. Indeed, one could easily argue that the counterculture, far than being a driving force for revolutionary change, was simply a symptom of the drive for change that has been recognized as central to the capitalist system since *The Communist Manifesto* and that has become even more so in the era that Fredric Jameson, among others, has called "late capitalism." Indeed, for Jameson (approvingly summarizing the insights of Jean Baudrillard), the failure of the counterculture was predictable from the very nature of late capitalism, given that "conscious ideologies of revolt, revolution, and even negative critique are—far from merely being 'co-opted' by the system—an integral and functional part of the system's own internal strategies" (1991, 203). In addition, Jameson also makes clear elsewhere that the political basis of the 1960s counterculture was never designed to take on capitalism at a fundamental level, noting that

> the values of the civil rights movement and the women's movement are thus preeminently cooptable because they are already—as ideals—inscribed in the very ideology of capitalism itself, . . . which has a fundamental interest in social equality to the degree to which it needs to transform as many [as possible] of its subjects or its citizens into identical consumers interchangeable with everybody else. (1992, 36)

In short, however convenient racism and sexism might have historically been as supports for capitalist exploitation, capitalism as a system can easily accommodate equality on the basis of race and gender because race and gender equality are not structurally incompatible with the workings of a capitalist economy.

Mad Men ultimately makes a similar diagnosis, if more haltingly and in a less theoretically coherent fashion. Among other things, what the series does do, quite effectively, is dramatize the historical evolution of subcultures/countercultures in the United States, thus adding an important piece to the puzzle of just what the 1960s were all about. As M. Keith Booker (2001) has argued, the historical period that we think of as the "1950s" really begins with the reorganization of global economic and political power immediately after World War II and extends at least through the Kennedy assassination near the end of 1963. By this reading, the decade of the "1960s"—with its distinctively remembered rock music, colorfully dressed hippies, and demonstrating college students—does not really begin until 1964, though of course the historical boundary between the 1950s and the 1960s is porous, with considerable overlap. The first three seasons of Mad Men are thus set in what Booker calls the "long 1950s," and their relationship to the context in which they are set needs to be understood accordingly.

Don Draper, the dashing (but troubled) central figure of Mad Men, is decidedly out of touch with the younger generation of the 1960s. After all, he was born in 1926, while freshmen entering college in 1964 would typically have been born in 1946, making them essentially a generation younger than Draper. What is clear, however, is that what we have here is far more than a failure to communicate based on the famed 1960s generation gap. Born in poverty and reared in lurid lower-class circumstances, the adult Draper is driven by a desire to attain respectability and affirmation by the mainstream culture he could only look at longingly from the outside as a child. As a result, his efforts to be accepted into the mainstream make his relationship with various subcultures and countercultures problematic to say the least. Among the many public allegorical resonances of his private story, then, is a meditation on America's strained relationship with countercultures in general, suggesting the way in which the national narrative of upward mobility and material success (offering opportunities to industrious immigrants and other outsiders) involves a dark subplot that involves acquiescence and conformism.

The first season episode "Babylon" (Episode 1.6) neatly encapsulates Draper's strained relationship with the American mainstream. Having taken a new identity in an effort to put his difficult childhood behind him, the talented and hardworking Draper is literally a self-made man, seemingly an embodiment of the American Dream—but it is a very 1950s-style American Dream. Set mostly during the Kennedy-Nixon presidential campaign of 1960, the first season of *Mad Men* remains very clearly rooted in the 1950s, and Draper (having already achieved considerable success in the professional world of high-stakes advertising) is very much the gray-flannelled corporate figure of that decade, even if he never quite feels at ease with the nice suburban home and pretty, well-educated wife that come with the territory.

Draper's sense of remaining an outsider in his new upper-class world can be seen in the obvious fascination he experiences when the Israeli tourism bureau enlists Sterling Cooper to produce an advertising campaign for them. The story of Jews in America—often growing up in poverty, widely rejected and despised, but also often achieving a great deal of professional success—would seem to be a perfect analogue to Draper's own position, and Draper seems to sense this connection. Meanwhile, given Draper's own personal proclivities, it probably comes as no surprise that one way he expresses his fascination with Jewishness is to take on a Jewish mistress in the form of Rachel Menken, the daughter of the owner of a successful department store and thus an embodiment of Jewish material success in America.

The complexities that underlie Draper's fascination with Rachel (which clearly include both her wealth and her Jewishness) make their relationship a particularly troubled one. Still, Draper's sense that, as a Jew, Rachel might have a special ability to empathize with his own rags-to-riches story becomes clear when, in a rare (for him) moment of genuine interpersonal connection, he elects a few episodes later (Episode 1.10, "Long Weekend") to make Rachel the first person (including his own wife) to whom he has told the story of his humble beginnings.

The relationship with Rachel ultimately goes nowhere, partly because they both have too many other irons in the fire. In the case of Draper, these irons include not only his wife and children but his *other* mistress, the artist type Midge, with whom his fascination seems to be driven by a desire to rebel against the chafing confines of the corporate world that has allowed him to buy a comfortable life by selling his soul. The self-consciously nonconforming Midge (a stereotypical version of the would-be individualist whose life is crafted from attempts to avoid stereotypes) offers Draper a sense of rebellion against the corporate world that allows him to maintain at least a flickering hope that he might still have a soul after all. However, his relationship with Midge ultimately has the opposite effect when it becomes clear how thoroughly unable he is to fit in with her and the bohemian Greenwich Village world to which she introduces him.

Indeed, the debonair Draper shows just how hopelessly square he is when he is so clearly out of his element when he hangs out with Midge and some of her friends in a Village club of the kind where Bob Dylan, one of the greatest icons of 1960s youth culture, performed on his way to prominence. When one of the friends, learning what Draper does for a living, asks him how he sleeps at night, a clearly offended Draper simply responds, "On a bed made of money." That answer, even though it makes Draper seem more comfortable with his materialist existence than he really is, neatly encapsulates the doomed nature of Draper's affair with Midge, which breaks off within a few more episodes.

Midge, incidentally, will resurface a few seasons later (in Episode 4.12, "Blowing Smoke") as a fallen and pathetic figure, a heroin addict who essentially seeks to prostitute herself to Draper, with the cooperation of her new husband, a starving playwright. By this season, the 1960s are beginning, and Midge's downfall can be taken as an emblem of the downfall of the 1950s subculture she represents. In any case, Draper beats a hasty retreat without completing the sexual transaction, though he does help Midge out by buying one of her paintings. He is, in fact, revolted by her offer of sex for money—no doubt partly because it evokes memories of his childhood growing up in a whorehouse—but perhaps because it also destroys his illusion that subcultures such as the bohemian world of artists might offer a genuine alternative to the venal world of which the advertising business is paradigmatic.

That latter world is quite consistently depicted in *Mad Men* as informed by a kind of prostitution—up to and including that pivotal moment when Joan Harris quite literally prostitutes herself in Episode 5.11 ("The Other Woman") in order to help the firm win a big account. Draper, not surprisingly, is the only partner who is opposed to allowing Joan to be used in this way: with his background, he seems to be able to sense the symbolic overlap between business and prostitution not only with a special acuity, but also with a particular disgust. It is not for nothing that he so consistently seems to want to think of his work in advertising as a form of art rather than mere marketing. Thus, it is no surprise when he is so powerfully disappointed when Midge and her world of art let him down so dramatically, revealing themselves to be just as thoroughly commodified as anything and everything else.

This gradual penetration of commodification into every aspect of American life is another of the main themes of *Mad Men*. This story, especially when couched in terms of the art world, can also be described as that of the rise of postmodernism. After all, Fredric Jameson, the leading theorist of the phenomenon of postmodernist culture, has famously described postmodernism as "the cultural logic of late capitalism." For Jameson, incidentally, this commodification of everything under late capitalism is pretty much completed, at least in the West, sometime in the 1970s, which would make the 1960s a pivotal transitional decade in his historical narrative—as well as in that of *Mad Men*'s. From Jameson's point of view, then, it is virtually inevitable that Draper's foray into the art world to find a refuge from late capitalism was ultimately bound to fail. After all, crucial to Jameson's theorization of postmodernism is the notion that postmodernist art is part of the "everything" that is commodified under late capitalism. For Jameson, with the rise of postmodernism, "What has happened is that aesthetic production today has become integrated into commodity production generally" (1991, 4).

Of course, in the case of *Mad Men*, countercultural protests against the inexorable advance of consumer capitalism tend to be ineffectual in general, and the counterculture sometimes comes in for what comes close to outright mockery. The clearest case of this phenomenon probably involves former copywriter Paul Kinsey, who, having formerly lost his job, resurfaces as a Hare Krishna in Episode 5.10 ("Christmas Waltz"). In this episode, Kinsey is clearly presented as a fallen and pathetic figure, while the Hare Krishnas are presented as comically ridiculous, not to mention mendacious and hypocritical. Kinsey, in fact, wants out of the movement, hoping to break into television scriptwriting with the help of Harry Crane, whom he feels might be able to help him hawk the new script he has just written for the original *Star Trek* series. Despite the movement's emphasis on sexual purity, Mother Lakshmi, who seems to have seduced Kinsey into the Krishnas in the first place, attempts to deploy her sexual charms on Crane to prevent him from helping Kinsey break free of the movement. He is, we learn, a very effective recruiter for the Krishnas (though a terrible scriptwriter) and thus a valuable commodity.

The Hare Krishnas, while a highly visible component of the 1960s counterculture, were very much a fringe group that represented a relatively small *sub*culture within the larger attempt to find alternatives to the soul-destroying advance of corporate-dominated consumer capitalism in America. As a whole, though, the youth-dominated counterculture was a much larger force that came to represent, for many, the central cultural memory of the decade. The counterculture was complex and multiple, of course, and a vaguely anti-materialist, anti-authoritarian hippie movement combined with more specific (and better organized) phenomena such as the antiwar movement, the civil rights movement, and the women's movement to produce an alliance of causes that became well-nigh hegemonic among Americans of a certain age (say, under thirty).

For these young Americans, then, the "counterculture" was arguably simply the "culture," and one that, if anything—given *Mad Men*'s reputation for effective presentation of the texture of American life in the 1960s—receives surprisingly little emphasis in the series. *Mad Men*, in fact, contains a number of such seeming gaps, leading Dana Polan to propose that the gaps in the "narrative project" of the series are used to "dramatize limitation and the forms of narrative struggle against it" (2013, 36). It is certainly the case that the oppositional political movements of the 1960s were marked by an incompleteness in the sense that they failed to carry their world-changing goals to the initially envisioned completion. *Mad Men*'s oddly incomplete representation of these movements thus might be taken to thematize the incompleteness of the movements themselves.

On the other hand, one could argue that *Mad Men* is simply not *about* the counterculture and therefore should not be expected to represent it with the vividness with which it represents its true subject, the world of advertising (and, by extension, the larger world of consumer capitalism). But these worlds cannot, of course, be so easily separated. All of the major oppositional political movements of the 1960s make forays into the corporate world of the Sterling Cooper advertising firm of one kind or another at various points in the series, though the intrusion is typically quite weak. For example, while *Mad Men* is notorious for the amount of alcohol consumed by its principals (including on the job), the emerging drug culture of the 1960s also creeps into the SC offices from time to time. In Episode 3.3 ("My Old Kentucky Home"), for example, Peggy Olson joins the guys in smoking a joint to relieve the tensions of a long weekend of work; this undertaking might be taken as a mild protest against the fact that the twenty-somethings involved are working all weekend while their older and richer bosses are partying, but it otherwise seems to have little in the way of political implications, other than perhaps to suggest Peggy's ongoing efforts to find a place for herself within the mostly male world of advertising.

It is, in fact, the women's movement that, of the oppositional political movements of the 1960s, plays the largest role in *Mad Men*, which makes the efforts of women such as Olson and Joan Holloway Harris to win respect in the advertising business a major part of its overall narrative. At the other end of the spectrum, the civil rights movement probably receives the least effective coverage in the series. There are no major non-white characters in the series: the most important black character is Dawn Chambers, who serves for a time as Draper's secretary, hired in response to a brief flurry of civil rights activism directed at the firm. Of course, one could argue, as does Clarence Lang (2013), that the marginality of black characters in *Mad Men* can be taken simply as a realistic commentary on the marginality of African Americans to the world depicted in the series. And it is certainly the case that the series shows an obvious disdain for the overt racism of characters such as the seemingly avuncular Bert Cooper, but this attitude stops well short of any real outrage or even detailed elaboration.

The most prominent appearance of the civil rights movement in *Mad Men* occurs in Episode 6.5 ("The Flood"), which deals with the April 4, 1968, assassination of Dr. Martin Luther King. Here, most of the white characters are shocked and stunned by King's shooting—and seem to feel that they must offer special condolences to Dawn, in a mode that seems sincere but also potentially suggests a veiled and unconscious racism. Mostly, though, the white characters just seem really awkward in their attempts to respond properly to the assassination—almost as if they are overcome with guilt that they don't really feel as saddened by the event as they think they should be. Their reactions thus thematize a certain awkwardness in dealing with race that runs through the series, though one could actually argue that this is a *strength* of the series, enacting an awkwardness that is a central fact of American society as a whole.

Awkwardness over race also rears its ugly head in Episode 3.5 ("The Fog"), when the generally smarmy Pete Campbell (who nevertheless seems to be one of the most liberal of the Sterling Cooper principals when it comes to race) decides to try to play the race card to his own advantage by suggesting that the Admiral brand could greatly increase its television sales by marketing specifically to African American consumers. Ultimately, of course, such racially targeted marketing would become a staple of American consumerism, but Campbell is here apparently ahead of his time—or at least pitching the idea to the wrong company. He is, in fact, harshly rebuffed by the horrified company reps in a reminder of just how deep racism still ran in America amid the civil rights fervor of the 1960s—a reminder that also sounds in the *really* awkward blackface performance by Roger Sterling in Episode 3.3 ("My Old Kentucky Home"). For that matter, Campbell's own research in pursuit of this project (which involves interrogating a black elevator operator as a sort of native informant) is itself extremely awkward.

If *Mad Men* thus conducts occasional critiques of racism, it also suggests that some of the white liberals who supported the civil rights movement might not have been quite as admirable as they at first appeared to be. Indeed, these antiracist liberals are sometimes treated less kindly than are racists such as the Ayn Randian Cooper or the sometimes clueless Sterling. A case in point is Kinsey's attempt to boost his liberal credentials by obtaining a black girlfriend (or perhaps he attempts to obtain a black girlfriend by boosting his liberal credentials). He then attempts in Episode 2.10 ("The Inheritance") to prove his virtue to said girlfriend by becoming a Freedom Rider, an attempt that Kinsey himself (hardly a paragon of courage and conviction) attempts to abort out of fear for his own safety, though he ultimately does make the trip.

Roger Sterling also takes trips in *Mad Men* in an apparent search for exotic sexual opportunities, though his fascination with LSD (and with the free-sex world of young hippie girls) does seem to contain at least a certain element of a genuine quest for new modes of experience that might take him beyond the soulless world of corporate capitalism. Of course, his (sometimes poignant) attempts to find meaning through drugs and sex with young girls mostly just end up making him look ridiculous, a point that is brought home when the hippie shoe switches to the other foot after his spoiled daughter, Margaret, bolts from her affluent life to join an agrarian hippie commune in upstate New York in the pivotal Episode 7.4 ("The Monolith"). Just as the Sterling Cooper offices are taken over by a soulless corporate computer, Margaret goes in the other direction, becoming a flower child and adopting the name Marigold, while leaving behind three generations of family (her parents; her husband, Brooks; and her son, Ellery).

Margaret/Marigold is seeking to opt out of the materialist system that has given her such a comfortable life—not to mention out of her conventional responsibilities as a wife and mother. As such, this moment in the series potentially makes a feminist statement of sorts, especially when her parents trek out to the farm/commune to fetch her back, only to be rebuffed when Marigold reminds her father that he never seemed to let his responsibilities as a husband and father get in the way of his personal ambitions and desires. Is a woman "abandoning" her family in the interest of countercultural "enlightenment" really any worse than a man ignoring his in order to pursue career and financial advancement—not to mention a string of affairs with secretaries who serve essentially as professional perks?

Mad Men, though, does not really follow through on the potential feminist implications of this motif, instead opting to focus on the generational differences between the ways Sterling and his daughter have sought personal fulfillment at the expense of family obligations. Neither generation comes off all that well, and both father and daughter appear vaguely ridiculous in this episode. Both, in fact, end up falling into a puddle of mud in a moment of slapstick. Meanwhile, the opposition between generations is complicated by the fact that Sterling himself has spent much recent time dabbling in the counterculture that Marigold has now joined in full force. This experience might explain why Sterling seems to react to the commune with surprising good humor at first—as opposed to his appalled, fur-coated ex-wife, Mona, who makes a quick assessment and immediately warns her daughter that "these people are lost, and on drugs, and they have venereal diseases." She then bolts, noting that she would think Marigold had been brainwashed, "except there is nothing to wash." Sterling, however, makes an effort to fit in, smokes some weed with the hippies, and even agrees to spend a night at their farm. There is, however, a limit to his open-mindedness, and he quickly reaches that limit when he realizes that Marigold is practicing the same sort of free-love lifestyle that he has already sampled in his own forays into hippie culture. So he demands that she return to capitalist civilization (and her son) with him, only to be sternly rebuffed and sent packing after both father and daughter take an inadvertent mud bath.

However—as is usually the case with *Mad Men*—it is Draper who is the central figure in the series' thematization of the cultural conflicts between mainstream capitalist culture and the youth-oriented countercul- ture. Indeed, while *Mad Men* has been widely lauded for its effectiveness as a period drama of the 1960s, Draper is very much a man of the 1950s, and one of the key narrative arcs of the series has to do with his struggles to make sense of the tumultuous new decade and to find a place for himself within the new world that it has brought into being. Thus, when Duck Phillips insists in the opening episode of Season 2 ("For Those Who Think Young") that Sterling Cooper needs to seek some younger creative talent in order to produce ad copy that will understand and appeal to younger consumers, Don (described in the episode as thirty-six years old) is highly skeptical. His response, in fact, is completely dismissive: "Young people don't know anything," he scoffs when Sterling brings up the idea of recruiting some younger talent. As the episode title (taken from a famous and highly successful Pepsi advertising slogan used begin- ning in 1961) indicates, others were already making great strides with youth-oriented marketing, so Draper is decidedly behind the times in this respect. He is also outvoted and thus forced to start interviewing some young writers and artists, most of whom appear ridiculous, appearing to prove him right. By Episode 2.7, "The Gold Violin," however, the Smiths (a seemingly gay writer-artist team who happen to have the same last name) manage to win the Martinson's coffee contract for the firm, sug- gesting that youth, after all, will be served. Draper is on board and helps out with the pitch, but he still seems completely out of his comfort zone. He thus opens his pitch to Martinson's by noting that "unsuccessful at- tempts have been made (puppets and so forth) to capture the attention of youth." "Youth" here sounds like an advertising business designation for some sort of strange, alien demographic with which communication is virtually impossible. And Draper's inserted "puppets and so forth" (sug- gesting that he can't tell four-year-olds from twenty-four-year-olds) is one of his most hilariously awkward moments as a pitchman in the series, a mode in which he is generally so smooth (when he isn't drunk or melting down).

Draper, having fought his way to the top of the mainstream culture, is in fact characteristically at his most awkward when attempting to deal with a youthful counterculture that threatens to render him obsolete just as he has finally found his place. Draper is, for example, very much confused by the emergent rock music of the decade, and his tin ear to the marketing possibilities represented by that music does not appear to bode well for his future as an ad man. On the other hand, by the end of the series Draper might well have finally caught on, though the exact implications of the closing moments of *Mad Men* are very much open to interpretation. After a cross-country road trip that clearly symbolizes his desire to escape the increasing routinization of the corporate advertising world, Draper meets up in California (homeland of the 1960s youth culture) with Stephanie Horton, the hippie niece of Anna Draper. To this point, Stephanie has been Don's principal firsthand contact with flower-child hippie culture, though his experience with that culture expands quickly when Stephanie takes him with her to attend a countercultural retreat of the sort that was becoming popular at the time, especially in California. Such retreats (the most famous of them was the Esalen Institute, founded in Big Sur in 1962 and still in operation as of this writing) were presumably designed to help struggling individuals find their way to the values of the counterculture and thus achieve enlightenment and nirvana.

Of course, one could argue that the organized, institutional (and rather commercial) nature of such institutes represented precisely the sort of commodification that the counterculture was presumably designed to oppose, so that Draper's attendance at this institute focuses the attention of the final episode of the series on the confrontation between capitalism and counterculture that had been crucial to the series all along, even if it often seemed to receive very little overt attention. This retreat, in fact, contrasts starkly with the hippie farm commune visited by Roger Sterling only a few episodes earlier. That commune eschews the strictures of Taylorization and the comforts of modern capitalism as much as possible, refusing even to use electricity in its quest to live at one with nature, while the members follow their own desires, free of assigned roles. The retreat visited by Draper in this final episode, on the other hand, is clean, modern, highly organized, and well-equipped; the nature with which it seeks to commune involves a Pacific Coast setting that might have come off a picture postcard in a tourist-oriented gift shop.

One can see this retreat as an emblem of the shift from the hippie culture of the 1960s (with its ostensibly more radical rejection of the competitive ethos of capitalism) to the more organized, institutionalized (and marketable) New Age culture of the 1970s. The prominent role played by this retreat (which Draper visits in November 1970) in the final episode of *Mad Men* can thus be taken as an appropriate farewell to the 1960s, in which the series was so firmly rooted, and an introduction to the 1970s. It can also be seen as a sort of farewell to the 1960s counterculture, the ultimate defeat of which is signaled in the sharp contrast between this efficient, therapy-oriented institute (with its posh setting and somewhat older demographic) and the free-form, youth-oriented hippie farm of "The Monolith."

At the retreat, Stephanie takes off from a group therapy session that only succeeds in making her feel worse about giving up the baby to which she recently gave birth. Draper chases after her and tries to comfort her, in what amounts to one of the most uncomfortable scenes in the entire series. He tells her not to listen to the others, whom he regards as too immersed in their own beliefs to be able to consider the feelings of others: "You weren't raised with Jesus. You don't know what happens to people when they believe in things." He, of course, is apparently not among such believers, but he proceeds to offer to move to California and devote himself to taking care of her, even though, in reality, he hardly knows her. She responds with an incredulous "What's the matter with you?" That, of course, is very much the question posed throughout *Mad Men*, and Draper himself provides an indirect answer by responding with a series of clichés that sound like advertising taglines: "You can put this behind you. It'll get easier as you move forward."

Not surprisingly, Stephanie is uncomforted by Draper's platitudes and instead opts to leave the institute altogether, leaving Draper there without transportation to get away himself. Draper, who seems completely lost and confused at this point, calls Peggy Olson, who insists that he should come home and return to their new corporate home at McCann Erickson, where he might have a chance to work on "Coke," among other high-profile accounts. He's not interested in returning, though, and instead proceeds to attend another group therapy session. In this one, a man called "Leonard," a sort of 1970 version of Gogol's Akaky Akakievich, complains that no one notices him or cares about him and that his life is totally devoid of real contact with others. He breaks into tears, and Draper (of all people) moves across the room to comfort him with a hug, breaking into tears himself.

Whether Draper has experienced a breakthrough or a breakdown is not entirely clear, but when we next see him walking toward the surf, we have to wonder whether suicide is on his mind. A quick cut to a sort of ocean-view yoga/meditation session in which he participates alleviates that fear, but the promise of the session leader that meditation can lead to "a new you" takes on a special irony given Draper's own personal history of switching identities. The camera then closes in on the face of a chanting Draper, who breaks into a gradual smile before the sudden shift to the brilliant final scene of *Mad Men*, which is simply the classic "I'd Like to Buy the World a Coke" ad, which premiered on TV in early 1971, just a few months after Draper's visit to the California retreat.

The final questions posed by *Mad Men* thus have to do with the way we interpret Draper's final smile. Has he finally found peace? Is he at one with himself? Does he himself finally believe in something? Or has he suddenly had his greatest and most profitable advertising idea ever? This famous commercial was, after all, produced by McCann Erickson only a few months after the events depicted in this final episode, events that include Peggy's call for Draper to return to New York to work on Coke commercials. Did he answer her call?

Whether one likes to imagine that Draper created the ad or not, the ad is a virtual summa of the attempted (and largely successful) conscription of 1960s youth culture by mainstream capitalist consumer culture. It features a multiracial group of young people singing of peace, love, and brotherhood—with the implication that a key strategy in the pursuit of these goals might involve the drinking of Coca-Cola. But the ad also assures the older generation that Coke can help to harness the energies of the counterculture for productive purposes. These young people, after all, look far more like the denizens of the retreat in "Person to Person" than like the hippie farmers of "The Monolith." They are both clean and clean-cut—sanitized, wholesome, chaste, and posing a threat to no one, including the capitalist juggernaut that has conscripted them for its own purposes. They look harmless from a mainstream perspective, though a critical observer might see something sinister in their placid, bland happiness: the Woodstock Nation has become the forerunner of the Prozac Nation.

Of course, the famous Woodstock Festival occurred in August 1969—in the space between the two halves of the final season of *Mad Men*. It is thus one of the key absences that mark the series' engagement with the counterculture throughout. Widely regarded as a sort of culmination of the youth-oriented counterculture of the 1960s, Woodstock might also be regarded as a sort of death knell for the counterculture. Heath and Potter, skeptical of anti-capitalist countercultures in general, see the culture represented by Woodstock as a protest against the mainstream that was full of sound and fury, signifying very little: "There simply never was any tension between the countercultural ideas that informed the '60s rebellion and the ideological requirements of the capitalist system" (2004, 3).

Of course, as Dick Hebdige has noted, even the most radical subcultures (much of his emphasis is on the punk movement) have a tendency to fall into the gravitational well of commodification presented by the mainstream: "Youth cultural styles may begin by offering symbolic challenges, but they must inevitably end by establishing new sets of conventions; by creating new commodities, new industries, or rejuvenating old ones" (1979, 96). In either case, the very countercultural forces that were supposedly meant to oppose the dehumanizing and spiritually impoverishing power of capitalism have themselves become simply another weapon in the arsenal of capitalist marketing. Particularly relevant here is the argument by Thomas Frank that the supposedly subversive counterculture of the 1960s and early 1970s was actually created—or at the very least substantially encouraged and enhanced—by corporate marketing strategies designed to help create markets for new, hipper consumer products as capitalism itself evolved into a new phase moving beyond the boom years of the 1950s. This phenomenon, for Frank, then led to "a new species of hip consumerism, a cultural perpetual motion machine in which disgust with the falseness, shoddiness, and everyday oppressions of consumer society could be enlisted to drive the ever-accelerating wheels of consumption" (1998, 31). And, given Frank's emphasis on advertising, it should come as no surprise that *Mad Men* ultimately seems to agree with his analysis, as well as with other skeptical analyses of the counterculture of the 1960s, from Jameson, to Hebdige, to Heath and Potter.

10

MAD MEN GOES WEST: CALIFORNIA DREAMIN'

On April 18, 1958, the Los Angeles Dodgers (formerly the *Brooklyn* Dodgers) defeated the San Francisco Giants 6–5 in a game played at the

Don Draper. *AMC/Photofest ©AMC*

Los Angeles Coliseum, a football and former Olympic stadium recently modified to accommodate baseball. It was the first major league baseball game to be played in Los Angeles, though the first MLB game in *California* had occurred three days earlier when the Giants hosted (and defeated) the Dodgers in San Francisco. It was the beginning of a new era for baseball and for America, marking the point at which California could truly be regarded as a full-fledged part of the United States, bringing the two coasts together as never before, and helping to usher in a new national sense of space and time as increasing numbers of Americans began to travel from coast to coast via the burgeoning airline industry. Meanwhile, the fact that both the Dodgers and the Giants had formerly been located in New York City gave baseball's move to the West Coast a particular symbolic resonance, signaling a shift in the nation's economic and cultural center of gravity away from Manhattan and the surrounding boroughs and toward the West, especially Los Angeles and the surrounding suburban sprawl.

This movement westward is one of the many national narratives that are central to the overall arc of the events related in *Mad Men*, which begins only two years after the initial move of baseball to California, so that this shift of power remains in its early stages as the series starts. California is thus still able to figure in the series as a mysterious and exotic locale, even if Los Angeles in particular is already a mighty media center, making it central to the media-oriented business in which the putative Don Draper and his colleagues participate.

The symbolic role played by California in *Mad Men* is nicely captured in Episode 6.10 ("A Tale of Two Cities"), the title of which already indicates the structural opposition between New York and Los Angeles (gradually emerging as the twin capitals of American capitalism) that emerges during the course of the series (and that emerged in real-life America beginning with the departure of the Dodgers and Giants from New York to California). Interestingly, though, this opposition is to some extent undercut in this same episode by the fact that the main historical events playing in the background (as they do in so many *Mad Men* episodes) take place in Chicago, America's *other* Second City, thus reminding us that the Midwest still exists in the midst of this newly bicoastal America. In particular, these events involve the 1968 Democratic National Convention in Chicago, including the August 28, 1968, Chicago Police Riots, which both Don and Megan watch on television, she back home in

New York and he in his hotel room in L.A. At the same time, Detroit figures prominently in this episode as well, creating additional uncertainty over the referents of the title, but also suggesting the way in which *all* American cities have by this time been penetrated by the same capitalist system, contributing to a growing homogenization that not only diminishes the once great differences between New York and Los Angeles, but also diminishes distinctive regional differences in general. It is the birth of postmodernism, and the death, as Fredric Jameson and others have argued, of any genuine sense of place in America.

In his recent book *Country of Exiles*, for example, William Leach sees the gradual loss of any distinctive sense of local differences among places in America as a consequence of the general instability and insubstantiality of everything under modern capitalism. For Leach, a key result of this loss of a sense of place is increased mobility among Americans who, one place being as good as another, become increasingly willing to relocate, especially in the pursuit of economic gain. From this point of view, it might be significant that so many of the principal characters of *Mad Men* have scattered about the country as the series ends. Meanwhile, another consequence, Leach notes, is the unique fascination of Americans with artificial environments (such as theme parks or the fictional settings of movies), which stand in for real places with increasing ease as those real places lose their distinctive character. This fascination, Leach also notes, is highly "subversive to taking seriously a sense of place, or the world people actually lived and died in" (1999, 13). At the same time, such invented worlds are very much the stuff of advertising—and to a large extent the stuff of California in the American imagination.

Much of the "Two Cities" episode deals with the bemusement of Draper and (especially) Roger Sterling at the goings-on in L.A., which they visit in the main narrative of the episode. This visit includes Draper's distaste for the convertible in which Harry Crane drives them around while they are out west and the misadventures of both Roger (who gets punched in the nuts by his former employee—and in-law—Danny Siegel) and Draper (who nearly drowns in the pool) at a stereotypical drug-infested Hollywood party. In this sense, the whole excursion reads like a riff on the trip of Woody Allen's Max Singer to an incomprehensible L.A. in *Annie Hall*, one of the many instances in *Mad Men* in which a sequence of events seems to refer to a specific cinematic predecessor (or at least genre). For example, Singer also has difficulties with a convertible and with a diminutive producer (though this time a *record* producer, in the person of Paul Simon's Tony Lacey).

However, the episode's most telling commentary on Los Angeles (and, in particular, on the relationship between Los Angeles and New York) is delivered by Sterling to Draper during the plane rides back and forth between the two cities of the tale. On the way west, he reminds Don that they are slick, sophisticated New York ad executives and that the yokels in California will no doubt be no match for them. He also compares Don and himself to conquistadors, coming to subdue the West Coast locals with their more advanced strategy and weaponry. With those locals clearly no match for them, their main problem, Roger suggests (extending the metaphor and also invoking the stereotype of California as a land of looser sexual mores), will be to avoid contracting syphilis while they are there. Then, on the way back east, Sterling seems only slightly chastened by the fact that events in L.A. have hardly supported his theory of the superiority of New Yorkers. Indeed, he now declares to Draper his ongoing conviction that New York remains "the center of the universe."

Sterling's pronouncement, of course, must be read in the context of the way in which the series increasingly depicts him and his attitudes as anachronisms whose time has passed, despite his sometimes frantic efforts to keep up with the times by exploring new frontiers in sex and drugs. It should be no surprise, then, that this episode undermines Sterling's confidence in the ongoing dominance of New York or that it also presents L.A. as a land of perverse pleasures and as a place where talentless opportunists like Siegel have a chance to make it big if only they have sufficient chutzpah. In addition, other events in *Mad Men* also work to undermine any sense of the superiority of New York to L.A., while continuing to show suspicion of the inauthenticity of L.A. as well.

Perhaps the most obvious motif in this sense is the suggestion that L.A. is the land of the future, while New York is the land of the past. This view is expressed most clearly in Episode 3.2 ("Love Among the Ruins"), in which the developers of the proposed new Madison Square Garden in New York run into trouble when opponents complain that the new facility will necessitate tearing down the aboveground portions of the original Pennsylvania Station, a grand old building that is a bastion of local tradition. This opposing argument is so convincing, in fact, that ad man Paul Kinsey (who functions in the series as a figure of pathetic and hypocritical liberal silliness) nearly loses the MSG account for Sterling Cooper by declaring right in front of their representatives that tearing down the station would be a travesty. Attempting to repair the damage and win the job of promoting the proposed facility for the firm, Draper—touting the power of what we have now come to know as "spin"—argues that they simply need to change the conversation to emphasize not the oldness of Penn Station, but the newness of Madison Square Garden. To make his point, Draper tells the MSG reps about his own recent trip to California. Out there, he says, "Everything is new, and it's clean. The people are filled with hope." By contrast, he tells them, "New York City is in decay. But Madison Square Garden is the beginning of a new city on a hill."

The pitch is a great success (until Sterling Cooper's new British masters, who appear to be idiots, pull the plug on the account because of its low potential for a quick income boost), suggesting the allure of the new in the 1963 setting of this episode—or at least suggesting the emphasis on the new in early-1960s advertising. But this extremely rich moment in the series also identifies California as a key locus of this emphasis on the new, while at the same time linking this cult of the contemporary with the distant prehistory of the United States. Draper, after all, here invokes Puritan leader John Winthrop's famed "city upon a hill" sermon, intended to inspire the colonists who arrived in New England on the ship *Arabella* in 1630 and remind them of the importance of their mission in the New World. The whole world would be watching the work of the new colony, Winthrop suggested, looking for evidence that their attempt to build a new world was either blessed or damned.

Winthrop's sermon, suggesting a special God-inspired mission for the new colonists, would become a key part of the American national narrative of struggling against a frontier composed of harsh natural barriers and inhabited by savage indigenous peoples to build a new, virtuous world. Of course, Draper (who has little formal education) probably remembers Winthrop's speech mostly because it had recently been invoked in another speech delivered on January 9, 1961, by John F. Kennedy, shortly before taking office as the new president of the United States. Speaking before the General Court of Massachusetts, Kennedy compared the task that lay before the United States at that time with the one that lay before the colonists on the *Arabella* 331 years earlier, one fraught with peril but rich with promise. "For those of us to whom much is given," Kennedy famously declared, "much is required."

The same spirit that animated Winthrop's sermon also helped to inspire the zeal with which the newly arrived colonists and their fellows would soon set forth across the continent, extending the frontier westward until it finally reached the Pacific, realizing what they saw as the Manifest Destiny of the new nation by helping it to span the continent, with California serving as the key focus of the westward expansion. This process made California the centerpiece of a crucial portion of the rhetoric of the American Dream, a dream that is, in a very real sense, the true subject of *Mad Men*. It is little wonder, then, that California plays a key symbolic role throughout that series as well.

In *Mad Men* Episode 2.11 ("The Jet Set"), Draper and accounts man Pete Campbell arrive in Los Angeles to attend a "Rocket Fair," where they hope to hawk their wares to the deep-pocketed defense contractors who are gathered there to tout their own high-tech products for use in the Cold War space and arms races. California, land of the new, is associated in the episode not only with the new high-tech aerospace industries that are centered there, but with the even more futuristic world of science fiction. Kinsey, himself a budding science-fiction writer, had in fact hoped to come along on the trip largely because he wanted to walk in the footsteps of Edgar Rice Burroughs, who had preceded the Dodgers by forty years in moving to the L.A. area to establish his Tarzana Ranch.

The episode, one of the strangest in the entire series, seems designed to highlight the status of California (especially Southern California) as a locale so alien and exotic that even the laws of physics might be different than back home in the logic-driven environment of New York City. That something out of the ordinary is going on in this episode becomes clear quite quickly when Draper and Campbell meet up poolside, where Don sends Pete off on his daily duties, despite the fact that the latter would prefer to spend his time playing golf, lounging by the pool, and soaking in the California sun. Don, in hat, gray suit, and striped tie, puts out his ever-present cigarette in an ashtray, on which the camera focuses. When the camera shifts back to Draper after one of the interesting cuts in which *Mad Men* seems to specialize, he is now wearing, without explanation, a blue sport coat, no hat, and a tie with a different pattern. There may, of course, simply be a time gap during which Don has changed clothes. But there is an air of strangeness about the moment, as if he has stepped into some sort of alternate reality, a description that might, in fact, apply to California in general as represented in the series. The latter interpretation is then reinforced when he sees a woman who appears to be his wife, Betty, then doesn't, then does, but she walks by him with no interaction as he, puzzled, continues to the bar to order his drink. In the bar, Don encounters a weird collection of (somewhat sketchy) jet-setters, including twenty-one-year-old Joy (Laura Ramsey), who will soon become his lover at the jet-setters' Palm Springs hideout, which itself seems almost to represent still another reality apart from the world in which ordinary people live.

At the hideout, where Don goes with Joy, thus skipping out on Pete, Don once again finds himself poolside, then suddenly collapses, apparently from heat exhaustion in the California sun—though Don is given to having various "spells" throughout the series. He awakes to a weird "doctor" about to inject him with something, but he refuses the injection and springs back on his own, later tasting his first Mexican food, the culinary offerings in various American locales having yet to be homogenized in the way they are today—as when we are reminded in the series that it is impossible to get a decent bagel in L.A. Don then samples the charms of the nubile Joy as well. Whatever we are to make of this whole sequence, it is certainly strange, suggesting that California is a place where strange things happen. It may be a land of rebirth and renewal, but it is also a land of charlatans, crackpots, and weirdos.

In Episode 4.13 ("Tomorrowland"), Season 4 ends with a series of new beginnings, the most important of which is Don's surprise engagement to his new secretary, the beautiful and ambitious French Canadian Megan Calvet (Jessica Paré). What is perhaps less surprising is that Don proposes (and Megan accepts) while they are on a trip to California, she having come along to help look after his three kids, who have come along for the journey. The "Tomorrowland" of the episode title ostensibly refers to the futuristic segment of Disneyland (the forerunner of all the invented environments Leach discusses), a destination that is scheduled to be a highlight of the trip for the kids, though it hardly features in the episode at all. But the designation "Tomorrowland" is clearly also intended to stand for California itself, which consistently figures in *Mad Men* as a signifier of the future and of new things to come. Don himself claims to see California that way (at least in certain moods), so it is entirely appropriate, then, that California is the site where his life suddenly and seemingly unexpectedly veers off in a new direction.

Of course, virtually nothing happens in *Mad Men* without irony or complication, and this fresh start for Don is no exception. For one thing, it is complicated by the fact that he is already involved in a fairly serious romantic entanglement with psychologist Faye Miller (Cara Buono), whom he later in the episode has to inform of the engagement in a rather awkward moment. Even Betty (now Don's ex-wife) shows a spark of regret when Don still later informs her of the engagement as well. Moreover, as signified by Joan's world-weary "This happens all the time," the stunning development between Don and Megan is not really all that stunning. It is, in the world of 1960s business, virtually a cliché. "He's smiling as if he's the first man who ever married his secretary," she tells husband Greg. "She's twenty-five! As if that's news." Moreover, it has been carefully prepared through the second half of the season, which has seen Megan increasingly fawn on her new boss, punctuated by a sexual liaison in Don's office on a fateful night.

Earlier in this same episode, Betty fires her children's longtime black nanny, Carla, in a snit after Carla allows the boy Glen (with whom Betty earlier had an awkward encounter) to say good-bye to Sally before she and the rest of the household move to a new house in Rye, another in the network of suburban enclaves that surrounds New York City. When her new husband, Henry Francis, expresses his doubts about the firing, Betty simply declares that she thought it would be good for the children to have a fresh start. "There is no fresh start," says Henry. "Lives carry on."

That Don's start with Megan is not entirely fresh is also signified by his characteristically nostalgic gesture of sealing his proposal by giving Megan the engagement ring that the original Don Draper had given to Anna upon *their* engagement, many years earlier, suggesting a kind of continuity with the past, even in the futuristic environment of California. Indeed, from this point (just a bit more than halfway through the series) forward, the figuration of California in the series will be a bit more complex. While it will continue to serve as a marker of the future (with New York continuing to serve as a marker of the past), the two cities will increasingly be interlinked, with no absolute historical rupture between them as place distinctions in America gradually begin to dissolve.

Don's relationship with Megan culminates late in the sixth season with a series of developments triggered by the firm's attempts to drum up new business in Los Angeles, in particular by their ultimately successful attempt to win the account of the Sunkist juice company. Having secured this important business, the firm decides to establish an office in Los Angeles, primarily to service this one major account, though with the secondary goal of winning additional business as well. This new office will be small, staffed primarily by one accounts executive and one "creative," thus duplicating in smaller form the administrative organization of the New York office. The choice of executives to go west, however, becomes the subject of much dispute, leading to some of the crucial events in the final episode of that season.

In fact, Episode 6.13 ("In Care Of") begins as their New York art director Stan Rizzo (Jay R. Ferguson) walks through the offices with Draper, trying to convince his skeptical boss to send him to California as the creative man there. Stan clearly sees California as much of *Mad Men* sees it, as a land of virtually unlimited new opportunities. He tells Draper that he believes he can build the small office there into a fully functioning agency with multiple accounts, while Draper (suspecting that the artsy Rizzo can't handle the business end of building a new office in California) attempts to persuade him that the idea is unrealistic and that starting anew in California is not nearly as easy (or as romantic) as the artist seems to believe. "Los Angeles is not what you see in the movies," Draper tells Rizzo, somewhat condescendingly, prefiguring Jameson and Leach. "It's like Detroit with palm trees." Rizzo then responds with a suggestion that his view of California might be even more romantic than Draper had suspected. "So it's the frontier," he tells his boss. "I don't even need running water. Just let me set up the homestead."

Rizzo thus undermines his own argument by making it clear that his vision of California is indeed (as Draper had already suspected) derived from the movies. Even worse, it seems to have been derived not from movies about contemporary California, but from Westerns about the initial rush to California in the second half of the nineteenth century in the Gold Rush days—even though that rush was aimed more at northern California, and especially at San Francisco. There is surely a certain amount of irony in his statement, and Rizzo clearly does not believe California is still like it was in the wake of the 1849 Gold Rush. Still, he makes it clear that he views 1960s California as a rough-and-tumble land of few rules and few limitations, a place where an enterprising young man might be able to make his own opportunities.

Unfortunately for Rizzo, his potential opportunity even to go west quickly dissolves amid a scramble at the firm to replicate the Gold Rush days as seemingly everyone suddenly wants to head to California in search of the riches there. In fact, Draper, despite having suggested to Rizzo that opportunities in California might not be all they are cracked up to be, decides to go to the Los Angeles office himself. Having spent most of season 6 in an alcohol-fueled downward spiral, Draper decides that he is very much in need of a new start of his own, so he surprises his partners by announcing that he wants to become the firm's creative representative in California.

Wife Megan greets Don's announcement of the planned move with great enthusiasm, especially as the move west would be beneficial to her own acting career, while Don (master marketer that he is) also wins her support by spinning the move as an attempt to resurrect their flagging relationship. Then, suddenly, Ted Chaough (Kevin Rahm), Draper's main rival (and co–creative director) at the firm, decides that he is the one who needs to move to California to save his marriage; having recently entered an affair with Peggy Olson (Elisabeth Moss), he has concluded that he wants to stay with his wife and kids and that the only way he can do that is to get as far away from New York (and Peggy) as possible.

Draper turns down Chaough's request, explaining that it is too late to change his own plans to move west. Then, Draper unravels during a presentation to representatives from Hershey's Chocolate and adopts a new strategy of facing up to things honestly. As part of this strategy, he decides to send Chaough to the California office after all. The problem is that he must also send Megan westward, as she has already made irrevocable professional plans to transfer to L.A. In short, the move that was supposed to renew and re-energize their relationship ends up placing an additional burden of distance upon it.

Much of the plotline of the seventh and final season of the series then involves Don and Megan's attempts to negotiate their new bicoastal relationship, an attempt that ultimately fails, ending in divorce. Megan, big teeth and all, has some success and begins to go L.A. all the way, though she also begins to unravel beneath the pressure, her behavior becoming increasingly erratic—to the point where her agent enlists Don to try to stabilize her, apparently not realizing that Don himself has recently been in serious need of some stabilization.

In the seventh and final season, the dialogue between New York and Los Angeles becomes central to the plot of the series. Don now in exile from SC&P after his Hershey's meltdown, hangs out in his posh Manhattan apartment, meanwhile flying back and forth to visit Megan in L.A., where she remains unaware that he has been suspended from his job and thus could easily join her in California full time. Episode 7.1 ("Time Zones") particularly continues this theme, including a memorable moment in which Pete Campbell, lamenting the fact that his apartment overlooks the La Brea Tar Pits, issues his summary judgment of Los Angeles. Possibly remembering the Beach Boys (emblems of California culture that they are) hit "Good Vibrations" from 1966, Pete, still acclimating to life out west, declares, "The city's flat and ugly, and the air is brown. But I love the vibrations."

By the end of the first half of Season 7, the plan to expand SC&P out west is pretty much shelved when Roger Sterling engineers a plan to sell a controlling interest in the firm to McCann Erickson, a (real-world) mammoth corporate advertising firm that represents precisely the sort of capitalist soullessness that most of the principals at SC&P (who tend to be nonconformists, even when they are nonconformist Republicans) have been working all their careers to avoid. The move saves the recently reinstated Don from being sacked in a shakeup at SC&P, but also requires that Ted Chaough return to work in New York. McCann, however, assures SC&P that they will remain an essentially autonomous subsidiary, controlling their own business and making their own decisions.

By Episode 7.11 ("Time & Life"), however, McCann's corporate inclinations rear their ugly heads when the behemoth moves to absorb SC&P altogether, stripping it of its identity as a separate entity. Sterling, Draper, and the others predictably react with consternation, but find that they have little recourse but to comply, until Don, always the most creative of the group, conceives of a plan to move the entire SC&P operation out to California, allowing them to operate with even more independence than before. By this time, of course, Don's penchant for California dreamin' comes as no surprise. And Don's plan is one of several moments in *Mad Men* when the series attempts to represent business as a sort of romantic adventure, with the principals of SC&P operating almost like swashbuckling pirates. In this case, however, the maneuver fails miserably and very quickly comes to nothing, with very little drama involved.

The leading example of this sort of business adventure occurs in Season 3, when the principals stripped their old firm of both equipment and clients in a successful effort to escape being acquired by McCann all the way back in 1963. By 1970, however, when the final episodes are taking place, no such escape appears to be possible. McCann's execs swat aside Don's proposal like a pesky gnat and instead offer lucrative jobs in their own firm to Don, Roger, Pete, Ted, and Joan, the surviving partners of SC&P, telling them to cheer up, because they have "died and gone to advertising heaven." At this point, capitalist routinization has proceeded to the point where even California cannot provide a romantic venue for escape from the process—as if it ever could—and heaven itself has been replaced by a corporate job with a fat paycheck.

Draper, however, is not so easily defeated. Lured by the promise of a big payout, he goes along with the plan and prepares to go to work for McCann. At his very first pitch meeting, however, which involves the presentation of some scientific marketing research, he decides he has had enough and bolts mid-meeting. For Don, advertising should be an art, not a science, and the data being presented simply serve for him as evidence that he will never be able to fit in at McCann. He takes off and spends the rest of the series on an almost surreal cross-country car trip, the goal of which is not really clear, even to him.

Still, almost anyone could have guessed by this time that Don's ultimate destination (after a variety of adventures along the way) would be California, which he has always envisioned as a land of renewal and as the place to go to seek a fresh start, which is something by this time that he badly needs. Arriving in L.A., he looks up his "niece" Stephanie Horton so he can give her Anna Draper's old engagement ring, which he has reacquired after his divorce from Megan. Stephanie, always a hippie type, ends up inviting Don to a countercultural retreat where various individuals have come to seek enlightenment and nirvana.

This retreat, of course, epitomizes one popular image of California as a haven for alternative lifestyles and New Age thinking, which is not exactly the kind of thinking with which Don characteristically feels comfortable. Not surprisingly, he circulates among the other attendees with a bemused air of detachment, clearly feeling out of place. Then (after Stephanie herself has taken off, leaving him there alone) Draper apparently experiences some sort of spiritual breakthrough during a group therapy session. When a man named Leonard complains of his feelings of being ignored and unnoticed, Don suddenly rushes to him and gives him a big hug of sympathy. When we last see Don, he is sitting with his back to us, yoga style, overlooking the surf of Big Sur, apparently transformed and having found peace at last.

Mad Men then cuts to its final scene, the classic "I'd Like to Buy the World a Coke" ad, which premiered on TV in early 1971, just a few months after Don apparently ended his retreat from capitalism by embracing the noncompetitive ethos of the hippie counterculture. In this famous commercial, a multiracial group of young people (looking very much like the young people Don encountered at the retreat and decidedly unlike the Madison Avenue types who created the ad) stand atop a hill (which one could easily imagine being in California) singing of peace, love, and brotherhood—with the implication that these goals can be significantly furthered by the drinking of Coca-Cola.

One is free to interpret this ending in at least two different ways, though both of these interpretations ultimately amount to pretty much the same thing. Perhaps the more interesting interpretation is that Don has not been transformed at all, but has simply recognized that the energies of the counterculture he has just observed at the retreat would make a terrific marketing tool. Consequently, he has returned to the "real" world of Madison Avenue and there created this Coke ad, which would be his greatest contribution to advertising history and would presumably put him back on top of the ad world. This interpretation, however, requires a certain amount of creativity, as there are no cues in the episode itself to suggest that Don has, in fact, returned to McCann—the firm, incidentally, that did in reality create the ad. A more straightforward interpretation would be that Don has genuinely found peace and that he remains at Big Sur contemplating his navel (or whatever), while the energies and imagery of the counterculture to which he has retreated are meanwhile in the process of being appropriated by the very advertising firm that he has left behind.

As noted in chapter 9, Thomas Frank's argument that the supposedly subversive counterculture of the 1960s was designed to help create markets for new, hipper consumer products, in fact, lies at the very heart of what *Mad Men* is all about. This complex, multifaceted series can be described in a number of ways, but the ending of this final episode suggests that a central project of the whole series is to tell the story of the confrontation between the nonmaterialist values of the 1960s counterculture and the ultra-materialist values of the consumer capitalism that arose in the 1950s and fully hit its stride in the 1960s. This confrontation, as the ending of *Mad Men* verifies, was clearly decided to the advantage of the latter.

It seems clear that *Mad Men* wants to portray the 1960s as a turning point in American history, most obviously in the way it suggests fundamental (and permanent) changes in the system of American consumer capitalism, including the spread of more and more sophisticated techniques of advertising and marketing. This same story, though, can be told in a variety of different ways, depending on which aspects of the narrative one emphasizes, such as a shift in media power from film to television or the growing power of technology as a determining factor in the texture of day-to-day American life. The Coke commercial ending, however, suggests that what is really being told is the story of the death of the American Dream, or at least the conversion of the American Dream into just another consumer product, ready to be packaged and sold, thanks to a process of commodification so thorough that nothing, even the most idealistic dreams, is immune to this process. California thus becomes the symbol of the completion and consolidation of the victory of commodification over all aspects of American life. Once a city of stern Puritans on a hill in Massachusetts, America is now a group of hippies on a hill in California, singing their hearts out and hawking Coke for all they're worth. And once California—long seen as the cutting edge of the American Dream—has been thoroughly conscripted into the capitalist system of modern America, then there is nowhere left to go for those, like Don Draper, who would seek to move west (literally or metaphorically) to find a new and better life.

Part IV

Mad Women

Betty Francis, Joan Harris, Peggy Olson, and Megan, the second Mrs. Draper (Jessica Paré). *AMC/Photofest ©AMC*

I I

JOAN: THE FEMININE IDEAL?

One of *Mad Men*'s most complex (and sometimes unpredictable) characters, the zaftig redhead Joan Holloway Harris (Christina Hendricks) is a virtual walking allegory of the various struggles faced by women in the

Joan. *AMC/Photofest ©AMC*

1960s, especially if they want to pursue professional careers. As such, Joan joins the ambitious and talented (but much less sexually attractive) copywriter Peggy Olson as the linchpins of *Mad Men*'s treatment of the theme of "women in the office." Indeed, the two women constitute a sort of dialectical pairing that enriches the treatment of that theme well beyond what could have been done with either character alone. Joan's arc through the seven seasons of the series certainly traces a narrative of the evolving role of women in American society from 1960 to 1970, though her pairing with Peggy emphasizes that her story is just *one* such narrative and that there are, in fact, many others.

Among other things, Joan is nearly a decade older than Peggy, which not only means that she approaches things from a perspective of greater experience and less idealism, but also that she thinks and acts in a style that was crafted in the 1950s, while Peggy (only twenty-two when the series opens in 1960) is a more modern woman of the 1960s. As Akass and McCabe put it, "Joan reawakens the 1950s Hollywood pin-up fantasy of a voluptuous female sexuality—combining erotic sex with a kitsch glamour" (2011, 181). The women characters of *Mad Men*, even more than the men, can often be read as historical allegories—as when Betty Draper begins the series as the ideal wife of a fantasy version of the 1950s, though this role quickly unravels. Reading Joan in this way is particularly valuable as a way of understanding her role in the series.

Joan's image as she moves into the 1960s is nicely summarized in Episode 2.6 ("Maidenform"), when Paul Kinsey conceives of a brilliant ad campaign for Playtex bras based on the notion that all American women want to be seen (by men) as either "Jackies" or "Marilyns," evoking Jackie Kennedy and Marilyn Monroe as the opposed paradigms of American femininity. Pointing out various secretaries in the office who exemplify this hypothesis, Kinsey notes the obvious fact that Joan is a Marilyn type, then corrects himself: "Well, Marilyn's really a Joan, not the other way around"—showing just how much she inhabits the role. But one of the ways in which Marilyn and Jackie were opposed was in the way Marilyn was really a 1950s paradigm, while Jackie's image was more suited to the new decade of the 1960s. Marilyn, in fact, would soon be dead, her death impacting the characters of *Mad Men* (perhaps Joan most profoundly of all) only three episodes later. One of the narrative arcs of Joan's struggles in the series, then, is her attempt to transcend her background in the 1950s and to move into the 1960s, a struggle that also marks the experience of Don Draper, among others, which might explain the odd connection that Draper and Joan seem to have throughout the series.

When we first meet Joan, in the opening episode of the series, she is showing Peggy, newly hired as a secretary, around the offices of Sterling Cooper. The rather cynical advice that Joan dispenses to Peggy during the tour has less to do with company policies and office supplies than with the sexual politics of being the new girl in a workplace. Joan's advice comes from ten years of working in the company, and she certainly knows what she is talking about. However, those ten years were also spent in the 1950s, and the world in which she acquired her wisdom is about to change. Joan's story through the run of the series is one of the markers of that change, as she ultimately moves from her position as an office manager on the lookout for a potential husband to the head of her own promotional film production company, ready to face the world on her own.

In Season 2, Joan, just entering her thirties, seems on the verge of living a stereotypically feminine version of the American Dream when she not only becomes engaged to be married, but becomes engaged to a handsome young *doctor*, in the person of resident surgeon Greg Harris. That this dream is clearly rooted in the 1950s, rather than the 1960s, is indicative of the way in which that earlier decade is the source of so much of the material from the early seasons of *Mad Men*, a series so widely lauded for its engagement with the historical context of the *1960s*. In general, Joan is depicted as confidant, poised, and seemingly in charge of every situation, especially at work. In the office, she is the one who really understands how things operate and the one to whom others automatically turn for help when something goes wrong. She is depicted, throughout the first season, as highly competent and professional, but she nevertheless displays herself in the office as a knowing target of the male gaze, a walking spectacle of feminine sexual allure. Moreover, she has not overcome the belief that, as a woman, her most likely path to success lies in marriage, even though she has already had one badly failed marriage before the events depicted in the series. Thus, her engagement to a doctor would seem to verify her ability to achieve her goals, to master all of life's situations and to come out on top.

Yet Joan can also be quite vulnerable, despite the fact that she herself tends to try to hide her vulnerability beneath a veneer of toughness. And her personal life is a mess. As the series opens, she has already conducted a long-term affair with her married boss, Roger Sterling. By the penultimate episode of the second season ("The Mountain King"), it is clear that the engagement to Dr. Harris will not automatically solve her personal problems, as it takes her into the center of one of the shocking (and often violent) moments that punctuate the ongoing narrative of *Mad Men*, upsetting plans and destroying lives. Here, Harris comes by the offices of Sterling Cooper to pick up Joan. While there, he meets Sterling; he knows nothing of Sterling's affair with Joan, but he senses that something might be going on between the two. Perhaps he also senses that the office is Joan's territory, and that there she is in charge, not he. Harris then follows Joan into Draper's office, where he forces her to the floor and rapes her. Apparently unsettled by Joan's seeming rapport with Sterling (and her mastery of the office environment), the good doctor reasserts his masculine power and his ownership of Joan in the only way he can think of.

Joan resists but is surprisingly acquiescent during the attack. What is even more surprising is that she decides to accept the attack as a sort of boys-will-be-boys moment and to continue her engagement with the young doctor, never again speaking of it. The strikingly beautiful and sensuous Joan knows that men regard her as a sexual object, and she realizes that, in the context of 1960s America, one of her most effective tools for achieving success is to accept this objectification and to try to use it for her own purposes. From this point of view, Joan's marriage to Harris, while wrapped in a conventional narrative of romance, is essentially a professional move of a kind that might easily be described as a form of prostitution, though in Joan's mind, she is simply following the course women are supposed to follow. Being a wife is the stereotypical goal of women of her generation, and her view of the world is most definitely "rooted in stereotypical gender roles" (Barkman 2010, 213).

After the rape in Draper's office, the romance of this stereotypical arc is shattered, but the presumed material advantage of marrying a doctor remains. By the time Season 3 opens, Joan has married her doctor. In the season, she also resigns from her long-time job at Sterling Cooper, a job that had been a key element of her personal identity. She then takes on a new identity as an all-American housewife, her own prospects now tied to those of her husband and his career. (Of course, one might speculate that her willingness to leave Sterling Cooper also comes about partly from her frustration at their inability to appreciate her talents, as when she served late in Season 2 as a television script reader [to help determine ad place-ment] only to be shoved aside in the role, replaced by a man.) These prospects seem considerable, given his profession. Unfortunately, it is gradually revealed that Greg is actually an incompetent surgeon, so that his prospects are not nearly as good as Joan herself had initially assumed.

Hints of Harris's incompetence as a surgeon surface during a key dinner party in Episode 3.3 ("My Old Kentucky Home"). Joan seems to take the news in stride, meanwhile providing entertainment by singing Cole Porter's "C'est Magnifique" while accompanying herself on the accordion. Ironically, the song is about an on-again-off-again love affair and can thus be taken as a commentary on Joan's former relationship with Sterling—which in fact will briefly flair up again in Season 4, leading to Joan's pregnancy with a child she will pass off as Harris's. "C'est Magni-fique," though, is all about the sweetness of the renewal of a former love, when, in reality, Joan conceives her child in a moment of rather rough sex fueled by the adrenaline rush experienced by Joan and Roger after they are mugged on a New York street. The song thus ironically anticipates the brief resurgence of the Joan-Roger affair, while reinforcing the notion that Joan's love life is not quite the stuff of songs.

After Harris also washes out in an attempt to switch to psychoanalysis, he then finds new life by joining the military and becoming an army surgeon in Vietnam, leaving a frustrated and infuriated Joan behind. Her husband seems to find success as a military surgeon, despite his seeming lack of any real ability. This success suggests that the military holds surgeons to far lower standards than does the civilian world, though the series does not follow up on the implications of this motif. In any case, given the events of "The Mountain King," it comes as no surprise that Harris doesn't turn out to be great husband material after all, and Joan essentially writes him off after he leaves for the military. By this time, she has already had to take a job in sales at the Bonwit Teller upscale depart-ment store to try to make ends meet, but she soon appeals to her former lover Sterling to try to get back into office management, a move she successfully makes after she helps Sterling, Draper, and others escape from the old Sterling Cooper when it is about to be sold to corporate behemoth McCann Erickson and to found their own new firm.

They couldn't have done it without her, in fact, and she becomes an indispensable part of the new company, Sterling Cooper Draper Price (SCDP). However, despite her savvy and skill in managing the company's offices, she continues to be regarded largely as a glorified secretary and to receive very little in the way of appreciation for her skills, no doubt largely because her gender and her spectacular looks have slotted her into a narrow set of predefined roles. The men in the office are happy to ogle her or to let her solve their problems for them, but they are not willing to take orders from her or even to treat her as an equal. As Mimi White notes, "She gives the impression that she fully controls her female masquerade, but she also endures the deprecation that comes with her carefully crafted image" (2011, 151).

Perhaps the pivotal episode in terms of Joan's role in the series is Episode 5.11 ("The Other Woman"), which is also one of the key episodes in *Mad Men* as a whole. Here, SCDP seems on the verge of finally hitting the advertising big time because they have a legitimate shot at landing the account for the British Jaguar automobile. Though not a big-selling brand in the United States, Jaguar is an expensive brand that carries a certain amount of prestige. In fact, as the episode makes clear, in the world of advertising *any* automobile brand carries a certain amount of prestige. Automobile accounts would seem to be the holy grail of the advertising world, with automobiles serving as the iconic commodities of modern industrial capitalism.

This episode is all about such holy grails, such ultimate objects of desire, and indeed SCDP's strategy for advertising the car is to depict it precisely as such an object—though advertising Jaguar is made somewhat more difficult by the fact that their cars are notoriously unreliable and thus ultimately undesirable as a practical means of transportation. So SCDP, with Draper taking the lead, decides to depict the car as a sort of gorgeous but fickle mistress, the desirability of which is, if anything, increased by its unreliability.

The notion of using sex to sell cars is nothing new, of course: it is, in fact, a virtual advertising cliché. What makes this episode special is the intricacy with which it explores the theme. For one thing, SCDP must win the account before they can sell Jaguars, which means that first they must sell themselves, a motif that becomes particularly literal when smarmy Herb Rennet (Gary Basaraba), a dealership owner who plays a key role on the committee assigned by Jaguar to choose an advertising firm, makes an indecent proposal by suggesting that he will help throw the business to SCDP in exchange for one night of sex with Joan.

With Pete Campbell leading the way, the partners at SCDP somewhat shockingly decide to ask Joan to carry out the deal, sacrificing her pride for the good of the company. Draper (for whom, given his childhood in a whorehouse, prostitution is always a particularly touchy subject) strongly opposes the notion and attempts to dissuade Joan from going through with it. The other partners, though, vote to offer Joan a partnership with a 5 percent stake in SCDP if she will spend the night with Rennet. Realizing what this partnership could mean for the financial security of her small son and herself, Joan accepts the deal, partly based on her understanding that the literal prostitution she will be performing is not really all that different from the kind of compromises that business people make all the time in order to achieve financial success. When Campbell first proposes the deal to her, she responds with appropriate outrage, "You're talking about prostitution!" However, Campbell coolly replies, "I'm talking about business at a very high level," and subsequent events suggest that his argument is more compelling than Joan at first lets on.

A moist-eyed Joan steels herself and carries out her end of the deal, while Rennet (apparently a very satisfied customer) keeps his bargain as well, helping SCDP to win the Jaguar account and completing the transaction. This link between business and prostitution is one that recurs at numerous points in *Mad Men*, though never quite so overtly as here. Indeed, one could argue that the link is so overt here as to be a bit heavy-handed. However, this intricately constructed episode is actually quite effective—partly due to the subtle acting skills of Jon Hamm and Christina Hendricks in conveying the emotional reactions of their characters and partly due to some of the most complex editing in the entire series.

The centerpiece of this editing occurs during Draper's official pitch to Rennet and the other Jaguar reps, which occurs the day after Rennet's night with Joan. It is one of Draper's most impassioned pitches of the entire series, partly because the stakes are so high for the firm and partly because of his own emotional reaction to Joan's prostitution, something he does not know has occurred at the time he makes the pitch. The pitch itself is a sort of masterpiece of denial, in which Draper seems desperately to want to convince himself (if not his audience) that he is talking about beauty, not sex, that he is proposing to market Jaguars as aesthetic objects rather than as objects of displaced sexual desire. It is an argument of which Nabokov's Humbert Humbert, always seeking to aestheticize his lust for young girls, would have been proud.

What makes the depiction of this presentation in the episode particularly effective is the editing, which produces a sort of Flaubertian counterpoint in which Draper's rhetoric of beauty is intercut with scenes of Joan's "seduction" the night before, making clear that sex is, after all, very much what the pitch is about. For example, Draper begins his pitch with a reference to all of the beautiful women he has known, declaring that "when deep beauty is encountered, it arouses deep emotions—because it creates a desire, because it is, by nature, unattainable." This pitch is intercut with Joan's arrival at Rennet's room the night before, suggesting that she is the truly beautiful but seemingly unattainable object of Rennet's desire.

Meanwhile, Draper's pitch continues, as he shifts to a variation on a theme that is central to his whole ambivalent relationship with the advertising business: "We're taught to think that function is all that matters. But we have a natural longing for this other thing." "This other thing" is that undefinable, unattainable beauty of which he has been speaking, but the idea closely relates to his own ongoing attempt to convince himself that, in creating ads, he is creating art, not simply hawking products.

But this particular statement also reveals the Lacanian strategy that underlies all of Draper's advertising campaigns. For Lacan, all individuals are propelled through life by a desire for something that they sense is missing, something unobtainable that they hope will overcome the sense of loss they experienced at the end of infancy when, upon learning language and entering the Symbolic Order, they gave up the sense of primal connection to the universe that is central to the Imaginary Order experience of infancy. This obscure, unattainable object of desire, labeled by Lacan the "*objet petit a*" is the elusive goal of all of our endeavors to attain satisfaction in life. For Lacan, these desires are, first and foremost, sexual, but later theorists, inspired by his work, have noted the applicability of the concept to other realms. Slavoj Žižek, for example, has combined Lacanian psychoanalysis with Marxist theory to describe the way in which this quest for an unattainable object of desire also well describes the mechanism that drives consumer capitalism.

Consumer capitalism is driven by the production of a desire to consume, rather than simply by the production of commodities. Firms such as SCDP and other advertising and marketing agencies are thus crucial to a consumerist economy because it is their business to generate this kind of desire in potential consumers. Moreover, the Lacanian notion of the *objet petit a* well describes this desire because consumerist desire can, by definition, never be fulfilled, lest the cycle of consumption come to an end, driving the consumerist economy into a state of collapse. In *Mad Men*, commodities stand in for the *objet petit a*, and Joan is treated by most of those she meets as the ultimate commodity.

By intercutting Draper's pitch to Jaguar with scenes from the encounter between Joan and Rennet, *Mad Men* essentially endorses a Žižekian analysis of the close correspondence between consumerist desire and sexual desire. Draper's pitch, however, goes one better by essentially arguing that consumerist desire, unlike sexual desire, *can* be fulfilled. Rennet cannot ultimately possess Joan, even though he rents her body for the night. However, the tagline (supplied by Michael Ginsberg) for Draper's Jaguar campaign is "At last. Something beautiful you can truly own," suggesting that, while a Jaguar automobile might be *like* a fickle mistress, it is better because it can be more truly and fully possessed than any woman.

What this somewhat misleading tagline leaves out, of course, is that possession of a Jaguar does *not* entail possession of the *objet petit a*, which is still hanging out there, just out of reach. The desire for a Jaguar can be fulfilled, but it will only be replaced by a new desire for some additional object, in a never-ending cycle. Meanwhile, this whole topic of the purchase and ownership of the objects of one's desires resonates strongly with the prostitution motif that is so central to this episode, but that in fact runs throughout *Mad Men*'s critique of consumer capitalism.

Joan's role in "The Other Woman" is obviously central to the question of the ownership of women, though the overt presentation of her role as prostitution is complicated. As Laurie Naranch notes, in *Mad Men* prostitution is typically figured as "an enterprise of economic survival in the context of an unequal, gendered, and raced world where structures of inequality constrain the choice" (2015, 103). Here, Joan's degrading objectification is also a clear form of empowerment, propelling her to the partnership that, after thirteen years of working at the firm, she still could not have hoped to achieve in any other way. It is, in fact, a more physical version of the strategy she has employed for some time in her career. As Akass and McCabe put it, "Joan consciously exploits the sex-bomb image that men, with their libidinous looks, impose upon her, while understanding the power (however limited) contained within that exhibitionist role" (2011, 183).

Other women characters in the episode are also used to explore the motif of women as property, though often in a less knowing way than is Joan. This is most obviously the case with Draper's new young wife, Megan, an aspiring actress who is treated like a piece of meat when she goes to audition for a role in a play, asked to turn and display her body from different angles while three men leeringly ogle her from a couch. Perhaps more important, though, is the way in which Megan is treated as a form of property by her own husband. Draper clearly feels threatened by the idea that Megan might be on the verge of career success that will lessen his power over her. In particular, her job as an actress might often include the specific presentation of her body as the object of the male gaze, and we know, from his reaction to her sexy musical performance at his birthday party in the opening episode of this season, that Draper does not particularly like other men looking at his wife. In addition, Megan's job could potentially bring her both fame and fortune, giving her complete economic independence from Draper's affluence. Finally, Megan's job might also involve considerable travel, as when Draper is shocked and horrified to learn that, if she gets the part for which she is auditioning in this episode, she will be away in Boston with the play for three months.

If Draper feels his control over Megan beginning to slip away in this episode, then one might say the same thing for his relationship with Peggy Olson, who has functioned as his protégée throughout the series but now appears ready to go out on her own. When Peggy expresses strong disappointment when Draper rejects her plan for a project that would take her to Paris on business, Draper throws a wad of money in her face and suggests that she should use it to help finance her own trip to France. The action is clearly a demonstration of power, a way of reminding her who is boss. It is little wonder, then, that Draper is shocked when Peggy responds by looking for employment elsewhere, ultimately accepting an offer from Draper's personal archrival, Ted Chaough, to become chief copywriter at the firm of Cutler, Gleason, and Chaough (CGC), one of SCDP's most direct competitors.

When Peggy meets with Chaough, they both try to pretend that it isn't about the money, but when Peggy asks for an annual salary of $18,000 and Chaough responds with a counteroffer of $19,000, the deal is sealed, seemingly on the basis of cash. Still, the point here is not so much about the money as the appreciation, the one thing Peggy feels that she is not getting from Draper. That money is not the issue becomes clear when a stunned Draper tries to make Peggy a counteroffer, assuming that he merely has to name a high enough number and she will stay. "There's no number," she tells him. Apparently unlike Joan, she has no price, though of course Draper was never going to offer her the kind of payment that Joan received for her prostitution to Rennet.

If this comparison seems to work to Joan's disadvantage, it is also true that much of the strength of the characterization of Joan in *Mad Men* lies in the refusal of the series to idealize her as a paragon of virtue. Though largely admirable and sympathetic, she is a character with many facets, and her ambition can sometimes make her at least as ruthless as any of the men she confronts on her path to success. She can, in fact, be downright mean-spirited when it seems in the interest of her own ambitions to be so. In fact, she has occasional bad moments, even when no ambitions are involved. In Episode 2.2 ("Flight 1"), Paul Kinsey hosts a bohemian party at his artist's digs in Montclair, which allows him to show off his new black girlfriend, Sheila White, who serves as a key marker of Kinsey's pretentious liberalism. Joan, who had once been involved in an affair with Kinsey herself, responds to Sheila with absolute condescension, at the same time making sure she reminds the younger woman of her own history with Kinsey: "It's good to see you and Paul together," she says, cattily. "When Paul and I were together, the last thing I would have taken him for was open-minded."

Late in the series, when Draper has unraveled to the point where Joan considers him a liability to the firm, she is among those most strongly in support of taking action to get rid of him, despite the fact that the two have shared a sympathetic personal connection of sorts at several points in the series. At times, in fact, the two have seemed on the verge of a potential romance, though this sort of relationship in fact never develops. In Episode 5.10 ("Christmas Waltz"), Joan throws a tantrum in the office after she is served there with divorce papers by Greg: she seems unable to bear the intrusion of her difficult personal life into the workplace, where she normally feels thoroughly in control. Draper intercedes and takes her with him on a "research" trip on which the two test-drive a Jaguar XKE, pretending to be a married couple. They then have a drink together, and Draper (himself newly remarried) tries to cheer her up by assuring her that there is life after divorce. He then leaves without making a move, though they definitely share a moment. This moment, in fact, is no doubt part of the reason why Draper reacts so strongly against the firm's decision to prostitute Joan to Herb Rennet in the very next episode. Joan, for her part, expresses appreciation for his attempts to prevent the exchange, tenderly telling him, "You're one of the good ones." We (and Draper) find out only later that her assignation with Rennet has already taken place.

In Episode 6.3 ("Collaborators"), Rennet resurfaces when he comes by the offices of SCDP to discuss their ongoing business with Jaguar, but first drops in on Joan to try (leeringly) to suggest an ongoing relationship. Her claws come out, and she has no trouble expressing her contempt for the man. She then stalks into Draper's office to get herself a drink, while Draper goes off to meet with Rennet, who proposes that the campaign developed by Draper and his team be modified to emphasize local radio ads rather than national television. He then suggests that Draper pitch the idea to the other Jaguar reps, given Don's skills with such things. Draper, already hostile to Rennet over the Joan situation, is furious—then responds by helping pitch the idea per Rennet's request, except totally incompetently, pushing Rennet's idea into the realm of the ridiculous (such as local flyers and mailers) and thus sabotaging the entire proposal. Confronted by Campbell and Sterling after the meeting, Draper responds that continuing to give in to Rennet's demands is like "Munich," referring to the attempt to appease Hitler before World War II.

Draper obviously takes the selling of Joan to Rennet quite seriously. His resentment toward Rennet finally boils over in Episode 6.6 ("For Immediate Release") when he "fires" Jaguar and announces that SCDP no longer wishes to represent them thanks to Rennet's ignorant interference. The loss of this key account, however, torpedoes a plan cooked up by Joan, Campbell, and Bert Cooper to take SCDP public, a move that would have made Joan's 5 percent stake worth a hefty amount of money. Draper thus manages to squander any good will he might have built up with Joan, instead drawing her ire because she feels he has cost her a considerable amount of money.

In the sixth season, this ire shows itself when Joan supports Draper's exile from the firm after his meltdown during a pitch to Hershey's Chocolate, and in the final season she will be among those who want to get rid of Draper altogether. On the other hand, she is not merely seeking some sort of revenge: she seems honestly to believe that Draper's behavior is costing her (and the firm) money, and her attitude toward him is clearly motivated primarily by financial self-interest. She didn't sleep with Herb

Rennet only to have Draper lose the proceeds of that transaction for her. It is perfectly consistent, then, that she reverses herself and allies herself with Draper and Roger Sterling after the latter arranges to sell a 51 percent stake in the firm to McCann Erickson (with the stipulation that Draper is part of the package) for a price that might make Joan's 5 percent worth more than a million and half bucks.

Joan seems to be riding high. As the newly reconstituted Sterling Cooper & Partners prepares for the future as an independent subsidiary of McCann Erickson, she is working primarily as an accounts manager as well as participating fully in partnership decisions. The deal with McCann Erickson turns out to be bad news in all sorts of ways, however, especially for Joan. When, in Episode 7.8 ("Severance"), she and Peggy meet with representatives from their new parent firm concerning SC&P's account with Topaz panty hose, the men from McCann use the nature of the product as an occasion to deliver a stunning stream of sexual innuendos. Peggy tries to ignore them and remain businesslike, while Joan mostly just sits and fumes, growing more and more angry at the leering sexist remarks. She then has a fight with Peggy in the elevator after leaving the meeting, as Peggy suggests that Joan should probably expect such experiences, given the way she dresses. It's payback, of course, for Joan's earlier remark that Peggy dresses like a little girl, as well as a sign of Peggy's resentment that Joan has become rich from the sale of the firm, while Peggy remains a mere employee.

This meeting at McCann is itself simply an indication of what Joan will face throughout her experience with the new company. After McCann breaks their noninterference pledge and absorbs Sterling Cooper altogether, Joan expects to bring her newfound accounts expertise to the new firm, but by Episode 7.12 ("Lost Horizon"), she finds that no one there will take her seriously—except as a potential target of what would now be called (especially overt) sexual harassment. When she complains to higher management, she is sternly rebuffed and offered fifty cents on the dollar of the half million dollars McCann still owes her from the purchase of SC&P if she will simply walk away.

Furious, Joan threatens to go to the press or perhaps the ACLU, but in reality she feels powerless in the face of her new corporate masters, especially after her old flame Roger Sterling appeals to her to take the money and run. She concludes that it really isn't worth the fight and takes Sterling's advice. Just as Peggy, the woman of the future, marches into the offices of McCann wearing a flashy dress and sunglasses, cigarette dangling from her mouth and Japanese erotic art piece under her arm, Joan (the woman of the past) prepares to exit the company altogether.

The symbolism seems clear, but the resilient Joan is not so easily defeated. In Episode 7.10 ("The Forecast"), Joan meets Richard (Bruce Greenwood), a somewhat older wealthy retired real estate developer, who is now divorced and determined to enjoy the rest of his life free of the constraints of either a business or a family. Richard and Joan strike up a relationship, which he quickly decides to leave when he learns that she has a son; Joan, in another of the problematic moves that complicate her characterization in the series, decides to send her son away so that she can be free to trot around the globe with Richard. The decision seems almost shocking, but Joan never seemed all that thrilled about being a mother. She is often good at helping others *manage* their problems, but this is a matter more of efficiency than of compassion. She's not really the nurturing type. For his own part, Richard has second thoughts and insists that she keep her son. They will find a way to work around the boy, especially as Joan's mother seems to provide most of his care anyway.

Retired from his own former life as a successful businessman, Richard wants now just to enjoy the rest of his life and he wants Joan to share that enjoyment with him. Unfortunately, he wants her on his own terms, available at any time to go with him wherever he wants. He wants her all to himself or not at all. So one might expect that, given Joan's unceremonious departure from McCann, she might simply retire and begin jet-setting around the world with Richard, having sex, snorting coke, and generally living the good life.

Joan, however, still has one more trick up her sleeve. In the series finale ("Person to Person"), Ken Cosgrove, now head of advertising for Dow Chemical, asks her to help him find someone to make a new promotional film. Joan grabs the opportunity to form her own company to produce this film and others like it. She attempts to convince Peggy to leave McCann and join her in the new enterprise as a partner: "Harris-Olson," she tells Peggy. "You need two names to make it sound real." Peggy declines, despite her own stated ambition to be a partner somewhere someday, but Joan approaches the new undertaking with relish, confidence, and enthusiasm nevertheless. Finally, she will be the boss, with no men to answer to. There is still Richard, of course, but he exits quickly when he realizes she will be devoting so much time to her new business instead of to him. "What are you doing?" he demands petulantly. "Don't you want to be with me?" Then he walks away, knowing that Joan's new business will take more of her time and energy than he is willing to relinquish.

Joan prepares to face the future alone, having learned once again the price that women must pay to succeed in the business world. She is not pleased by Richard's departure, but she still has something to prove and some new worlds to conquer in business, even after Sterling announces that he is changing his will to leave a sizable portion of his estate to her (and his) son, Kevin, thus securing the boy's future and removing one of Joan's major motivations to try to make more money. As if to punctuate her independence and the fact that she needs no one but herself, she even gets the desired second entry for the name of her company by adding her maiden name to her married one. "Holloway-Harris" will enter the 1970s with momentum and energy; it is not likely that Joan, always a force to be reckoned with, will fail, despite the special challenges that she will face as a woman whose sexual allure makes it hard for men to see her other talents for what they are. As the series ends, Peggy seems poised to move forward with both the man and the job of her dreams. Joan has only the job, but somehow it feels like Joan is the big winner of the two. The 1960s have become the 1970s, and Joan (the bombshell of the 1950s) has become the entrepreneur of the new decade.

12

PEGGY: CREATING THE MODERN WOMAN

Greater development of women's potential and fuller use of their present abilities can greatly enhance the quality of American life.— "American Women: The Report of the President's Commission on the Status of Women" (1965)

The women's ladder was one person wide. No woman could ascend unless somebody else was kicked off it. It became a lethal catfight and caused some very bitter competition.—Laurel Cutler, former advertising executive, 2008

Bertram Cooper, the venerable advertising leader who founded the original Sterling Cooper with Roger Sterling's father, uttered his last word in July 1969 as Neil Armstrong spoke to the nation from the surface of the moon: "Bravo" (Episode 7.7, "Waterloo"). The moment carries weight, symbolizing that Cooper's generation and its ideas will not make the transition beyond the 1960s. Their antiquated views no longer matter, viewed by the youth swarming around the office as old-fashioned and simple as the senior leader's demand that people entering his office remove their shoes. The era of figureheads is over, and the youngsters storming the gates are pulling down statues as they smash their way inside.

At the other end of the spectrum, and in contrast to the senior partner's demise, is Peggy Olson's ascendancy. Even Don, at yet another impasse in his attempt to return to full power in the agency he created, decides that

Peggy. *ABC/Photofest ©AMC*

it is Peggy's time. He is willing to sacrifice his power in order to assure hers. It is as if the baton is being passed from the past to the future, not only in the agency, but also across the advertising industry.

While Cooper's death overtly symbolizes the changing of the guard, Don and Peggy unfurl their status in Episode 7.6 ("The Strategy"), a deeper moment that is transcendent in the *Mad Men* oeuvre. Prepping late at night in an attempt to develop a pitch for the Burger Chef fast-food chain, their discussion moves from business to personal, even though Sterling Cooper's fate may rest on the ideas they amplify.

Peggy, wearing her emotional life on her sleeve, admits that she turned thirty years old several weeks earlier and, with no family or even significant relationship, has no business attempting to sell Burger Chef on a family-related theme. How can she make such a case if she does not know what it is like to be a mother? Opening up, Don responds with his own list of fears about aging and losing his family: "that I never did anything and that I don't have anyone."

A few minutes later, Peggy is ready to give up and tears flow. Her emotional life and work pressure are too much to handle. Don, the gentleman, hands her his handkerchief. His words of encouragement set the stage for reconciliation after months of ill will. Draper, now in the role of subordinate, looks her in the eyes and provides the acknowledgment she has always desired: "You're doing great." Peggy's eyes brighten and she ad-libs a new campaign. Don's support enables her to break through the clutter, and a winning pitch comes to life.

In the background, dark night sky contrasted against the false whiteness of the office, Don hears the strains of "My Way" by Frank Sinatra. Viewing the song as an omen, Draper stands and puts out his hand. He reaches out to her for a dance, but she momentarily hesitates, giggling, then stands to join him. At first, they are awkward, the intimacy of the atmosphere causing them to keep a safe distance. After about ten seconds, though, Peggy places her head on Don's chest. A little stunned, but full of pride, he bends down and kisses her head.

Although it is initially awkward, the dance between mentor and mentee—often a relationship filled with contention and anger—melts away as he realizes that the future is hers. There may not be a more heartfelt moment in *Mad Men*'s ninety-two hours. Don and Peggy have evolved full circle. She is not only recognized for being a powerful, important part of the team, but he is wise enough to help her get to a point where she can develop the winner. Don goes a step further, seeing that the only way to save the agency and the Burger Chef account is to have Peggy lead the effort. The show's history—the deep, challenging relationship between Peggy and Don—culminates in the way Jon Hamm and Elisabeth Moss portray the characters and the scene is filmed. Their glances contain multitudes, and sly smiles indicate depth that they understand and the faithful audience appreciates. Draper's approval is what Olson has coveted, to be valued by him specifically, and almost no one else.

This small moment speaks volumes.

PAVING A WAY

Peggy, like her mentor Don, is a conflicted and contradictory character, but as *Mad Men* unfolds, it is clear that she is the straw that stirs the drink. In various interviews, Matthew Weiner outlines a master plot that makes it fairly clear that Peggy is the show's chief spark. He certainly does not want to alienate viewers or underplay Don's centrality, so he discusses it as a joint effort, a kind of partnership that really would not work without the other. Weiner explains, "To me, their [Don's and Peggy's] stories are being told in parallel. The conflicts between them and their interactions with each other are definitely running side by side" (March 11, 2014).

Peggy's journey from office girl to Burger Chef pitch is a fictionalized amalgamation of the lives of many women who paved the way during the real-life mad men era. She first appears on the program in a brief glimpse barely discernible within the framework of the pilot, the 6:41 mark of the first episode. The peek of Olson is from the back as she enters an elevator. She is just one of many people (mostly men) crammed into the tight space.

Weiner and his team, however, might be giving away Peggy's future importance by the way she is contrasted from the white-collar men on the elevator. They are in dark suits, wearing or carrying overcoats. The elevator operator is a black man in a uniform. What sets Olson apart, besides her sex, is her light brown topcoat and wide-brimmed tan hat. Although she seems like an extra in the scene, her youth and appearance distinguish her in that space.

The treatment Peggy receives the rest of Episode 1.1 ("Smoke Gets in Your Eyes") is what the viewer might expect at the hands of early-1960s young executives—she is demoralized, bullied, and given bad advice about how to act in the workplace. Joan Holloway, the head secretary, even sends her to a doctor to get a prescription for birth control. Dr. Emerson, the chauvinistic physician, embarrasses Peggy, essentially chastising her for wanting the pill and cautioning her against becoming a whore because she is on it. He even claims that he will take the prescription from her if she has too much sex. In the drab examination room, featuring earth tones and brick that seem straight out of a mid-century insane asylum, Emerson talks down to Peggy (literally as he stands over her as she lies on the examination table). His lit cigarette is a cue to modern audiences that this is a shady doctor, clearly willing to overlook the health hazards at a time when ads of physicians endorsing smoking filled magazine pages.

Peggy receives similar treatment at work, particularly at the hands of Pete Campbell, an aristocratic account man who is clearly attracted to her. However, he also has to retain his reputation among "the boys" by harassing her like a middle-school bully. Pete, engaged to a well-to-do socialite from a rising family, wants to keep his crush a secret. Like a kid, he resorts to calling her "Amish," based on her dress, as a way to mask his true feelings. Pete clearly views women as sex objects to be dominated. His aggressive posturing is starkly contrasted to Don's smooth demeanor. The joke is so biting, obvious, and childish that Draper actually apologizes for the young man's rudeness and chastises him.

Paving her way at Sterling Cooper, Peggy's role is continually secondary, even after she gets elevated to copywriter. Simultaneously, her insight into advertising and intelligence are on display. She seems to have some of the street smarts that enabled Draper to become a creative whiz. Early in the series, Peggy's primary part is to serve as the counter to the era's many problematic issues, ranging from workplace sexual harassment to pervasive gender inequality. Her character is not like the other secretaries or telephone switchboard operators. Nor does she burst onto the scene, like the real-life Mary Wells (one of the models for the Olson character), a pioneering female advertising leader in the 1960s. The petite, blonde Wells could light up a room by the force of her will and stunning charisma. She disarmed her male counterparts by concurrently being beautiful and witty, but then hitting them with knockout ideas.

In Peggy, though, the viewer is asked to make decisions. Is she the lamb being led to slaughter in the big-city world of advertising or the vamp that lets smarmy Pete into her apartment late at night? Olson is continually caught up between doing what she thinks is expected and a desire to be respected, more than another girl in a skirt.

Years later, after Peggy has left Sterling Cooper for rival agency Cutler Gleason and Chaough, Peggy puts on a Draper-like mask, bullying and berating her subordinates and generally terrorizing them (Episode 5.11, "The Other Woman"). Writer Willa Paskin explains:

> Peggy has always been the kind of demanding, oblivious boss who makes her employees stay late on holidays, qualities she inherited

from her own boss, Don. But those traits in a woman mean she is lacking the very thing we expect female bosses to have: emotional intuitiveness. (2014)

Peggy acts like "Don Jr." and is given a number of sexist monikers that are reserved for women (especially in the business world) who act as shady, immoral, or aggressive as their male counterparts. She has learned from her boss, even as she charts a course different than his. Their notions of work coalesce. "You can relate to her wit and ambition and yet see that can she sometimes be cold, self-centered—human," says cultural critic James Poniewozik (2014).

It is clear—and Weiner confirms in interviews—that Don and Peggy are both unfolding and transforming, often on parallel paths and sometimes diverging. While Don is consistently the buttoned-up business executive at work, Peggy presents a wider array of emotions. For much of the series, she does not replicate Draper's cool ease with her coworkers, clients, family members, or the people in her personal life. As she realizes her power and talent, though, she becomes more Draper-like. Fans went nuts at the emergence of the new "badass" Peggy who walks into McCann Erickson smoking, hungover, and carrying an extremely inappropriate, obscene octopus painting (Episode 7.12, "Lost Horizon").

Initially, Peggy's fundamental contrast to Don and her role as protégée and underling serve as reasons for the audience to root for her—she is the harassed worker that so many people can relate to and whose troubles they may have experienced themselves. Yet, the intensity of their relationship propels the small moments and contextualizes the large changes across the turbulent 1960s. Weiner divulges his feelings about the character, explaining:

> Peggy is my favorite. I identify with her struggle. She is so earnest and self-righteous and talented and smart, but dumb about personal things. She thinks she's living the life of "we." But she's not. And every time she turns a corner, someone says, "You're not part of 'we.'" "But you all said 'we' the other day." "Yes, we meant, 'we white men.'" (Spring 2014)

The audience comprehends what Weiner outlines above. Peggy becomes such a sympathetic figure that even when she is difficult, viewers are still charmed by her down-to-earth sensibilities. More frequently than any major character on *Mad Men*, Peggy is most often compassionate, friendly, and "normal" in a way that audiences appreciate. She possesses that magic "relatable" characteristic that people respond to in a really personal way.

MAD WOMEN

One of the common early criticisms against *Mad Men* centered on its portrayal of women, particularly in excluding the pioneering females who played a critical role in advertising history. Although there is speculation that the Peggy Olson character is based on industry legend Mary Wells, Peggy will really have to put her career into warp speed to match that of her real-life counterpart, one of the true giants of the industry.

Wells parlayed her creative talents as a copywriter to the top of the agency world, working for both McCann Erickson and Doyle Dane Bernbach, before founding her own agency Wells Rich Greene. At the heart of Wells's vision, according to writer Mark Tungate, was seeing television advertising as "a form of theater." "Arguably," he writes, "she was the first advertising executive to unlock the potential of TV advertising as spectacle" (2007, 60). Bill Bernbach, one of modern advertising's founding fathers (and at least in part a role model for *Mad Men*'s Don Draper), valued Wells and at one point called her "the agency's dream merchant" (qtd. in Tungate 2007, 61).

Dubbed "chic, blonde and successful" in a 1969 *New York Times* article, Wells and her creative staff pushed the boundaries. In a speech at a meeting of the Association of National Advertisers, Wells lectured the assembled agency leaders on the need to be creative with television commercials, despite the cost, and then provided a return on investment analysis that pulled the ideas together. The money spent resulted in commercials that could be aired longer, as well as campaigns that would generate publicity. Essentially espousing integrated communications efforts long before the term grew popular, Wells explained, "We don't get publicity by accident; we get it by design" (Dougherty 1969). Her high-flying, outsized personality became part of the marketing mix. Wells Rich Green clients counted on her promoting them as she herself drew headlines.

Wells's true talent focused on combining creativity with the snappiness television commercials afforded. She led the efforts that turned chalky antacid Alka-Seltzer into a lifestyle product based on commercials that mixed humor with iconic taglines, like "plop, plop, fizz, fizz, oh what a relief it is." Wells's ideas were even more revolutionary for Braniff Airlines. In this case, the "dream merchant" turned the drab airport terminals and planes themselves into vibrant symbols of the new age by having the planes painted in bright, rainbow colors. Wells also had the company redesign the interiors, moving away from drab earth tones and adding an array of colors. Stewardesses too, who had traditionally worn outfits that made them look more like nurses than anything else, underwent a noteworthy change, donning bright, patterned leggings and mod designs representative of the era.

Wells understood the link between advertising, products, and the desires and aspirations of modern consumers. Her creative team used artistry and creativity to link the goods and services provided by their clients to notions of what it meant to live at the upper reaches of the American Dream. She drew deeply from the cultural revolution taking place around the globe. Wells saw these transformations as colors and images that, in turn, promoted and created new strands of culture.

For Wells, the connection boiled down to storytelling. "Advertising, in any form, is about telling stories that captivate readers or viewers and persuade them to buy products," she explained. "You can tell stories in many ways, with or without words. But knowledge is the fuel that ignites your talents in the advertising business" (Lawrence 2002, 70). Later, Wells wrote about her infatuation with television's potential for reaching the 1960s consumer, admitting, "I was giddy with the thrill of making movies out of advertising commercials" (qtd. in Maas 2012, x). These ideas were not necessarily revolutionary; many agencies had the same aspirations, yet it took someone of Wells's insight, talent, and leadership to build an agency based on satisfying dreams.

Under Wells's guidance, Braniff launched a commercial called "The Air Strip" that immediately brought attention to the newly colorful and exciting brand. Designer Emilio Pucci created uniforms for the reminted stewardesses, now called "hostesses," that could be easily removed as a route moved from cold weather to a warm weather port. Pucci's idea focused on the hostess removing or changing clothes while in the air, which would equate air travel and elegance in the passenger's mind.

"The Air Strip" begins with a plain white background and a heavy percussion beat, but then a female dances into the frame, long and lean, looking like a model on the runway. Dressed in bright orange, she begins tossing small clothing items as the music changes to a whistling tune reminiscent of a burlesque show or strip joint. "Braniff International presents The Air Strip" appears, and a husky male voice describes how the hostess will be dressed at various times during the flight. His voice drips with sex and innuendo as the stewardess continues to remove clothing. He later intones, "Ssshhe'll ssslip into something a little more comfortable" and that even an airline "hostess should look like a girl."

Although the commercial "shocked" many people, Wells recalls, "we ran it on the Super Bowl [and] it was a sensational hit. . . . Braniff hostesses [were] the most exciting ones in the world and businessmen went out of their way to fly Braniff to see them" (Lawrence 2002, 36–37). To modern eyes, the Braniff commercials are hopelessly dated and overtly sexist. Yet, for Wells and her creative team, the notion of turning "hostesses" into runway models and creating an air of excitement about the airline and act of flying itself provided the mix of glamour and artistry they craved. More importantly, the new branding effort had important ramifications for their client. Writer Charlie Moss next came up with the tagline: "The End of the Plain Plane," which symbolized the transformation at Braniff. Wells explains the outcome, saying, "Airline advertising and marketing and design would never ever be the same. . . . In less than a year we received more publicity in newspapers and magazines than we paid for advertising in over ten years" (39).

The reason the Braniff ads and others of the era worked so well is that they capitalized on "the Big Idea." Writer Steven Heller explains that creative leaders in the 1960s "realized that to truly capture an audience's attention and impart lasting messages they had to continually amuse." As a result, he continues, advertising then became "cleverer, funnier, and more enjoyable than ever before" (2012, 342). Simultaneously, though, advertising grew more deeply ingrained in American life. One could no longer look past commercials or print ads. The collision between the advertising business and television created a landscape primed for the kaleidoscope world facing consumers and businesses in the mid- to late twentieth century. Although print ads and radio spots seemed powerful when introduced, television commercials pushed advertising forward by matching the energy, emotion, and vibrancy of real life like never before. A TV ad might provide drama, titillation, sex appeal, humor, horror, sadness, or various mixed emotions designed to solidify a product in the buyer's mind.

Almost fifty years later, for example, the Braniff campaign still influences the airline industry and many others based on its success in brand creation and management. There is a reason, for example, that Southwest Airlines has colorful airplanes and it spends countless millions of dollars annually so that consumers equate it with the idea of "fun," a decidedly ironic emotion to feel when it comes to describing modern airline travel. Similarly, Mary Wells Lawrence, David Ogilvy, and other advertising titans still serve as role models for today's practitioners. These legendary figures demonstrated that advertising could concurrently create and reflect culture across society at large. They transformed the way people interacted with products, goods, services, and organizations by demonstrating that brands could possess humor, passion, drama, and suspense.

Money poured into advertising in the 1960s because corporations, particularly in consumer goods, realized that traditional purchasers were savvier and had a broader array of choices. Yet, as the consumer base tacked toward a younger demographic, agencies and clients had to combine information with entertainment. Essentially, the impetus stood, "give them a reason to buy and do it with style." Later, when the culture seemed in the midst of change brought on by free-spirited youth, antiwar demonstrations, and the fight for women's and minorities' rights, ad agencies jumped aboard the current trends, aping the styles coming out of San Francisco and college campuses. Edward P. Morgan explains, "Madison Avenue's co-optation of sixties dissent for profit was deliberate. . . . The rising counterculture of the mid-sixties was probably the first of the newly visible social groups to attract major marketing attention" (2010, 224). What Wells and other young stars of the advertising game could do is take in the style and popular culture influences swirling in the air and package them into beautiful little gifts that consumers wanted (or perhaps demanded) to open.

A STEP FORWARD, A STEP BACK

Assessing *Mad Men*'s portrayal of working women in the business in the 1960s, the trade journal *Advertising Age* interviewed several women who worked in the big agencies at the time. What the discussions uncovered is that the series nailed the big vices perfectly, like how much people smoke and drank. The women interviewed were mixed, however, on just how restrictive the industry could be for women who wanted to get ahead.

Laurel Cutler, who started at the bottom ranks as a clerk/typist at J. Walter Thompson (JWT) in the late 1940s (reminiscent of Peggy's initial status), viewed the industry as repressive and limiting for females, who all had to fight for the few spots anywhere near the corporate ladder. In her early years as a copywriter, she explained that women could only write for clients in the "four 'F' areas: food, faces, furniture, fashion" (qtd. in Giges 2008). Women were also confined to copy roles, not the account jobs that men could hold. This important detail makes Joan's treatment at the hands of her McCann Erickson bosses authentic. Although Cutler later rose to vice chairman of Foote, Cone & Belding/Leber Katz Partners, her route out of copywriting and into management took years to achieve.

In contrast, the other women interviewed—also high achievers via the creative side—found the workplace less sexist. Janet Wolff, for example, who worked as an executive at JWT and William Etsy Co., said that the male copywriters who worked with and for her were great teammates. They even covered for her if the duties of being a mother of four children meant that she had to go to school functions or the like. Wolff recalls the workplace being a fun environment and accepting.

What separates Peggy from some of the original Madison Avenue groundbreaking female leaders is that she entered a little later than they did. Many of them, such as Phyllis Robinson, had already attained great success by the early 1960s. Her work with Bill Bernbach led to her becoming the industry's first female copy chief when Doyle Dane Bernbach launched in 1949. Robinson inspired a generation of women who wanted to do more than be secretaries.

On *Mad Men*, Peggy and Don's relationship seems constantly in flux, particularly as the 1960s move from Camelot to the Age of Aquarius. Peggy is young and popular but stands a bit outside the free love and marijuana-smoking people in the mainstream of the youth movement. Her desire to please Draper and be taken seriously as a creative force ties her to seemingly outmoded ideas of work, just as she seems enamored of traditional romance and consumer trapping. Peggy and Don are *Mad Men*'s oppositional forces, but at times they come together based on their shared love for the agency and advertising. Weiner explains, "Peggy is always thinking about the agency. Peggy's ambition and desire to fix the agency is always on her mind" (2010).

Visually, Peggy's modest wardrobe and plain hairstyle point to her conservative nature. In contrast, her closest work friend (and much later, lover), Stan, is wholly representative of the counterculture 1960s ethos. He grows his hair and a full beard, so that by the late 1960s, he is fully adorned in a typically hippie style. Even though working at the agency might place Stan in the mainstream, he smokes dope, listens to rock music, and demonstrates characteristics of the era's rebellious young people. He is clearly not Don or Peggy.

The yin and yang aspects of Peggy and Don emerge in Episode 4.13 ("Tomorrowland"), the Season 4 finale. Despite the challenges the new agency faces, Peggy's office (that she shares with artist Stan) is colorful, with a mauve wall offsetting the traditional workplace gray and equally drab dark blue couch. She has taped magazine ads to the walls. The ads, the creativity of competitors worthy enough to be added to this mini-shrine, represent Peggy's commitment to new ideas and thinking (very 1960s counterculture), but also the work world that keeps her tied to mainstream values. In other words, ads are simultaneously art and the output of work in the agency/organizational arena. Viewers might also interpret her confines as the young woman in the thralls of creative work, doing her part to "fix" the agency, as Weiner claims.

When Don flies off to California to take care of the house that Anna, his pretend ex-wife, left him and vacation with his beautiful, young secretary/nanny Megan and his children, Peggy is the rock that holds together the crippled agency. She has real power and authority over the men in the office, like television head Harry Crane, who have positions higher up the food chain.

The physical transformation from secretary Peggy (mocked by Pete in the series pilot as dressing like an Amish woman) to powerful Peggy is startling. Even in a situation where men do not trust her instincts because she is female, she wears her clothing like a superhero's costume. In a new business meeting with Topaz panty hose executives, she sports large gold earrings and bright lipstick. Her black mock turtleneck with brown vertical stripes makes her seem a high-ranking ad executive and casts an aura that is much classier than the dingy office where the appointment takes place. As a matter of fact, the office itself is so pedestrian that it seems as if Peggy may be the only woman to have ever entered it.

Given the chance to make up for Ken's mistakes in the meeting, Peggy relies on what she knows—delivering, as Weiner says, "her version of Don" (2010). In donning her Don mask, Peggy essentially saves the company by bringing in essential revenue. Her success, however, is short-lived (a quick hug from Ken after she impulsively jumps into his arms), since Don had just announced his engagement to Megan minutes earlier. As Peggy and Ken stride toward Don's office to share in the news of the new client win, they are overwhelmed by the boss's announcement. Draper and Megan hug and kiss. Again, as the heart and soul of *Mad Men*, Peggy's bewildered reaction—a mix of jealousy, disbelief, and curiosity—mirrors the audience's feelings.

Draper and the young agency have been in a free-fall. When it is time to right the ship, Peggy goes out and earns new business. On the other end of the spectrum, her boss grabs for a young, beautiful life raft. He is male in a male-dominated world, so he wins. Peggy's power is sucked up and virtually eradicated in a split second of applause and sly smiles as Draper and the soon-to-be Mrs. Draper bask in approval. Episode co-writer Jonathan Igla explains, "Peggy is disappointed in Don because he has grown as a person over the course of the season and their relationship has obviously grown into something different and more intimate. . . . She feels something of a betrayal" (2010). The engagement creates a schism that Peggy immediately senses but Don overlooks in his general post-announcement bliss.

Peggy needs a sounding board and turns to Joan. The two women share their first real moments of kinship as they discuss the shortcomings of these much-flawed men that, for better or worse, they have dedicated their lives to serving. Peggy sums up the situation, stating, "A pretty face comes along and everything goes out the window." Joan concurs and reports that she has been given a promotion, but with no raise in salary. When Joan claims that she told herself long ago to not expect any real satisfaction from the job, Peggy calls her out: "That's bullshit!" Then they share a long, conspiratorial laugh, both realizing that they are stuck with these men and this place.

The scene above is a powerful affirmation of the strength of *Mad Men*'s female leads. Joan's office is the perfect setting for the détente, since it exudes her newfound power. Joan's striking orange hair contrasts with the equally striking mod red chair she uses, in juxtaposition with her black dress and red lipstick. The office is large, publicly displaying

Joan's growing influence, yet the women are filmed at the desk, making the scene feel smaller. The cramped framing intensifies the conspiratorial aspects—the strong women are marginalized to the outskirts, while the celebration of the boss and weak secretary rages outside. They both smoke, drawing on its intimacy as an act one does with another person and the bond developing between them as they talk about their roles in the office and as women.

Yet, the office is also a place where work gets completed, more or less what seems to be the hub of core functions that keep any workplace running. While Joan enjoys soft lights and demure furnishings, the office central piece is a project flow chart, most likely related to billing or project completion cycles. Across the early seasons, Joan stood as the central repository of female power at Sterling Cooper; her office in the newly formed agency, though, transitions her from gossip and courtier to genuine authority. Peggy needs her as an ally and friend, since both are becoming players in a male-dominated game with constantly shifting rules and measures.

As Peggy transitions from office girl to copywriter to protégée then boss and back to writer and underling, her career takes shape and seems on a solid trajectory, even if that professional path did not really exist for many women in the era. In contrast, Draper's career often careens from one thing to the next as he deals with both personal challenges and past demons.

Slowly, in Season 6, as Don falls apart, then finds ways to piece his life back together, Peggy charts a course with a bit more deliberation. "Peggy's story is a constant mix between what is good for Peggy as a person and what is good for Peggy's career, and they have not gone together at all," Weiner explains. "I think she only knows how to pay attention to her job. And that may become a story for this season. [Peggy] would probably say she's not a political person, but everything she does is pioneering. She's reaching a point in her life where she's going to have some choices" (Romano 2014).

Typical of Weiner's quote above, after years of yearning to prove herself as a leader, Peggy does one of the most stereotypical things a 1960s female can do: fall in love with her boss, Ted Chaough, even though he is married and has a family. Interestingly, he is another in a line of average-looking men that Olson falls for, not the dashing types, like Draper or Roger Sterling.

In the season finale, Episode 6.13 ("In Care Of"), Peggy's personality and outward appearance reveal her newfound happiness with Ted, despite his marriage and family. As she types away in her cramped office, the energy flows through her. Her hair is pulled back, revealing large, stylish earrings. Peggy wears a colorful scarf and low-cut dress, all more playful and daring than her typical work outfits. Her outward façade reflects bliss. The night before, Ted promised to leave his wife, which changed her outlook, simultaneously seeing a future that she had not imagined.

The next day, however, Ted backs out of his bold declaration after talking Don into letting him go to California, which Draper had planned to do. The confrontation with Peggy is intense and brief, with Ted attempting the moral high ground, explaining, "You can stay here and have your life and your career, and let this be the past." Peggy's retort is filled with disgust and resolution: "Well, aren't you lucky, to have decisions." Once again, her love life is dictated by others.

Meanwhile, Draper has been suspended after the Hershey's pitch debacle and telling the truth about his horrific childhood being raised in a whorehouse. Don's fall, though, literally opens a door for Peggy to ascend. The scene opens in his (former) office; the door is open and his name is prominent, as well as an outdated photo of his daughter, Sally, from when she was little (and he still controlled her). Standing, Peggy is looking through files. She is back to her more typical clothing style—turtleneck, tartan matching pants and vest. As usual, her attire is buttoned-up, but with a little flair and a bit of smugness.

Meanwhile, Draper takes his three children to the brothel where he spent some of his youth. The children are old enough to understand that it is a horrible part of town and they are a bit afraid. A black child sits on the steps, eating a Popsicle—perhaps a slight updating for the era of the way Dick/Don at one time sat alone eating a Hershey's chocolate bar. Don exchanges a look with Sally; now she understands him better.

Season 6 ends with "Both Sides, Now," Joni Mitchell's anthem to love's hold over one's thinking and its consequences. This is the Judy Collins version, the first of many artists to turn the song into a hit. The everyday life, according to the song, is illusionary and changes as people transform in their day-to-day existence. It is as if love is impossible to understand as are people in the midst of its hold over them.

Peggy walks into Don's office and sits at the desk, then, as if deep in thought, turns to her left, mimicking the back-of-the-head camera angle that Draper is in during the opening credits. The iconic shot only lasts about two seconds, but signifies the up-and-down relationship between Draper and Olson. From a larger perspective, her replacing him as the icon of the new era symbolizes the wider societal transformations that will sweep his generation out the door in favor of the next, just as he had done with older leaders like Bert Cooper. It seems as if Peggy has finally ascended to replace her mentor. In the real world, women were revolutionizing advertising as well, from the flamboyant Wells to the steady, pioneering leadership of Robinson. The sixties mentality and cultural transformation would not wipe away sexism, racism, homophobia, or other societal ills, but the era did open up new avenues for women like Peggy to live more fulfilling lives.

13

BETTY: DIARY OF A MAD HOUSEWIFE

I knew this woman wasn't going to live long, and we love the idea of her realizing her purpose in life right when she ran out of time. . . . I think there's a lesson to be learned about the randomness of things.— Matt Weiner, 2015

*The women of this country are tired of being prisoners. . . . The image is of the moronic housewife whose sole aspiration in life is to have kitchen sink and husband's shirts.—*Betty Friedan, 1970

A typical scene: Betty (whether Mrs. Draper or Mrs. Francis) sits alone, staring off into the distance, arms crossed, right arm cocked straight up and holding a cigarette. The vibe feels as if the cigarette could burn down to her fingers and she would not even notice. Betty is absorbed—in her thoughts, feelings of loneliness, disillusion, herself. Then, an oddly appropriate song that illuminates the week's theme begins and a million or so viewers watch the credits, waiting for the preview to next week's episode.

Despite a myriad of creepy characters and odd individuals that flicked into, then out of, the picture, Betty became *Mad Men*'s most polarizing figure (people loved "hating on" Betty, in the parlance of our times). From the show's earliest days, it seemed as if fans either loved or despised Betty (and soon, in turn, January Jones). While viewers seemed to forgive Don for his many foibles, his wife never received similar absolution. Writer Ali Trachta explains: "In the earlier seasons, Weiner observed a hostility toward Betty for being so beautiful and being cheated

Betty. AMC/Photofest ©AMC

on. Audiences perceived her as an idiot, he thought, or felt she deserved it somehow" (2013). After Betty and Don split, the character then drew fire for being a horrible, disinterested mother and gaining weight. Then the real tragedy struck as the series ended. Despite the horrific sendoff, many fans viewed Betty's cancer and imminent death as a fitting end for someone that they often viewed disapprovingly.

Ironically, for a character seemingly stuck ten years behind the actual calendar date, when Betty finally steps into the modern 1960s—asserting her individuality by returning to school for a master's degree in psychology and then gaining a deeper appreciation for the horrors of Vietnam—she is stricken with terminal lung cancer. Unlike many characters that wander out of focus or simply vanish, Betty prepares to die, the token demise that propels the story arc as *Mad Men* hurtles headlong into the 1970s. Her death is a symbolic representation that some of the excess of the 1960s would not make it into the next decade. Betty never quite caught up to the era, so the rest of the world just passed her on the road to the future.

And, despite how fans reacted, Betty's downfall really is a tragedy— she has a teenage daughter who will be without a significant female role model and two young boys that will grow up without ever being old enough to really know her. As viewers, we can only make assumptions about how Don will interact with his children. Via Sally we learn that her mother wants their uncle to take care of the children, but there is no guarantee there either. These children will have to overcome the trauma of Betty's early, horrible death after watching her deteriorate. No matter how one might judge her life, the end is brutal.

Betty's death symbolizes real heartbreak, perhaps even a cruelty, particularly when one considers the predictions regarding Don's conceivable demise leading up to the end of the series. All those rumors and tricks to get viewers contemplating his death, though, came crashing down in the effervescent glow of Don and the famous Coca-Cola commercial that capitalizes on his newfound enlightenment. Although he is an awful, damaged human being, his atonement for seven years of sins—if it ever comes to fruition—can only be imagined. Betty, on the other hand, takes hers to the grave.

The Betty discussed at the beginning of the chapter is more than simply lost in the space of her own mind. Her character is complex. Many critics and commentators would argue that audiences consistently underrated her importance. Sometimes, an aura of sadness encases Betty: she is a beautiful, refined, yet overwhelmed woman, wondering what became of her life. Other instances, she is alone with the children, feeling the burden of being a mother forced to raise her kids virtually alone. And Weiner demonstrates that Betty is human: she can be depressed, overweight, and eating ice cream from the carton, essentially drowning her sorrows to escape the unease she feels in her own skin. One reason why viewers tended to dislike Betty is that her anger and simmering rage probably struck a nerve with those who had experienced similar reactions from their own mothers. It might be shocking to watch now, but the cringeworthy moments were realistic to the age and the kind of parenting that dominated the period.

As a character (perhaps in spite of the anti-Betty feelings of viewers), Betty is essential in exploring the lives of 1960s women, a goal Weiner often explained stood at the heart of *Mad Men*. The juxtaposition of a person who externally seems to have it all versus the internal demons and emptiness she feels provides nuance, especially in contrast to the way the show examines the lives of Peggy, Joan, and other women who are dealing with issues they confront in the business world.

From a cultural history perspective, Betty represents both the supposed or surface-level stability of the 1950s and the discomfort much of the middle class experienced during the 1960s. All these versions of Betty and all the others we do not see (characters have a "life" outside of what is shown, since it is a show built around the progression over a specific timeline) reveal the many challenges that women confronted.

Women are in constant negotiation, never able to just exist on an equal footing, and must be willing to make sacrifices or tradeoffs to gain some imaginary foothold. For example, Peggy and Betty exist on different planes, yet each must strategize a path and then plot to achieve an end. In the workplace, Peggy never gets the benefit of being a man, like her longtime friend Stan, who instantly is accepted and viewed for his professional talents. Betty, a long way from the hubbub of Manhattan, has her own goals. She cannot simply be a divorcée with three kids and no life, so she must find a parachute. Given her situation, political operative Henry Francis, who kind of creepily asks to touch her pregnant belly in Episode 3.3 ("My Old Kentucky Home"), is her best bet for rebounding from Don and maintaining what she considers an acceptable lifestyle for her and the children. Finding a new husband is an important objective given what she knows about Don as a potential loose cannon and his past. She probably bet that she could not count on him to support them forever.

Betty's cancer diagnosis, then, could be Weiner's metaphor for the death of the 1950s-tinged view of women and their secondary status. Her impending demise could also represent the payment for the sins of American overindulgence during the tumultuous era. For Betty and all women, though, *Mad Men* demonstrates the struggles they faced across the spectrum of womanhood in the 1960s. Nearly every episode delves into this topic or at least makes reference to it. In assessing Weiner's comment about the "randomness of things," it is surprising that Betty is the token death at the end of the series, despite what we now know about cancer and smoking. Sometimes, though, victims are innocent and their deaths may galvanize those left behind. Viewers might assume that this will happen with the Draper children as they confront the future.

THE DELUSIONAL FIFTIES

Although journalists, historians, and cultural studies scholars have chipped away at the sketch of 1950s America as a happy-go-lucky era presided over by the grandfatherly Dwight Eisenhower, the image persists in the popular culture mindset. The premise is common in comedy and drama films, as well as television shows and books. One is almost forced to conclude that there is something wonderfully comforting in this persistent misrepresentation of the decade, one in which people willfully let nostalgia wash over them (see chapter 8 for an extended discussion of nostalgia). Or perhaps the "gray decade" moniker is just one that enables people to encapsulate their thoughts in a shorthand fashion without necessitating more critical or contextual historical understanding.

Regardless of our current interpretation of the 1950s, however, one cannot overlook the conformity that infused the era's advertising. Leafing through magazines from the decade reveals a striking focus on glamour, novelty, sparkle, and exhilaration. It seems as if advertising served as a kind of mass lobotomy, ramming these ideas into consumers as a way of inculcating the positive messages coming out of a postwar, happy, healthy United States. Advertising's message—happy, happy, buy, buy—matched the relentless optimism of the mass exodus to the suburbs where new homes awaited, ready to be filled with shiny gadgets for upwardly mobile families as they pursued the American Dream.

Given the ideological unity among the growing legion of white suburbanites based on acquiring goods aimed directly at them by America's consumer goods industry, the companies and the ad agencies they hired created images that equated buying things with a life well-lived. Unlike today, the phrases "keeping up with the Joneses" and "suburbanite" were not necessarily negatives.

In portraying Betty's day-to-day life, the show excels at revealing her insulation from what seems like the rest of humanity. Early in the show, tucked away in the suburban enclave of Ossining, New York, she is far removed from the frenetic vibe of New York City. When Don returns home, often far into the evening or late at night, he rarely brings her into what he experiences, most likely since much of his life is wrapped tightly in lies and deception. She seems to yearn for basic adult interaction, but he certainly does not want to be tied to explaining his days. Betty can expect little—a peck on the cheek, quick question about her day, and her husband's beeline for the whiskey cabinet.

Although college-educated (Bryn Mawr, anthropology) and multilingual (Italian), Betty stews with the other housewives out in Ossining, but her barely educated husband enjoys the superstar career in the Big Apple. As a matter of fact, the idea that Betty might continue working after giving birth is laughable, if not outright ludicrous. When she attempts to get back into modeling, she cannot overcome the stigma of being a mother and Don's wife. It is clear that her successes will only come via his hand.

According to Laurel Cutler, a former typist at J. Walter Thompson in the late 1940s and a suburban wife, *Mad Men*'s picture of life for women in this age is true. She explains, "What most impresses me is how extraordinarily accurate the details are, and it's as dead-on for the wives in the suburbs as it is for us in the office" (qtd. in Giges 2008). Cutler later rose up the ranks to serve as creative director at McCann Erickson during the era portrayed on the show.

Betty and Don initially follow the prescribed roles society would have them play in the 1950s. He is the dominant male breadwinner, while she raises the children. Her life centers on the home and his on the office. On the surface, one would assume that the Draper clan is winning in the postwar race to fulfill the American Dream. Weiner calls Betty part of America's "wasted generation," at the time the best educated in the nation's history, yet doing little on a daily basis beyond childrearing and minor household upkeep. The Drapers, for example, have Carla to watch after and entertain the children (qtd. in Trachta 2013).

Advertisers and marketers capitalized on the conspicuous consumption habits of the new suburbanites, eager to provide them with the technological innovations and other gadgets designed to make life more enjoyable. These young people filled their homes with consumer goods and brought children into the world at a quick clip, thereby ensuring the capitalist machine would continue to thrive. The transition from radio to television amplified the advertising message, blurring the line between nightly entertainment and selling goods and services. The ads urged people to live a specific lifestyle, which reinforced their desire to conform and adapt to newfound wealth and the leisure time that went with it.

CAMELOT TO KENT STATE

Betty Draper evolved gradually in the 1960s, a slow path from bored housewife to the more enlightened student she becomes in the last season. Her protracted evolution is akin to the changes in another fabled Betty—the iconic Betty Crocker, the symbolic representation of Gold Medal Flour. Turning what stood as essentially a company logo into an internationally known brand demonstrated the growing power of advertising and mass media in the twentieth century. Betty Crocker, like a real-life celebrity, soon starred around the world—on a national radio cooking show, in recipes and cookbooks, and later endorsing other food products.

Created to provide a human response to consumer inquiries about cooking with flour in the early 1920s, "Betty Crocker" existed solely in name for fifteen years. During that period, the company expanded the use of the brand name, first for a string of cooking schools and then on radio. As consumers grew to trust the brand name, company executives decided to give the moniker an actual human face. In 1936, she appeared as a nondescript female, close to middle age and sporting a red turtleneck sweater.

The plan to grow the brand and turn the logo into an icon worked. Reportedly, by the end of World War II, some 90 percent of American women recognized Betty Crocker. It was reported that the "First Lady of Food" stood second in the nation in terms of familiar women, behind only First Lady Eleanor Roosevelt. Based on the extensive recognition, the company loaned out the Crocker visage for a number of socially conscious programs, from ration programs on the war home front to healthy eating projects. Later, when television exploded onto the advertising landscape, Crocker appeared on numerous shows.

Over time, Betty Crocker gradually transformed, mirroring the zeitgeist of the era. For example, in 1955, she was pictured as a slightly older female, with gray highlights and a representative housewife's blouse. A little fuller in the face and a bit friendlier than the 1936 model, the new Betty could have stood in for many of the nation's middle-class housewives. Neither a grandmother nor a spry young newlywed, this Betty exuded the confidence of the era and the respect for heritage as typified by Dwight and Mamie Eisenhower. The logo reflected the conservative age.

It is the 1965 Crocker image that most closely resembles Betty Draper, not necessarily in looks—one with dark brown hair and the latter a classic blonde—but in attitude and grace. Emerging from the Camelot era, the new Crocker is a sophisticated woman. Gone are the red sweater and frock, replaced by a smart blazer that looks as if it could have been pulled from Jackie Kennedy's closet. Like Betty Draper, the new Crocker is smartly sophisticated. Her hair flips on the ends exactly the way it should and she accessorizes with a string of pearls. The two Betty figures also share a fresh-faced glow and vigor that makes them look younger than perhaps they should. The younger Draper accentuates her youth with longer hair than Crocker's, still sporting a kind of long bob. This version of the advertising icon is completely in line with the television character and the mid-1960s era. It is as if one could simply walk into the kitchen of the other and strike up a conversation over a cigarette flittingly held and swung about, punctuating their sentences, as they commiserated about their analogous lives.

The change the Crocker image experienced provides an example of how advertising firms got smarter in the 1960s. They implemented new technology and built research capabilities that enabled them to better understand what American consumers wanted, desired, or hoped to buy. One of the primary criticisms the leaders of Sterling Cooper & Partners have against the McCann conglomerate that eventually gobbles them up is that it has a large and expanding research department and an advanced computer system, which attempts to capitalize on making advertising more scientific, something few of the senior SC&P execs believe is possible or warranted. For them, advertising success is built on creativity grounded on filling the client's specific need. The sci-fi element of using computers to do the hard research labor seems otherworldly to creative leaders like Don Draper.

Three synergistic areas converged in the 1960s that made advertising a more ingrained part of American culture. First, people in general were smarter, more educated, and creative. An improved national transportation network of roadways and airplanes enabled that creativity to spread nationwide. Rarely, if ever, in history, for example, could someone like Bob Dylan emerge from the Hibbing, Minnesota, iron range to become a national superstar so quickly. In the early 1960s, Dylan enjoyed the luxury of quick travel and a creative explosion in Greenwich Village that enabled the singer to maximize his vast talents. And let's not forget the impact of radio on the young man's development, first as a fan and then later in spreading his own music. Advertisers realized that what was considered "average" in the early postwar years would not work as well with a more educated and sophisticated audience. Jerry Della Femina, one of the real mad men of Madison Avenue, explained that the success of Bill Bernbach's agency resided in the way it thought about its audiences: "Doyle, Dane's advertising has that feeling that the consumer is bright enough to understand what the advertising is saying, that the consumer isn't a lunkhead who has to be treated like a twelve-year-old" (1970, 29).

Television and technology served as the second leg in the trifecta, standing as critical foundations of the change in advertising and culture in general, as well as a means of solidifying people's smartness and creativity. Television viewers might not be strictly engaged with highbrow entertainment, but the programming did (to a large extent) lift the veils of provincialism and greatly expand the kind of information available to the audience. Critics can lament the medium, but the programming that developed in the 1960s changed the nation. People grew less gullible, and that had important ramifications for the advertising business. Realizing the power of ads on television revolutionized advertising and fueled its creativity as more and more companies wanted fresh, new commercials. Agencies and their clients spent about $171 million on TV ads in 1950, but by 1967 that figure rocketed to $2.9 billion (Shaffer 1969). Clients and consumers yearned for more sophisticated ads, at least in theory, which caused production and creative costs to increase.

Finally, in the 1960s, advertising grew into a central component in the blossoming American consumer culture, one that could be regulated by the federal government but was so tightly wound into the business landscape that it could not really be impeded. Writing in 1969, H. B. Shaffer contends, "Though most Americans are comfortably attuned to the ubiquitous presence of advertising in their daily lives, they tend to be cynical about its operations." Ironically, according to the writer, advertising had a "curious public relations situation." Few people had a favorable view of the industry, but people still enjoyed watching commercials and accepted that ads were not going away. A report analyzing the consumer's reaction to ads by Raymond A. Bauer and Stephen A. Greyser noted that American audiences "generally enjoy advertising" and do not deny that "advertising has a legitimate role in American life" (qtd. in Shaffer 1969).

Like the pervasive acceptance of a corporate capitalist and consumer culture, people assented to the role advertising played in their lives, perhaps the epitome of the well-known phrase "necessary evil."

While advertisers continued to nod at traditional values in the 1960s (like Betty Crocker's ode to home and hearth), the "creative revolution" in the business enabled young writers, designers, and creative leaders to take risks. In less than ten years, advertising transformed wholesale, which more or less pulled the corporate world along too. Many ads and commercials featured content viewed as witty, ironic, sexy, daring, and visually appealing. As the 1960s ended, writer Rodney Campbell summed up the period, saying, "Never has advertising been so honest, free and pleasantly outrageous" (qtd. in Shaffer 1969). Della Femina, ever quote-worthy, sums up the feeling of the age: "I like to think the work that I do is good—I know damn well it sells the product because my clients wouldn't have anything to do with me if I didn't move the product. . . . And I honestly believe that advertising is the most fun you can have with your clothes on" (1970, 254). *Mad Men* delivers on Della Femina's vibe, not only showing the fun in the work, but the high drama of an industry central to the American experience in contemporary history.

BAD MOM

Henry, arriving home from another rough-and-tumble day of work in the New York City political machine, walks into the middle of a familial Cold War, but this one not between two superpowers that can wreak havoc on an equal footing. Instead, this scene is seemingly a page out of the Soviet Union's dominance over its Eastern European neighbors. One side has all the power and has flaunted it at the other's expense. Asked what happened, little Bobby Draper looks up at Henry with big doe eyes, completely distraught, and says, "I wish it was yesterday." Henry rubs the boy's shoulder in a show of male solidarity, but this seems like a familiar place for them both. Betty is mad, the children are unhappy, and Henry is puzzled. Welcome to the Draper/Francis house!

Earlier in Episode 7.3 ("Field Trip"), the audience gets the full-on Betty treatment. First, she has a lunch date with Francine, her newly employed friend from their old neighborhood. After bragging about Henry and his relationship with New York Governor Nelson Rockefeller and the possibility that Henry might become state attorney general, Betty asks Francine about her job in "real estate," indicating just how unimportant it is, since she knows the woman works in travel. Overcoming the ennui of living in the suburbs, kids self-sufficient, and living like roommates (rather than lovers) with her husband, Francine sees her position at a local travel agency as "a reward," which Betty immediately questions, replying that she thought the children were the reward.

The back-and-forth between the two old friends is consistent with the way they used to converse. Betty never lets Francine believe that they are equals and rarely lets her think her upper-middle-class life is anything but fabulous. They glare at one another for a heartbeat at various times in the discussion, which seems to reveal their true feelings, no longer stuck together as neighbors, but both struggling to establish an identity in suburban society that would gladly define it for them. Francine no longer meekly gives in, though; her life might not be perfect, but she did not suffer through a divorce and remarriage, so she does have some high ground over her friend. Betty, attempting to save face, claims confusion and calls herself "old-fashioned," which Francine concedes: "That is indeed how I would describe you."

The scene ends as Francine turns to order dessert and Betty's glare turns cold. Lighting another cigarette, she takes her traditional Betty pose—arms crossed, deep exhale, and shooting daggers. It seems as if she cannot figure out her friend, herself, or exactly why she is so upset, but there is no doubt she would like to strangle Francine with her bare hands.

Later, as if atoning for the exchange with Francine by attempting to be a better mother, Betty walks in on the black housekeeper, Loretta, helping Bobby with his homework. She snaps off the television—as if that is the worst thing in the children's lives—and chastises the maid for having it on. When Loretta says the children "were little angels" in response to Betty's question about the day, the looks the two exchange indicate that this is a common dance. Each pretends to placate the other—the maid that she was not watching television and Betty that she has a handle on the homestead.

Again, as if the specter of Francine hangs overhead, Betty shocks Bobby by saying that she will chaperone his upcoming field trip. His excitement is palpable; a huge smile crosses his face as his mother walks away. Like so much of Betty's life, though, the whole thing seems fabricated to put on a show of competent mothering and lacks sincerity. On the bus to the farm, mother and son small talk about movie villains. Both seem happy, until the teacher interrupts. Her youth, good looks, and lack of a bra offend Betty as she glances at the young woman's unbuttoned shirt. When Bobby exclaims that the teacher really likes her, Betty snarkily replies, "Well, that blouse says that she likes everyone" and continues puffing away, flicking ashes out the bus window. Even as her son looks at her with love and admiration, Betty cannot help but reduce her world to appearances and decorum. This is where she feels safe, in the "old-fashioned" world that allows her to be a half-hearted mother, cruising in and out of the children's lives because her family is wealthy enough to have "a girl" to manage the hearth and children on a day-to-day basis.

The idyllic day on the farm, Betty turns on the charm when it plays to the adults present. She lights another mom's cigarette and they share a laugh about the latter's quip: the "farmer's daughter needs a bra." The comment gives Betty a brief moment of self-satisfaction as she inhales deeply. Next, after Farmer Cy hand milks a cow, Betty is the only one willing to drink from the old tin pail. Bobby is shocked, and his mother demurely wipes at her mouth with the back of her hand as she gives the container back to the teacher.

The idyllic day on the farm ends abruptly when Betty returns from washing her hands. This scene (and many others where she is callous and cold) speaks to the general disgust viewers have for the character. Basically, Betty lets loose on Bobby, who does the kind thing by trading the second sandwich he finds to Susie Rogers, a classmate who does not have one (though she does have gumdrops?). From a pro-Betty perspective, perhaps she sees this "trade" as Bobby lying to her—acting like his father—and shuts down in an attempt to nip the boy's deceitfulness in the bud early in his life. Betty haters, however, need no more evidence of the woman's repugnance than the way she belittles the child. Reaching for yet another cigarette and making the process a grand spectacle, her look of contempt wilts the boy's joy of having his mother there. "Eat your candy," she sneers, as if reacting to a decade of Don's infidelities and a lifetime of being a second-class citizen in a man's world. In a final display of loathing, Betty turns away from her son, pulling her dark sunglasses down over her eyes as a means of telling the boy, "You are invisible to me now." He slowly chews the gumdrops, quickly glances at her, and then looks away.

When Henry arrives home, he asks Betty if she has eaten, and looking at Bobby, who picks over his dinner, she says, "I'm not hungry. I was hungry, but now I'm not." The poor boy bears the brunt of the psychological battering, never looking up from his meatloaf and rice. He twirls his fork through the food, suffering every moment under Betty's glare and coldness.

After Henry attempts to console Bobby, he asks Betty what happened. She says, "It was a perfect day and he ruined it." But then she asks Henry if he thinks she is a "good mother," clearly questioning her earlier conversation with Francine and whether children are the "reward." If she believes her own rhetoric, then she must feel dissatisfied with her day with her older son. The question hangs in the air as her youngest child, Gene, clings to her bosom and sleeps. If Betty doubts the idea, then her whole world is probably spinning off-kilter. Too old to be a flower child and feeling out of her league with the women's liberation movement, females in Betty's generation learned to equate success with motherhood and marriage. In her eyes, she must view her marriage to Don as a failure, even if just subconsciously. Thus, the children hang in the balance—society's self-worth scale for Betty and others like her that most likely scares her to death.

BETTY AND THE AMERICAN CENTURY

The word "sheltered" holds many connotations. When applied to the "typical" 1960s housewife, like Betty, it can mean anything from being deliberately ignorant of events taking place to occupying a secondary status to one's husband, who demands control of the household. She seems like the kind of person that men completely underappreciated because of her looks, thereby forcing her to endure a lifetime of "Oh, honey, you don't need to worry your pretty little head about that."

Breaking from this role took courage for women of Betty's generation (which those viewers who vilified the character should reconsider). While Henry treats Betty so much better than Don did, neither man is a surrogate for her empowerment as an individual. In fact, one could argue that she was a trophy wife for both: arm candy that fulfilled Don's desire for a beautiful wife to match his handsomeness and the photogenic, educated supporter that would help Henry in his political pursuits, particularly within the housewife/mother demographic.

Betty's response to Don marrying a much-younger, hip wife is to rebel against her own pretty girl image and privileged youth. Weiner explains, "When her ex-husband, whom she rejected, married a woman 10 years younger than her, that was a crushing blow to her self-esteem" (qtd. in Trachta 2013). As the world around her shifted mightily in the 1960s, Betty responded with her own version of a sit-down strike via a significant weight gain. Consciously or not, she destroyed the beautiful blond bombshell version of herself. Eventually the thrill of the negative attention she receives wears off, though, and she returns to her beautiful shell. Betty does not really understand how to function outside of her flirty blond bombshell persona, so her overweight days are quickly forgotten as she returns to what she knows well.

Since Betty really cannot count on either of her husbands to support her growth, she learns from (often odd) outside sources. Since she uses her sexuality in many of these instances, there is also an accompanying tension. In the premiere of Season 2, Episode 2.1 ("For Those Who Think Young"), viewers get the full Betty experience. Early in the action, she flirts with misguided, burgeoning equestrian Arthur, a much younger, engaged man. Later in the episode, there is a stranger interaction with a rugged mechanic who stops to help Betty when her car breaks down. Almost throwing herself at him but in a coy fashion, she flirts to get his attention and a discount, since she does not have enough cash to cover the bill. In a moment of seeming clarity, but tinged with a notion of "what if," Betty hands the man the money and he holds onto her hand for several long moments. The gesture seems like an unspoken acknowledgment of what could happen sexually, as well as his understanding of how she used her good looks to her advantage.

Another strange talisman for Betty is Glen Bishop, who we first meet as a neighborhood child, the son of her friend Helen, and then as one of Sally's confidants. Even as a little boy, Glen possesses special insight about Betty and her needs. The oddity of their partnership is solidified right away in Episode 1.4 ("New Amsterdam") when the boy asks for a lock of Betty's hair, which she gives him. Helen discovers the token, which leads to a physical confrontation at the grocery store, when Betty slaps Helen (Episode 1.7, "Red in the Face"). Much of the series, he also has strange relationships with Sally, sometimes acting like an erstwhile boyfriend and others like a big brother. He pivots between trying to impress her and giving her advice for dealing with her disinterested parents.

When Glen appears as an eighteen-year-old young man in Episode 7.10 ("The Forecast"), he forces a confrontation between Sally and Betty as each yearns for his attention. Yet, in the end, it is Betty that the much younger man wants. On his second appearance darkening the Francis door, Betty lets him in, but only so far. Glen pushes and attempts a physical closeness, which causes viewers to experience a moment of "will she or won't she." Betty, however, is not Mrs. Robinson from *The Graduate*. Glen becomes another in a long line of men that Betty draws in and then ultimately rejects.

Instead of skyrockets in flight and afternoon delight, Glen confesses to Betty that he is going to Vietnam, not out of bravery or bravado, as he intonated earlier in front of Sally and his girlfriend, but because he flunked out of college. The flash that spans the potential horrors and possible death that Glen may face is too much for Betty to accept, particularly losing her confidant in such a grisly fashion. Like a person who rethinks her own racism by actually engaging with someone outside her ethnicity, Glen's precarious situation brings all of Vietnam home to Betty. What she sees on television and hears about the war is suddenly personalized.

The interesting question is why viewers cut Betty so little slack for the accurate portrayal of the difficult life of stay-at-home mothers/wives in the 1960s. She is shackled in so many ways. Early in the show, she is stuck with a cheating husband and raising her children; later, she is still childrearing and wound tightly to Henry's aspirations, but hardly an equal partner like many political couples would publicly enjoy several decades later. Betty's job—what she trained for her whole life—is to be a trophy wife. She did as she was told by her own female role models and followed the path they devised for her. Yet, she lived up to society's expectations and found the result lacking.

Unlike the career women on *Mad Men*, Betty has no independent agency except in exchanging one handsome, wealthy, powerful husband for another. She is not young and aggressive, like Peggy, or a kind of win-at-all-costs striver like Joan. Her path should have been the most recognizable to many *Mad Men* viewers, which may have elicited some sympathy, but instead she never found solid ground with audiences. Show regulars and critics followed as her life unfolded, but never gave her the benefit of the doubt for acting like a woman of her age, which they seemed to do for just about every other character on the show.

Because Betty's storyline drew so much condemnation (arguably at the center of most of the criticism related to the show), Weiner's killing her off at the end seemed either contrived or cruel. Writer Sarah Seltzer explains, "Weiner is killing off Betty to remind us that we care about her, despite all the hate, to prove that we've connected with her . . . but what a manipulative thing for the writers to do to the viewers, and to the character. Surely there was a way to make us understand . . . without simply offing her" (2015). One could argue that the insensitivity indicative of the way the character was treated across the series simply continued through to the end, but that does not negate the feeling that Betty Draper (though compelling) could have been better.

CONCLUSION

Some people think money is our national religion. I think it's selling, and it's beautiful, and we do it better than anyone.—Matthew Weiner, 2006

I realized that these people who ran the country were all from these very dark backgrounds, which they had hidden, and that the self-transforming American hero, the Jay Gatsby or the talented Mr. Ripley, still existed.—Matthew Weiner, 2014

Matthew Weiner clearly loves the advertising industry, particularly as it developed over time. He understands the psychological significance of the advertising game and how it helped construct American culture.

Via television, which enabled him to present ninety-two "filmic" episodes, Weiner explored and interrogated advertising's task as a means of getting at the people who ran the business and lived in the era. The examination then opens the contemporary viewer's eyes to the current state of advertising and the way daily lives have transformed over the past fifty years.

In a sense, at *Mad Men*'s core is the chaos of that daily life. Similarly, historian Warren I. Susman spoke of American culture and its multiple dualities as producing "tensions" that "provide both the necessary tensile strength to keep the culture stable and operative and the dynamic force that may ultimately bring about change or complete structural collapse." These warring factions inherent in Susman's definition of culture might be most evident in contemporary advertising and its curious grip on the

Don Draper, 1970. AMC/Photofest ©AMC

modern world. Few topics exude such intense dichotomies (1984, 288). *Mad Men* explores these frictions in two ways: by demonstrating the challenges of living in the 1960s and by revealing to the viewer that there is always a large gap between fiction and reality, which is created by the lived past and the re-created historical.

In our modern iteration of advertising, we experience the significance of advertising's play on life's tensions. For example, recall the way commercials can bring viewers to tears by exploiting passions on one hand, and then in the very next thirty-second space, be utterly hilarious or completely factual. A spot showing abused puppies and caged kittens in an attempt to solicit donations for an animal shelter may be followed by the randy, middle-aged man playfully interacting with his wife, demonstrating the potency of the latest erectile dysfunction pill. Susman cogently discussed the inherent tensions in contemporary life, which Weiner accentuated on the series.

Mad Men skillfully shows how critical commercials became in the 1960s, not only to pump money into the networks, but in creating programming sponsored by corporate interests. The immediacy of a famous variety show performer directly pitching a product to consumers—looking them right in the face, as if through the screen itself—created a relationship between viewers and sellers of goods and services. One might go so far as to proclaim that the advertising industry—via commercials—taught Americans how to watch television. Susman caught this link, particularly from an emotional viewpoint, explaining that advertisers and their clients could "seize and manipulate all the possible instruments of persuasion the culture provides: symbols, central icons, devices to achieve laughter and those to create tears, rhetorical flourishes of all kinds including the enormously effective use of key words or phrases" (1984, 288).

Mad Men demonstrates how clear-minded (despite the prodigious amounts of alcohol, cigarettes, and drugs consumed) agency leaders were in fulfilling the needs of their corporate clients. Draper and Olson, *Mad Men*'s dynamic duo, fully understand they are manipulating the viewer's emotions to sell products or tying a brand to some familiar feeling or impulse.

Weiner does not flinch from presenting the business in this fashion, actually regaling in the creativity, whether it occurs like a bolt out of the blue or by difficult bouts of research and brainstorming. David Strutton and David G. Taylor pick up on Draper's relevance to the business today and its timelessness, saying, "Prominent behaviors and ideas—particularly those associated with managing creativity, client or prospective client relationships, and leadership decision-making processes within the agency—appear timeless in their relevance and practical significance" (2011, 469). The beauty Weiner mentions in the chapter epigraph is clearly a motivating tenet of *Mad Men*—one might even conclude that the series is a love story to the advertising industry.

MAD AGE

"Mad age" is an apt title for an era that seemed always teetering on the contrasting ideas between reality and illusion. On one hand, for example, American economic prowess in the postwar years gave the nation unprecedented wealth and power. Between 1945 and 1970, gross national product expanded from $212 billion to $900 billion. From this perspective, U.S. corporations created a production and sales juggernaut, despite the occasional weak moment, that every other nation on earth would envy.

Yet, on closer inspection, so much of the nation's wealth remained in the hands of the lucky few—similar to today's economic disparity. The lowest 20 percent of the population continued to wallow, if not in abject poverty, at least in a relentless struggle to achieve some semblance of a healthy, productive existence. The illusion of America as a democratic bastion is offset by the realism of people at the bottom of the economic system, futilely clinging to life in an organism gamed against them.

Looking back at the role of the mass media in maintaining an aura of American dominance, Edward P. Morgan explains, "The mass media are capitalist institutions that not only produce our diversionary media culture but help to keep serious discussion of capitalism outside the common ground of mainstream discourse and therefore off the political agenda" (2010, 8). So while we trumpet a free press, that force is determining how we interpret the news and how those engaged with media outlets challenge or defend the status quo. In the sixties, the creation of an "us versus them" mentality regarding race, antiwar activism, and women's rights essentially deflected people's attention from the root cause of the antipathy: capitalism's relentless creation of economic inequality.

This mentality plays a starring role on *Mad Men*, seeping noisily in to question the traditional family dynamic. At the dining room table—or increasingly in overly lit, high-gloss booths at Burger Chef, as imagined in Peggy and Don's campaign for the fast-food chain—fathers who fought in World War II and Korea sat in amazement as their sons and daughters renounced the foundational ideas their dads had served to preserve. Morgan points out: "Between a sense of hopeful empowerment and a sense of feeling helpless in the history of the times, ideological backlash against and commercial exploitation of sixties' social movements were becoming more pronounced" (9). *Mad Men* makes use of the contradictions between capitalism and democratic values. However, the program usually portrays the divergence in starker personal challenges based on differences between the generations rather than the capitalist system. This makes sense for a dramatic television series, but raises questions about how viewers will interpret the interpretation.

The paradoxes between democracy and capitalism continue to haunt American society today and tightly tie the 1960s to the contemporary world. In the Mad Age, however, this contradiction (although supremely significant) stood as one of many inconsistencies. Even though race relations, antiwar activism, and the battle for women's rights may have been the primary focus of the mass media to divert people's attention away from capitalism, these challenges existed and created situations that many people felt were outside the bounds for a democratic society.

From a casual perspective, *Mad Men* might seem like a love letter to the advertising industry and the corporate world that increasingly came to dominate the cultural landscape. Weiner adorns Sterling Cooper with beautiful and interesting characters. He repeatedly demonstrates Don's heroism in the business realm, even when his personal life is shattered. This reading focuses on the pretty drapes and not the bones of the series. Assessing the show's relation to capitalism, one might deduce that Weiner views the corporate world with disdain. According to writer J. M. Tyree, Draper "becomes a cultural metonym for the inherent tolerance embedded in American capitalism but also its cruel utilitarianism—all are welcome to consume and be exploited, to be self-made and self-unmade" (2010, 35). From this view, Don is handsome but full of wickedness that points to the moral and ethical corruption at home in corporate America.

As a history-based series, *Mad Men* must balance its own incongruities as a depiction of life in the 1960s with its reality as a television program aired in the twenty-first century. As a result, the program worked in the challenges of the 1960s as the characters experienced them as part of the ongoing plot (though critics argued that Weiner might have pushed this notion to explore greater depths). Simultaneously, the characters and action must be presented in a manner that will be supported by corporate advertisers and viewed by audiences. As such, Weiner is a historian re-creating the past, but also an entertainer who must be responsible to the network, production house, and other partners in the studio system, including the actors themselves, who take large risks committing to a new series.

As a form of entertainment, the energy of a television series is that it provides an avenue for enabling audiences to feel that they "know" the characters, thus the fictional pain they experience is more genuine. Even a character as generally disliked as Betty Draper provides ample opportunity for today's viewers to understand the ennui of the 1960s housewife, trapped by social norms and the economic system.

Alternatively, when she learns that her young confidant Glen Bishop is about to ship out to Vietnam because he flunked out of college and cannot face his stepfather, the look on Betty's face that reveals the fear that the boy might die does more to convey the horrors of the war in Southeast Asia than scenes of blood and gore (Episode 7.10, "The Forecast"). She is awoken to the potential ending for an enlisted soldier in Vietnam on a personal level, like real-life Americans who might have tacitly supported the nation's involvement, until the war touched them in their own homes, neighborhoods, or towns.

The Mad Age is an era of contradictions and chaos. One senses that despite the countless books, films, documentaries, TV programs, shows, and other mass media pieces written about the sixties, the era will never be fully captured or understood. Even for those who lived through the decade, their experiences only seem to capture a part of the larger portrait, as if each carries a jigsaw puzzle that might have a couple matching pieces but no real continuity. This is a burden of history that is rarely examined—people live through and experience the past on very individualized and small-group levels. It takes historians to create a record from the bits and pieces they can unearth from all those disparate lives.

HISTORY OF THE MAD AGE AND OUR OWN

If one digests the contemporary reviews (professional and academic), then the early returns overwhelmingly rate *Mad Men* as one of the most important television series ever created. As such, the show has had a role in determining how viewers interpreted the decade, which will almost certainly continue into the foreseeable future. The program, though, is only one of countless tools that a person might employ to get a better comprehension of the 1960s and its legacy.

To reveal the Mad Age, set in the recent past, the audience must rethink either what it actually experienced or what it learned about the time frame. As discussed in previous chapters, *Mad Men* and other forms of public scholarship raise questions about television's role in depicting history. According to Keith Jenkins (2003), history at its essence is what remains, from documents and photographs to film and tapes, which lacks real meaning until the historian supplies a framework for interpretation. There may be a commitment to objectivity and diligent primary resource research employed, but historians certainly still bring pieces of themselves into the work either consciously or subconsciously.

Historian Alun Munslow explains that the past is "what actually happened but which is now gone" and quite different than history, "only ever its narrative representation." Thus, Weiner and his team of writers, directors, and producers wield a deft scalpel in fashioning a grand narrative that becomes *Mad Men*, essentially determining "truth" or some version of it. According to Munslow, the historian plays an active role filtering through numerous personal and cultural lenses that then are reflected in the representation of the past (2002, 18–19). For *Mad Men*, although on the surface slavish to historical authenticity, the sexism, anti-Semitism, and cruelty within the confines of the narrative are presented in a manner that allows the audience to rebuke its characters in contrast to today's (supposedly) higher standards. Elisabeth Moss addressed this point, saying, "We know it's a good script when we do our table read and the heads lower, like, five times. I definitely cringe at the sexist things the guys say. The guys cringe too" (qtd. in Schwartz 2008).

As Moss's comment indicates, we should also consider the important role the actors play in (re)creating the era. They perform a role similar to the audience by crafting an interpretation based on their own internal experiences (built through varying degrees of formal education, popular culture, and other stimuli, including the direction and input of the creative team). Whether he knew it when he earned the role as Don Draper, Jon Hamm is now a cultural artifact, a twenty-first century representation of the turbulent mid-twentieth century.

Peggy plays a significant part in *Mad Men*'s aesthetic vision of the decade. As Weiner has suggested, the series is not really about Draper; it is about the female leads and their transformations. From our ultra-knowing, post-postmodern perspective, we are supposed to look down at the endless misogyny Peggy faces on an episode-by-episode basis. The concurrent feeling, then, is rooting for the character and the desire for her to succeed—despite all the obstacles. The viewer's distance from the 1960s (even the supposedly more enlightened days of the late 1960s) promotes assessment, or in the case of those who experienced similar discrimination, reassessment.

Interpreting Peggy's travails gives critics and viewers multiple readings, including a means to deconstruct the show's signs and symbols and compare and contrast these ideas with today's world. For example, the viewer who prides herself on condemning the harsh sexism and other shortcomings of the mid-1960s can use the portrayal as a benchmark for looking at what women face in the twenty-first-century corporate world. The commitment to authenticity and its resulting influence on viewers is critical in creating an atmosphere in which the audience can root for often-vile characters. Comparable to motion picture cinematography, every aspect of what would normally be considered background comes alive in *Mad Men*. As such, careful viewers recognize nostalgia and history having a role in both creating and propelling the story.

Given the darkness inherent in so many *Mad Men* plots, one must surmise that the portrayal of life's challenges is appealing. Weiner created characters that enabled pretty depressing plots to be turned into quality television. Peggy is particularly important here too. She has problems and internal demons, but as a guide to the series in general, Peggy stood out as a ray of hope amid the carnage.

At various times in the series, Peggy seemed on the edge of breaking, but in her resilience, she revealed that these weak spots are part of life. She was not a broken soul, like her mentor Don. Peggy could make poor choices and be forced to live with the results (like her secret pregnancy and child with Pete), but she also served as the link to what viewers know is on the horizon, such as improved workplace rights for women and the end of the Vietnam War. Peggy is the optimism that people carry when they look to a positive future, whereas Don and his generation flailed at the changes sweeping them into history's dustbin.

For *Mad Men*, the artful aesthetics and strong narrative work together, not only connecting the intimate moments with the broader cultural and historical era, but also creating a story that seamlessly jumps between characters and lives as they unfold. Writer Todd VanDerWerff discusses the link between the 1960s and today, explaining:

> In placing a remove between us and the screen, in setting this in the comfortable past, the series is able to deconstruct our own lives, to show us how the relationship between the haves and have nots, between races, and especially between the genders haven't really changed all that much beneath our veneers of political correctness. (2013)

Weiner's window into this specific past has purpose but is enacted subtly, enabling today's viewer to reassess contemporary society.

The intimate flashes, sometimes seemingly unimportant, exist to provide cultural and historical context for the enormous transformations rocking the nation across the 1960s. As a result, large events, like the astronauts landing on the moon, are encapsulated in the facial expressions of characters as they witness the events in what for them would be real time. The wonder and awe of an age is reduced to a tense nod, shocked expression, or general amazement.

MAD CRITICS

Popular culture that endures often faces stiff criticism, particularly as time passes and specialists wrest critical control from journalists and others who often rely on quick judgments and assessments. *Mad Men* is no exception and, frankly, generated quite a bit of controversy and criticism across its entire run. One can imagine that writers and scholars will continue to pore over the show, searching for an elusive key to interpreting it and what it all means in analyzing its representation of the sixties and how we use it to reflect on our own era. *Mad Men*'s long-term critical reputation seems in many ways tied to the way commentators consider the ad business.

In the 1960s, critics debated the inherent evil that advertising represented, questioning its use of scientific methods and technology to dig deeper into the consumer's psyche. In 1969, H. B. Shaffer reported:

> Advertising grew more clever. It catered to the individual's desire to be young, beautiful, rich, admired. Consumers learned from advertising of such previously unrecognized menaces to their health, beauty and success as halitosis, pink tooth brush, tattletale gray, and they simultaneously learned of the one product that would banish the threat to their happiness.

Shaffer's summary of the challenges at the heart of the ad game continued to plague the industry into the contemporary era. Strains of this argument are revealed as today's advertising insiders and critics challenge the ubiquity of Google- or Facebook-sponsored ads that employ advanced algorithms to essentially spy on the user and feed her commercial content based on information that most people would consider private.

This notion of privacy that bedevils modern users is related to American values and what is considered within the bounds of good taste. The advertising industry blew some of those ideas out of the water and continued to do so well past the Mad Age. For example, the rampant hyper-sexuality in ads from the 1970s and 1980s and commercials for erectile dysfunction pills in the 2000s and beyond demonstrated how far the business world could push cultural norms. According to writer J. M. Tyree, *Mad Men* reveals "an American paradox": "The much-vaunted Emersonian characteristic of self-reliance dovetails rather nicely with the goals of big business to create a nation of isolated, vulnerable, and greedy selves who can be persuaded that buying products is a form of self-expression" (2010, 35).

The criticism against advertising, which seems to have developed alongside the industry from its earliest times, sets the tone for the approach some critics adopted to critique *Mad Men*. In other words, some commentators viewed the program as an overt celebration of corporate power and the advertising industry's ubiquity. The latter brought rampant consumerism to the fore, essentially locking the nation into hyper-capitalism and its intrinsic evils. Weiner discussed this idea with NPR's Terry Gross, explaining:

> The show is about, on some level, the contemplations that we have about what we want versus, you know, what we can get. And happiness is always that gap in between there. Happiness becomes this weird invention, you know, just something that's sought out of that other people have, and you're like, how do they get that? (2015)

Critics bemoan the ad game's role in creating an aura in which people should measure themselves against others based on consumer products, goods, and services. Advertisers killed whatever innocence once resided in the American Dream by making life worth based on who had the most toys.

Another common reproach Weiner faced centered on *Mad Men*'s depictions of vice, race, gender, gay rights, and other societal ills. For many critics, the program did not address these topics often enough or push them enough to satisfy modern sensibilities. Ironically, an offshoot of this reasoning also blossomed. For example, writer Peter Suderman censured *Mad Men* for serving up its characters for judgment by modern audiences. He labeled the show "passionless," explaining, "*Mad Men*, though, is too timid to let its viewers in on the fun, choosing to judge its characters safely and subtly, through the lens of modernity" (2007, 54). For some critics, it seems, *Mad Men* either had too much or too little history or historical accuracy, as if that could be measured by anything other than an individual's opinion.

One of the most interesting controversies surrounding *Mad Men* focused on whether the show's overt wickedness in some ways gave viewers an avenue to condone the repulsive behaviors on display. For example, journalist Susannah Breslin labeled the show "man porn," explaining that male viewers secretly watched the show to revel in Don's decadence (qtd. in Weinman 2008). Writer Jaime J. Weinman supported the notion, saying, "Don Draper may live a lie, but if we didn't enjoy that lie, we wouldn't be watching" (2008, 78).

What Breslin and Weinman tap into is a notion that many people simply are not willing to contemplate—are people in contemporary society less racist, sexist, or homophobic than in the past? Perhaps at the heart of this deep-rooted angst is the idea that modern society has not only not really advanced but in many areas receded. Whether or not we secretly applaud Draper taps into the often conflicted and hidden feelings about socioeconomic and cultural challenges. It might be impossible to ever prove, yet is intriguing—like the answers one would get conducting a survey on racism or sexism in which respondents give the answer they think the interviewer desires, rather than the truth that asks them to contemplate their most complicated attributes. There is an air of snickering, "Weren't we naughty boys?" in the comments of advertising greats interviewed about the veracity of the show, as if they get a free pass because people "back then" did not know any better.

From the beginning, Weiner realized the slippery slope *Mad Men* traveled, particularly in using vice as a marketing tool. Asked whether he wants viewers to like Draper, the showrunner responded: "No one wants to look in the mirror and see the warts. I'd say just wait and stick with the story and see what happens, but I hope that the source of the entertainment is not judging these people. Everyone has a reason for what they're doing. It all comes from a human place. . . . I'm trying to talk about what it is to be a person" (qtd. in Whitney 2009).

There seems to be an interesting duality at work when one assesses *Mad Men*. On one hand, the show excels in representing American history as something life-altering for its characters. In essence, these are significant turning points on an intimate and societal level. As viewers, though, we already know (or assume we know) the outcomes or how events unfolded. All the handwringing over Armstrong's moonwalk, for example, is to heighten suspense for a situation that viewers know (in reality) went successfully.

At the same time, though, *Mad Men* urges people to do more than watch, enjoy, laugh, cry, criticize, or the many other reactions people have to most television programming. The opportunity exists for the audience to engage with the series almost as if wearing a historian or sociologist hat. Interrogating the issues Weiner raises allows viewers to consider what the show says about the cultural, economic, or political values we value today, as well as how those topics transformed over time.

END OF AN ERA

There is a strangely endearing moment on the audio commentary for Episode 5.6 ("Far Away Places"), which features Weiner and Hamm giving insight into the show and its characters. At several points during the commentary—each time Elisabeth Moss's Peggy Olson walks into Draper's office when the character is not there—Hamm jokingly barks: "Get the f#@k out of my office!"

Known far and wide for his understated humor, Hamm plays the occasion for a laugh, but on closer inspection, one senses a deep intimacy and attachment between Moss and Hamm that makes the moment possible. There would not be any angry words exchanged after Moss heard the audio, and nothing about it would end up in a tabloid. Instead, it offered an instant of real affection, even if in a mock-angry tone. This might have been the happiest f-bomb ever dropped!

In addition, Hamm's exclamation demonstrated how intertwined *Mad Men*'s actors were with their parts and the show. A viewer could imagine Draper shouting an expletive at Olson, particularly if he were in a bad mood or experiencing something that forced his Draper and Whitman identities to collide. To Hamm, Moss walked into "my office," showing his deep commitment to being Don Draper. That space—completely fabricated to look like a 1960s executive's office—came alive to Hamm as his and not another character's. Just like Don and Dick sometimes smash together, Hamm and Draper came together in an instant, thus merging identities, if just for a second. Life and reality blurred.

Weiner chuckled at Hamm's outbursts, but one might wonder if he recognized the undercurrents. Past, present, fact, and fiction swirled in a flash: while the audience watches and listens, an actor who plays a person from the past both discusses the show and moves into character to comment to another actor on the show, also playing a history-based role. Like so much of *Mad Men*, the looping in and around itself is delightful. Yet, others question how any piece of popular history can present the past. Historian Jerome de Groot wonders about these mass media channels, particularly something like a TV series, explaining:

> History is the misrecognized reflection of now seen in a glass darkly; something connected but misunderstood, a moment of trauma to be constantly returned to; the cycle that cannot be escaped or avoided; a problematic representation of an imagined past that never existed. All historical work, then, is an attempt at surmounting this or avoiding it. (2011, 275)

As historical content re-created by Weiner and the creative team, *Mad Men* unfolds across the lives of characters from three generations. The intimate perspective gives the audience a sense that life carries on, just as it does in reality. As viewers, we know this is not reality, but it feels authentic. Is the audience simply passive here, allowing Weiner to fill us up with a version of history of an era that people know well, or does the audience work and think to actively partake in the process?

The audience joins in the notion that what happens on screen among a group of actors imitates life. As such, Sally, the offspring of Betty and Don, reveals traits that a child might inherit from her parents. Sally mimics her mother in the way she looks and the poses she strikes, including the movement of her arms and hands when she smokes cigarettes. At the same time, Sally is quick-witted and insightful like her father, with more than a little angst around the edges. We root on the evolutionary aspects of the show as we live out our own times. The audience gets the notion that children eventually supplant their parents, grow older, have families, and continue the human cycle. History then, unfolding in forty-four-minute snapshots on television, helps us contextualize the past, present, and future by demonstrating that life's themes and arcs contain universality across the contemporary world. Or it doesn't.

One point Weiner emphasizes is that history evolves along a continuum that does not always make sense at the time. Looking back now, it might seem to be more linear, but that is simply because historians and others establish timelines that appear logical when analyzing the past. The details, as *Mad Men* demonstrates, are much stickier. Some aspects of the decade seem to flow into the next, as if the self-help and meditation of the 1970s had to be the outcome of the free love and activist 1960s. We know, though, that this kind of equation is never the straight line it might appear on paper, film, or digital media.

What can never be shortchanged is that *Mad Men*, like the endless stream of mass media meant to entertain, is a rendering of a historical vision, created out of events that sometimes mirror the past but are never actually past events. Weiner's early accomplishment centered on portraying the era with an eye toward authenticity, which enabled him to market the show as accurate, in as much as any history can be true. Success here allowed Weiner to bring his vision to the screen, win multiple awards, and run for seven seasons.

Writing around the time Madison Avenue began its ascent half a century or so ago, it is as if the eminent historian Arthur M. Schlesinger Jr. had a crystal ball that would explain Weiner's show so far in the future: "Our greatest new industry is evidently the production of techniques to eliminate conflict, from positive thoughts through public relations to psychoanalysis, applied everywhere from the couch to the pulpit. Our national aspiration has become peace of mind, peace of soul" (2008, 46). The irony is that as the nation developed its capacity for "peace of mind, peace of soul," it also perfected a form of vicious capitalism that expanded and solidified economic inequality. Advertising facilitated selling via the depiction of life as a bright, sunny day in a nation unable to make sense of its foibles. Weiner revealed that the people behind the happiness industry in the sixties did their jobs while contending with messy, chaotic personal lives. This turmoil—a kind of societal madness—is at the heart of *Mad Men*.

The most surprising revelation for some regarding *Mad Men* after seven seasons and ninety-two hours of programming is that the series actually undermines the very system that it seems on the surface to promote—another duality wrapped in a pretty bow. Similar to F. Scott Fitzgerald's *The Great Gatsby*, *Mad Men* is an exploration of the evil inherent in the American Dream narrative.

Mad Men articulates Weiner's vision of the wide gap between real and imagined across American society in the 1960s and today. Furthermore, the series undermines many of the values that most people would view as foundational and essential, but the same ones that they may feel have been sold out by a nameless, faceless "them"—the invisible hierarchy that dictates contemporary American life. We cannot actually know the past via *Mad Men*, but under Weiner's skillful touch, we can join in his vision of a nation fueled by its dichotomies.

Weiner also delivers this worldview—*Mad Men* in a Mad Age—with a sense of optimism. Don Draper, our long-suffering antihero, the mystery man with a hidden past, escapes the decade that he only partially understands by creating a commercial to sell dark, fizzy water. Ironically, the commercial he develops employs replicas of the free spirit youth who (in part) are rebelling against people like him who represent the corporatization of America. So one could deduce that the optimism is also tinged with more than a little pessimism.

How appropriate, then, is this as the concluding moment of the show? Weiner, as he predicted, is presenting a logical conclusion of seven years of watching Don careen through life, alternatively on top of the world and often closer to the bottom. Weiner is essentially asking the audience: "Come with me now on a journey through time and space." He revealed that time machine in Draper's triumphant moment selling Kodak his magical carousel.

What Weiner exposed, though, did not just center on Don's winning moment. At the end, he is sitting on the steps, alone and deserted. He has just imagined a triumphant moment—arriving home in time to accompany his family on a trip to spend Thanksgiving with relatives. Yet the flashback is a dream. Don's pain at realizing the space between dream and reality drives that moment and the series. People can climb aboard the spaceship or wheel or whatever Weiner wants to call this ability to look back into the past, but it only allows snapshots into lives filled with commotion. We must decide what is authentic and what is imagined.

THE EPISODES: AN OPINIONATED COMPENDIUM

EPISODE 1.1: "SMOKE GETS IN YOUR EYES" (JULY 19, 2007)

Who is this guy smoking? Why is he alone? Boy, he is handsome. *Mad Men*'s impressive debut launches the series, introducing a rich array of characters and motifs in the space of a single episode. The audience glimpses Peggy, the new secretary, off to work in the scary big city. She gets bad advice from Joan and worse treatment from a sleazy doctor and sleazier account man Pete Campbell. Don begins to clash with Pete as they both try to sell cigarettes. Don has a lovely wife—and an offbeat mistress—and an eye for any other interesting woman who might come along (except Peggy and Joan).

EPISODE 1.2: "LADIES ROOM" (JULY 26, 2007)

The second episode of *Mad Men*, appropriately entitled "Ladies Room," is somewhat low-key relative to the spectacular opening episode. It focuses on the question of gender, rather than introducing everything. Nice moment: Betty looks at the head of a sleeping Don and asks, "Who's in there?" The exchange helps develop the theme of Don's problematic identity. Mostly, the focus is on Betty's travails, Don's infidelity (including not only adultery, but conspiring with Betty's psychiatrist behind her

Pete, Don, and Roger. *AMC/Photofest ©AMC*

back), and Peggy's realization of the gender dynamics at Sterling Cooper, where (as Peggy puts it) if men take female coworkers to lunch, they expect the women to be dessert. Don already shows both mean streak and creative genius. He is skeptical of linking an aerosol spray can for deodorant to the space age.

EPISODE 1.3: "MARRIAGE OF FIGARO" (AUGUST 2, 2007)

Don whores himself out to department store heiress Rachel Menken to get the advertising account for her father's store amid a constellation of motifs involving anti-Semitism. Then he runs away from home and gets drunk in the middle of daughter Sally's birthday party, taking her cake with him. And he's the most *likeable* of the men in the episode. The women, meanwhile, are mostly gossiping harpies. These people are the ones Tom Brokaw calls the "Greatest Generation"?

EPISODE 1.4: "NEW AMSTERDAM" (AUGUST 9, 2007)

More tensions between Don and Pete, as Pete begins to show his weasel side more clearly. The newly wed Pete reluctantly accepts help from Trudy's father to buy a new Manhattan apartment. Betty continues to unravel. In an example of the loaded dialogue that runs throughout *Mad Men*, after an unfortunate encounter with creepy neighbor kid Glen, Betty tells her psychiatrist, complaining of Glen's hot mom, but by extension commenting on Don's situation as well, "The person taking care of him isn't giving him what he needs." Don's wandering eye focuses on Rachel beyond just winning the account.

EPISODE 1.5: "5G" (AUGUST 16, 2007)

This might be the episode when it became clear that *Mad Men* offered something truly special. Here, there are more developments and jealousies at the office, while Don's infidelities nearly get him in trouble at home. Pete practically whores out Trudy to get a short story published in a magazine, mainly out of jealousy that Ken Cosgrove got a story in the prestigious *Atlantic Monthly*. These people desperately want to be creative, but Don seems to be the only truly creative one, and his creativity is, in many ways, that of a particularly brilliant pimp. The heart of the episode concerns the motif in which Adam Whitman emerges from Don's murky past and identifies Don as his half-brother, Dick Whitman, whom Adam had long thought to be dead. This further develops the idea that began when an ex-army buddy had already identified Don as Dick on the train in Episode 1.3. Don's sense of panic is palpable when Adam finds him. Lots of details remain to be filled in, but it becomes clear that Don's early family background was pretty horrible and that he wants to get as far away from it as possible. He offers the shocked younger man, who seems to idolize Dick/Don, $5,000 to get out of town and forget he ever found him. It's a cold move on Don's part, but one that, at least for us, wins him considerable sympathy as well. There might be good reasons for his dysfunction in personal relationships. It is clear that one's reactions to the characters in this series are likely complex. Even Pete, the anti-Don, is, in many ways, more pathetic than despicable. Meanwhile, the gradual revelation of Don's underprivileged past helps explain his animosity for Pete: born to privilege and coasting on it ever since. Class issues are more prominent in *Mad Men* than in virtually any other major American television program.

EPISODE 1.6: "BABYLON" (AUGUST 23, 2007)

With so many plotlines, Mad Men sometimes presented bridging episodes, filled with lots of stuff and many different subjects. The Drapers celebrate Mother's Day. Don experiences flashbacks to his awful childhood. The Jewish theme continues, as Don ponders ways to advertise tourism in Israel, seeking suggestions from Rachel. People in the episode actually read books, including a search for Israel ideas in Leon Uris's *Exodus*. Don's (other) mistress Midge introduces him to friends (beatniks in Greenwich Village), at which point we realize how hopelessly square the dashing Don really is. Asked how he sleeps at night after spending his days in advertising, he says, "On a bed made of money." Peggy shows an ability to turn a phrase as she and the other secretaries test a lipstick line. It begins her journey into copywriting and becoming Don's protégée, rather than just his secretary. Office knockout Joan Holloway gets it on with ad scion Roger Sterling and reveals her cynicism about relationships.

EPISODE 1.7: "RED IN THE FACE" (AUGUST 30, 2007)

Betty continues to deteriorate, slapping Helen Bishop in the supermarket. She confesses her awareness of being the object of the male gaze. Don continues to get secret reports from her psychiatrist. Don is jealous when he has Roger over for dinner and Betty seems a little too friendly. Roger makes a pass, which Don doesn't see, but suspects. He gets his revenge by bribing the elevator operator to pretend the elevator is out of service, so Don and Roger have to climb the stairs to their high-rise office. That climb is, for us, one of the iconic moments in the series. Nixon continues to hover in the background. Pete returns a wedding gift, gets rebuffed when he flirts with the clerk, then soothes the bruises to his masculine pride by buying a small-caliber rifle. Weirdly, his gross hunting fantasy arouses Peggy, who apparently is *really* in need of some stimulation beyond cheese Danish.

EPISODE 1.8: "THE HOBO CODE" (SEPTEMBER 6, 2007)

The title refers to an extended flashback of Don's Depression-era childhood. A hobo visits the Whitman farm and Dick's dad proves to be an asshole. Peggy succumbs to Pete's feeble charms; she may be smart and talented, but her taste is seriously questionable. At least she has her first creative success with the lipstick ad. Lois the telephone operator is impressed by Sal's Italian masculinity, so Peggy isn't the only one who has trouble reading men. The seemingly amiable and charming Bert Cooper proves to be a fan of Ayn Rand, showing questionable tastes of his own. Don is a master of the hard sell; he may be an artist, but his specialty is the art of the con. He also fails to fit in with Midge and her bohemian crowd in the Village, having cultivated his persona as a paragon of middle-class respectability.

EPISODE 1.9: "SHOOT" (SEPTEMBER 13, 2007)

McCann Erickson, an international powerhouse in advertising, attempts to lure Don away, partly by hiring Betty (once an aspiring young model, as she keeps reminding *everyone*) to model for them in a Coca-Cola campaign. The shoot goes well, but the job falls through after Don nixes the recruiting attempt. Peggy gains weight. Pete sucker punches Ken Cosgrove after he makes a rude remark about Peggy's fatness. A neighbor threatens to shoot the Draper dog after it attacks one of his pigeons. The increasingly unstable Betty ends the episode in the backyard, cigarette dangling from her lips, taking aim at the pigeons with a BB gun, as the theme of shooting and killing things continues to run through this first season of the series. It is, after all, the American way.

EPISODE 1.10: "LONG WEEKEND" (SEPTEMBER 27, 2007)

Betty meddles in her widowed father's love life. Roger and Joan clearly have a real connection. With their families away for the Labor Day weekend, Roger and Don are still in town, in the mode of Richard Sherman in *The Seven Year Itch*. Instead of Marilyn Monroe, Roger scores a pair of identical twin sisters for a tryst, though Don's participation is half-hearted. Roger's, however, is whole-hearted, so much so that he has a near-fatal heart attack. Don, rattled by Roger's brush with death, turns to Rachel for solace. Post-coitus, Don gives Rachel details of his almost ridiculously bad childhood (which eventually left him an orphan raised by two not-so-great parental surrogates). Rachel now knows more about "Don" than Betty.

EPISODE 1.11: "INDIAN SUMMER" (OCTOBER 4, 2007)

Peggy is tasked with developing an ad campaign for a problematic weight-loss device that turns out to have, uh, other uses. Many appliances, in fact, can have multiple uses, as when we learn that Betty *really* loves her automatic washing machine. She kinda likes her air-conditioning salesman too. Roger is dragged in from the hospital for a pitch to Lucky Strike—and promptly has another heart attack. Don is made a partner in order to stabilize the firm in the light of Roger's shaky condition. Bert continues to extol the virtues of Ayn Rand. Pete tries to figure out how he can profit from recent events. He then intercepts a package sent to Don by Adam Whitman shortly before Adam's suicide.

EPISODE 1.12: "NIXON VS. KENNEDY" (OCTOBER 11, 2007)

The Kennedy-Nixon election finally takes center stage at Sterling Cooper, as it should, given its significance as a marker of the growing importance of vision and the media in American politics and American life. The firm is inhabited mostly by obnoxious Republicans. They stage an election-night party in the office after Don leaves. They get too drunk to really notice or care who wins. Harry Crane, separated from his wife, gets it on in a booze-fueled encounter with Hildy, the straitlaced secretary. Peggy proves too businesslike for the shenanigans. Pete uses information from the intercepted package to try to bribe Don to make him head of accounts. Don rebuffs him and Bert backs Don, saying he has no interest in the information Pete reveals to him. Instead, Duck Phillips gets the accounts job. Duck is an awful human being. More extended flashbacks to the Korean War flesh out the details of the Dick/Don switch.

EPISODE 1.13: "THE WHEEL" (OCTOBER 18, 2007)

Duck begins to assert himself. Duck is an awful human being. Pete is still pondering a baby with Trudy. In the meantime, Peggy delivers her own baby (presumably fathered by Pete) in secret and refuses to even hold it. She also officially becomes copywriter. Betty discovers that Don has been conspiring with her psychiatrist, so she reveals Don's infidelities, knowing the info will be relayed. In another of the key moments of the entire series, Don delivers perhaps his greatest sales pitch in his classic invocation of the Kodak carousel slide projector as a nostalgia-fueled time machine. The pitch is a success, and Don has an attack of family-oriented nostalgia. He decides to join his wife and kids on their Thanksgiving trip to visit family. He rushes home, but they have already left. Families do not work well in this series, except as ad copy, suggesting that American family values are basically just an advertising slogan.

EPISODE 2.1: "FOR THOSE WHO THINK YOUNG" (JULY 27, 2008)

Sterling Cooper gets a huge photocopy machine in another example of the way in which the series marks the advance of technology in American business and American society. Duck insists that the firm needs to hire some younger creative talent to be able to develop ads that appeal to younger customers. Duck is an awful human being. Don begins to interview young writer-artist teams, even though he thinks young people don't know anything. At 36, he's developing into an establishment type. In this case, he might have a point, though. Betty, meanwhile, is starting to flirt (or at least think about flirting) with anything in pants. Don reads Frank

O'Hara's poetry collection *Meditations in an Emergency*. We even get to hear Don read aloud from an appropriate poem.

EPISODE 2.2: "FLIGHT 1" (AUGUST 3, 2008)

The crash of American Airlines Flight 1 (a real-world event that occurred on March 1, 1962) causes Sterling Cooper to dump Mohawk Airlines so they can go after American, which is now going to need a big-time PR campaign. This attempt to cash in on the deaths of ninety-five people on the plane suggests just how venal and ruthless American capitalism really is, though this is again one of those times when Don (who just wants to stick with Mohawk, which he worked so hard to land in the first place) shows much greater integrity than Roger and most of the firm leaders. Pete learns that his father had been on the plane. Even more shockingly, he learns that his seemingly rich dad had been broke. Paul Kinsey hosts a raucous bohemian party at his digs in Montclair, which allows him to show off his black girlfriend. Joan shows her claws. Peggy visits her family. They urge her to rejoin the Catholic Church.

EPISODE 2.3: "THE BENEFACTOR" (AUGUST 10, 2008)

Insult comic Jimmy Barrett grossly insults the overweight wife of a pota-to-chip magnate, triggering a small crisis. Don manhandles Jimmy's wife, Bobbie Barrett, with whom he is having an affair, and forces her to get Jimmy in line. Ironically, Don also for once deploys Betty, having her accompany him to a dinner with the Barretts and the chippers. Harry Crane intercepts Ken Cosgrove's paycheck and is shocked that Ken makes more than he. Harry jumps to action after taking an ear beating from his wife. He winds up the head of Sterling Cooper's TV department, even though the company still, even in 1962, doesn't seem to have real-ized how important television is in advertising. Arthur, the klutzy young man at the stables where Betty rides, comes on to her, telling her she seems profoundly sad. Betty's reply (though meant entirely seriously) is one of those hilarious moments when the dialogue of *Mad Men* gets really funny: "No, it's just my people are Nordic."

EPISODE 2.4: "THREE SUNDAYS" (AUGUST 17, 2008)

Easter season 1962. Peggy has a weird flirtation with a young priest who looks like he should be a serial killer on *Dexter*. She helps him with a sermon, indicating a kinship between religion and advertising/marketing that Leopold Bloom understood well more than half a century earlier. The firm hires a call girl to help schmooze a client; Roger decides to use her services too, given that his affair with Joan is over. Don and Betty seem to be getting on better, though Bobby gets out of hand. Betty is inpatient with Don's reluctance to employ corporal punishment, leading him to share with her a story of the violent abuse he himself suffered as a child. This seems to bring the Drapers closer. Bobbie Barrett develops a TV-show idea for her husband.

EPISODE 2.5: "THE NEW GIRL" (AUGUST 24, 2008)

Trudy and Pete struggle to conceive. Don and Bobbie go on an account, get drunk, and wreck his car. Peggy goes to Long Island to pay Don's drunk-driving fine, getting him out of jail. She also takes in and helps care for an injured Bobbie. Bobbie gives her advice on how to win Don's respect (act like she is his equal), something Peggy is desperate for. The dazzling Jane Siegel shows up as Don's new secretary, though neither she nor anyone else seems interested in her typing and clerical skills. Oddly enough, Don seems rather oblivious to her charms. More details unfold regarding the days after Peggy gave birth, including a period when she was confined to a mental facility after a supposed breakdown. Don visits her there with some very supportive advice. The whole episode surrounding her child and its fate remains mysterious and downright weird, suggesting the difficulty of early-1960s American society in dealing with such matters.

EPISODE 2.6: "MAIDENFORM" (AUGUST 31, 2008)

Impressed by Maidenform's ad campaign, the stodgy folks at Playtex ask Sterling Cooper to come up with an ad campaign that has more pizzazz. Paul comes up with a brilliant Jackie-Marilyn idea, but the Playtex folks decide to stick with their conservative campaign since they already dominate the market. Don is horrified by Betty's sexy new bathing suit, which he claims looks "desperate." Duck, with his ex-wife about to remarry and other tensions mounting, dumps his beloved dog on the street in Manhattan and decides to hit the booze. Duck is an awful human being. Don shows signs of serious stress in his relationship with Bobbie and in life in general.

EPISODE 2.7: "THE GOLD VIOLIN" (SEPTEMBER 7, 2008)

Don considers buying a Cadillac—and flashes back to his time selling cars (the perfect prep, of course, for his time as an ad man). The Smiths (the new young talent at Sterling Cooper) present Don with a copy of the Port Huron Statement, hoping to convert it into new advertising strategies. The episode also features a new technological advance: Pampers disposable diapers. Bert Cooper shows more Ayn Randism, buying a Mark Rothko painting, not for the aesthetics, but for the investment. He also assures Don that "philanthropy is the gateway to power." Don buys the Cadillac. Jane nearly gets fired, but Roger rescues her (she will soon "rescue" him as well). In the meantime, Jane, counting on Roger's support, faces down the formidable Joan. For a twenty-year-old, she's a force to be reckoned with. The Smiths' hip new approach wins the Martinson's coffee contract. The Drapers go on a family picnic. Sal reads Ken's latest story and has him over for dinner to give him feedback. Sal's wife feels neglected. Duh. Betty is flattered by the attentions of Jimmy Barrett, who hints to her that something is going on between Don and Bobbie. Afterward, Betty pukes in the Caddy. Brenda Lee's "Break It to Me Gently" is an excellent example of the way *Mad Men*'s ending credits music plays a crucial part in the series.

EPISODE 2.8: "A NIGHT TO REMEMBER" (SEPTEMBER 14, 2008)

Mad Men at its most soap operatic. Father Gill reappears and practically twists Peggy's arm to get her to design a flyer for the church dance. The church ladies, of course, find it too sexually suggestive. Poor ad placement triggers a crisis in Harry's TV department when a Maytag ad touting the virtues of their agitator is placed right after a segment in which a Communist spy is referred to as an agitator. Joan helps out with reviewing scripts in order to avoid a repetition but is then pushed aside. She will, in the series, repeatedly show talents that are not fully utilized because of her gender. Betty, on the edge of a nervous breakdown, murders a dining chair and later confronts Don about the affair with Bobbie. She calls him at work and tells him he is no longer welcome at home.

EPISODE 2.9: "SIX MONTH LEAVE" (SEPTEMBER 28, 2008)

Marilyn's death (August 5, 1962) casts a shadow over the whole episode, casting it firmly in its historical setting. Freddie Rumsen hits the booze hard leading up to a big presentation, then pisses his pants in the office beforehand. Peggy pinch-hits and knocks it out of the park, winning Freddie's place on the account and, ultimately, his job. Don takes up residence in exile at the Roosevelt Hotel, while Betty continues to unravel. Jane tries to be supportive of Don, but he's not particularly interested in sharing. Roger and Don take Freddie out for a night on the town prior to sending him off for a six-month leave that is likely permanent. In a development both surprising and predictable, Roger leaves Mona so he can pursue Jane.

EPISODE 2.10: "THE INHERITANCE" (OCTOBER 5, 2008)

Paul and Pete prepare to attend a "Rocket Fair" convention in Los Angeles, still a relatively exotic destination in 1962. A science-fiction fan, Paul fantasizes about making a visit to Pasadena, land of Jet Propulsion Laboratories and Ray Bradbury. (The trip also gives him a chance to bail out on his plan to become a Freedom Rider with Sheila.) Don reminds him that the trip is business, "as much as I'd like to indulge your *Twilight Zone* fantasy of being shot into space." Astronauts will definitely be at the convention. Sterling Cooper hopes to make connections there to cash in on the space and arms race. Betty's father, Gene, has a stroke, bringing Don and Betty together to visit. Dad seems relatively okay but repeatedly mistakes Betty for her mother and grabs her breast. Don decides he'll go to L.A. in place of Paul, who now heads off on the Freedom Ride, claiming he changed his mind. A family crisis causes Glen to run away and hole up in the Draper kids' playhouse. He seeks solace from Betty, announcing that he has come to rescue her and run off with her. Instead, Betty turns the boy back over to his mother. Betty confides in Helen about her separation from Don. Helen's advice: "The hardest part is realizing you're in charge."

EPISODE 2.11: "THE JET SET" (OCTOBER 12, 2008)

One of the strangest of all *Mad Men* episodes, the focus is the view of California as a place where strange things happen (which runs through the series). In California, Pete meets scientist Caleb Sawyer, who shares his "Optiman" thesis, concerning the engineering of human beings to function better in space: "new organs, super strength, you know the Soviets are working on it." Don seems to step into an alternate reality (of course, in *Mad Men*, California *is* an alternate reality), where he meets some strange jet-setters, including twenty-one-year-old Joy, who becomes Don's lover, then reads *The Sound and the Fury*. The nefarious Duck, warned by Roger that he might be in trouble at Sterling Cooper, secretly suggests that his old British firm should buy Sterling Cooper. Duck hits the sauce. Duck is an awful human being. Kurt Smith, having openly declared his gayness to his shocked coworkers, goes with Peggy to see Bob Dylan in the Village, but first, being gay and all, he has to style her hair for her. Don arranges a mysterious meeting, jotting down the address on the last page of *The Sound and the Fury*. What a jerk move for the next person reading it . . .

EPISODE 2.12: "THE MOUNTAIN KING" (OCTOBER 19, 2008)

Attempting to sell popsicles, Peggy compares them to Communion, then channels Leopold Bloom, noting that "the Catholic Church knows how to sell things." Her campaign to sell the eating of popsicles as a family ritual goes over well. Bert ponders merging with the Brits, though the Brits would definitely be in charge. Don goes to see Anna Draper (the real

Don's widow), with whom he had previously established an acquaintance and to whom he has long been sending money. Pete, back in New York, goes home angry when he finds that Trudy has signed up with an adoption agency. *The Day the Earth Stood Still* plays on the TV. Joan unsuccessfully tries to get it on with Greg. Then later, Greg, seemingly the ideal dream man, rapes Joan in Don's office. Things are seldom what they seem on *Mad Men*. The partners vote to merge with the Brits, though Don is still AWOL in California. Anna reads tarot cards for Don, with vaguely apocalyptic resonances. Betty, apparently afflicted with hysteria, becomes more and more erratic. Peggy moves into Freddie's old office and is accused of trying to be the next Don. Duh.

EPISODE 2.13: "MEDITATIONS IN AN EMERGENCY" (OCTOBER 26, 2008)

Betty gets the news that she is pregnant; she is less than thrilled. Meanwhile, the entire episode is dominated by the Cuban Missile Crisis, which obviously distracts everyone. But life goes on. Don returns to Sterling Cooper to find the firm sold to the Brits; the news that he will make $500,000 from the deal mitigates the shock. Duck, brokering the deal, has also managed to have himself made president of the New York branch of the new firm. Duck makes Pete his replacement as head of accounts, a position that apparently requires one to be a weasel. Duck is an awful human being. Betty plays Don and has a quickie assignation with a man she meets in a bar. When that isn't very satisfying, she starts to chow down. Father Gill makes his move, trying to scare Peggy with the fires of hell. She doesn't fall for it. Duck's vision for the new company is highly TV-oriented. Don isn't interested and walks out. He goes home wondering if the world will survive the weekend. Peggy, meanwhile, drops a bomb on Pete after he declares his love for her. The season ends as Betty tells Don she is pregnant, once again descending into soap opera. Of course, it also pretty much replicates the ending of part I of *Madame Bovary*. The line between high and low culture isn't always clear.

EPISODE 3.1: "OUT OF TOWN" (AUGUST 16, 2009)

Don reigns ascendant at the British-controlled Sterling Cooper, Duck having been sent packing because of Don's opposition and Lane Pryce having arrived from England to take the helm. Duck is an awful human being. Bert Peterson has been made head of accounts but is quickly sacked. Pete and Ken become co-head of accounts. Don makes hot milk for the pregnant Betty and has a weird flashback to his own birth and infancy, including his prostitute mother's death in childbirth. The highlight of the episode is a business trip to Baltimore, where Don and Sal pitch to London Fog. They both have sexual encounters, Don with a stewardess and Sal with a bellboy, though they are interrupted by the hotel fire alarm. Don sees Sal in flagrante, but says nothing other than issuing an oblique warning to Sal to keep his proclivities to himself by telling him of his new "Limit Your Exposure" ad campaign for London Fog. Don has a moment at home with his family.

EPISODE 3.2: "LOVE AMONG THE RUINS" (AUGUST 23, 2009)

Sterling Cooper hopes to land the account for "Patio," Pepsi's new diet soda, using an Ann-Margret musical performance from the then-new *Bye Bye Birdie* (released in New York on April 4, 1963). Don hasn't seen the film. Shown the clip he understands it immediately: men *want* Ann-Margret; women want to *be* Ann-Margret. The firm tries to land the account for the proposed Madison Square Garden; Don steps in when Paul blows the pitch with his opposition to tearing down Penn Station to build the Garden, but SC's British masters pull the plug and order the firm to drop the MSG account. Roger's daughter is planning a wedding, made more complicated by Roger's switch of spouses to the dazzling young Jane, with which ex-wife Mona is not too happy. Peggy is forced to admit that she yearns to have the sexual allure of Ann-Margret in *Bye Bye Birdie*. She has a one-night stand. Don boots Betty's smarmy brother and wife out and keeps Betty's father (and his Lincoln) with the Drapers. The Drapers attend the Field Day celebration at Sally's school. Don is hot for teacher, who might just have a bit of the allure of a youthful Ann-Margret herself.

EPISODE 3.3: "MY OLD KENTUCKY HOME" (AUGUST 30, 2009)

Paul, Smitty, and Peggy have to work the weekend to come up with new ideas for hawking Bacardi Rum. Instead, they just spark it up, which leaves the boys pretty much wasted but stimulates Peggy's creativity. Don, Betty, and most of the Sterling Cooper accounts execs attend the Derby Day garden party at Roger and Jane's estate. Jane gets drunk and seems on the way to train-wreck status. In one of those weird, jarring, estranging moments at which *Mad Men* is so good, Roger performs "My Old Kentucky Home" in blackface. The rich attendees at the party pretty much seem like a collection of obnoxious, privileged assholes. However, Don slips away to the bar and meets up with a folksy, down-home rich guy—who turns out to be Conrad Hilton. Connie on his rise to wealth: "It's different on the inside." Joan and Greg host a party of their own, at which there are hints that Greg might not be any better at being a doctor than he is at being a fiancé. Sally steals some money from her grandpa, triggering a minor domestic crisis. Betty meets dashing politico Henry Francis. Don discourses on class warfare: pissing in the trunks of the rich when he was a car parker at a club attended by "fancy people."

EPISODE 3.4: "THE ARRANGEMENTS" (SEPTEMBER 6, 2009)

Peggy wants to move from Brooklyn (near her ma) to Manhattan because she's one of "those girls." She seeks a roommate to share the high rent. A rich idiot wants to pay Sterling Cooper a million bucks to promote jai alai. They move ahead with the account despite Don's reservations. Grandpa Gene makes arrangements for his death and its aftermath. Betty asks him to keep it to himself. Gene becomes more and more of a problem in the household. Then he dies—in line at A&P. Sal directs the Patio TV ad. He's thrilled, but less thrilled by Kitty's new nightie. The Pepsi reps reject Sal's ad, even though it's exactly what they asked for—an exact copy of Ann-Margret in *Bye Bye Birdie*. Roger puts his finger on the subtle problem with the ad, which no one else can articulate: "It's not Ann-Margret." Sally watches a TV news report of the self-immolation of Buddhist monk Thích Quảng Đức, which occurred on June 11, 1963, in

South Vietnam. The U.S. imperial adventure in Vietnam is picking up steam in the background.

EPISODE 3.5: "THE FOG" (SEPTEMBER 13, 2009)

Another filler, extremely busy, and filled with miscellaneous events, many setting the stage for later developments. Sally gets in a fight at school, causing Don and Betty to conference with Don's favorite teacher, Miss Farrell. Betty gives birth to a baby boy while Don shares a moment in the waiting room with another expectant dad, a Sing Sing prison guard. Don does some dad time with Sally while Betty is in the hospital. Pete comes up with a plan to boost Admiral sales to black consumers and is harshly rebuffed. Duck, now working for a rival firm, tries to recruit Pete and Peggy. Duck is an awful human being. Considering the offer, Peggy asks Don for a raise but is denied due to Lane's penny-pinching management. Betty comes home with the new baby to a newly domestic Don, though he's not much help when the baby cries at night, reminding Betty of the difficulties to come.

EPISODE 3.6: "GUY WALKS INTO AN ADVERTISING AGENCY" (SEPTEMBER 20, 2009)

The British are coming . . . the British are coming. They visit (appropriately) during the July 4 holiday, apparently to make a point. Pleased at Lane's performance, they promote him to head their operation in India. British accounts genius Guy McKendrick will take over the New York office. However, while he might walk into the New York office, he doesn't walk out. In a mayhem of blood spray worthy of *Dexter*, Lois chops off his foot with a runaway John Deere tractor (a quintessentially American product), a present from Ken's new account score. Brits apparently shouldn't mess with Americans during the July 4 holiday. The moment is one of the strangest, most shocking, and funniest in all of *Mad Men*. Most of the second half of the episode is informed by the black comedy of the aftermath of the bloody event, including the rumination by McKendrick's British boss that Guy is probably ruined as an accounts man because, footless, he might never golf again. Lane remains in New

York. Meanwhile, Connie Hilton woos Don, and Joan leaves the firm to be with Greg in his lucrative new life as a surgeon—except that he washes out of his residency and now needs to do another year. Sally is convinced that baby Gene is the ghost of Grandpa Gene.

EPISODE 3.7: "SEVEN TWENTY THREE" (SEPTEMBER 27, 2009)

Hilton agrees to give Sterling Cooper the ad business for three New York hotels, with Don in charge, but only if Don will sign a three-year contract. He resists, valuing his independence, but eventually gives in. Betty's misadventures with home decorating are accompanied by an uptick in her flirtation with Henry Francis. Peggy refuses Duck's offer of a job but accepts his offer of sex. Duck is an awful human being. Don gets drugged and mugged by a young hitchhiking couple, seeing a vision of his dead dad along the way.

EPISODE 3.8: "SOUVENIR" (OCTOBER 4, 2009)

As the residents of the city flee the August heat, Trudy visits her family, leaving Pete behind. He executes a seduction of the neighbor's German au pair, then gets warned off by the neighbor. In the process, Pete discovers Joan now working at a department store. Hilton summons Don (who has been touring Hilton hotels) to Rome; he takes Betty along, even though they're only there one night. It turns out to be a romantic one, at least momentarily distracting her from Henry.

EPISODE 3.9: "WEE SMALL HOURS" (OCTOBER 11, 2009)

Hilton continues his Don man-crush, asking him to wow him with some ideas for a new ad campaign for his international business. For Hilton, it is the mission of America to take its ideas and values everywhere, even to the moon, and he wants his chain of hotels to be a central player. He is, however, disappointed by the campaign that Don comes up with, which he feels lacks the dazzling flights of imagination he had hoped for. Betty, meanwhile, continues her halting flirtation with Henry, while Don continues his flirtation with Suzanne Farrell. He asks her to have coffee with him, but she declines. Lee Garner Jr. meddles with Sal's production of a TV ad for Lucky Strike, then tries to meddle with Sal but is rebuffed. In response, Garner demands that Sal be fired. The request is granted, and Don refuses to step in to save Sal, given the importance of the Lucky Strike account to the bottom line.

EPISODE 3.10: "THE COLOR BLUE" (OCTOBER 18, 2009)

Don finally gets it on with Suzanne, whose basic idealism clearly attracts him as much as her basic prettiness. He has an interesting encounter with her epileptic brother that shows Don's basic decency, despite his serious flaws as a human being. Betty reads Mary McCarthy's *The Group* in the tub. A grumpy Don rejects Paul and Peggy's ideas for an Aqua Net ad. A drunken Paul comes up with what he thinks is a brilliant ad idea for Western Union, but he cannot remember the idea once he sobers up. Betty finally gets a peek at Don's private drawer, just as Molly Bloom did with Leopold's. It's full of cash and relics that reveal his identity. However, she can't seem to get a chance to confront him about it as SC's fortieth anniversary party turns into a showcase for Don—and for the firm, which Putnam, Powell, and Lowe has put up for sale.

EPISODE 3.11: "THE GYPSY AND THE HOBO" (OCTOBER 25, 2009)

Film once again impacts *Mad Men* as Annabelle Mathis, a long-ago flame of Roger Sterling, hires the firm to help rescue her struggling dog food company. Its sales have plummeted in the wake of the recent film (starring Clark Gable and Marilyn Monroe) *The Misfits* (1961), which cast a bad light on the industry. Joan asks Roger for help finding a new job. Greg struggles to switch his specialization to psychiatry but eventually joins the army, where he can be a surgeon after all. The Drapers have a family crisis as Betty finally confronts Don about his secret past, leaving Suzanne Farrell out in the cold. As the episode ends, Don and Betty take the kids out trick-or-treating, despite their recent difficulties. Sally and

Bobby are dressed as the gypsy and the hobo of the episode title, which a man who answers the door at a house acknowledges. Then the man looks at Don and asks, "Who are you supposed to be?" Good question.

EPISODE 3.12: "THE GROWN-UPS" (NOVEMBER 1, 2009)

Another *Mad Men* moment when history takes over. The crucial episode is dominated by news of the Kennedy assassination, bringing the nation (and SC) to a halt. Meanwhile, Duck and Peggy have a nooner as the news comes in. Duck is an awful human being. Pete, informed that he has been passed over in favor of Ken as head of accounts, cries and considers leaving. The wedding of Roger's bratty daughter occurs the day after the assassination. Don tries to be on his best family-guy behavior, but Betty is clearly more interested in the aristocratic Henry. Don, despite all his charm and talent, just doesn't have the right bloodlines for the pretentious Betty.

EPISODE 3.13: "SHUT THE DOOR. HAVE A SEAT" (NOVEMBER 8, 2009)

The mighty McCann arranges to buy Putnam, Powell, and Lowe. Don, Roger, Bert, and Lane all decide to bolt and form a new agency. Pete, Harry, and Joan join in, but Peggy balks, not wishing to be taken for granted by Don. He talks her into it anyway, apologizing for seeing her as an extension of himself. Then *Mad Men* becomes a sort of heist film as they make off with as many Sterling Cooper accounts and resources as they can, under cover of night. Sterling Cooper Draper Pryce sets up shop in a hotel suite. Betty decides to seek a divorce, and things get real ugly real fast in the Draper household, though Don and Betty manage to put on a civil face in front of the kids. She and Henry head for Reno with the baby, leaving the older kids with Carla; Don agrees to cooperate with the divorce. The season ends with many new horizons looming and many older bridges burning.

EPISODE 4.1: "PUBLIC RELATIONS" (JULY 25, 2010)

Don Draper is interviewed by *Ad Age* magazine and asked the classic question: "Who is Don Draper?" He responds with evasion, supplying no info and leading to an article that is a total dud. Don the PR master has missed an opportunity to toot his own horn and that of the new Sterling Cooper Draper Pryce, which has now moved into nice but cramped offices in the Time Life building. Don has had a great year and is more of a star than ever, partly due to his brilliant campaign for Glo-Coat floor wax. Riding high, he tosses the reps of Jantzen bathing suits out of his office because of their puritanical (and hypocritical) attitudes. Don and Betty are divorced; Betty and Henry are married but still living in Don's house, despite an agreement to vacate it. Pete and Peggy concoct a stunt to promote Sugarberry ham. Don doesn't approve, even though they are successful. Roger fixes Don up with Bethany, a young friend of Jane's, but he gets his rocks off with a regular prostitute. Don gets another shot at an interview, this time with *The Wall Street Journal*. He pulls out all the stops, using the old Draper magic this time to sell himself. Don learns from his mistakes—at least some of them.

EPISODE 4.2: "CHRISTMAS COMES BUT ONCE A YEAR" (AUGUST 1, 2010)

Who else but *Mad Men* can get away with a Christmas episode that was broadcast in August? Of course, Christmas is largely beside the point, which sees Don finally starting to succumb to his excessive drinking. Freddie, though, resurfaces, having joined AA. He returns to SCDP, bringing along the Ponds cold cream account. SCDP boosts its Christmas party to impress the smarmy Lee Garner Jr., whose Lucky Strike ads account for 69 percent of the firm's business, so they have to kiss his ass. Glen reconnects with Sally. Don *really* connects with his secretary, Allison. Psychologist Faye Miller brings her expertise as a consultant to the firm—and catches Don's eye, though he (unsurprisingly) refuses to fill out her questionnaire about his childhood.

EPISODE 4.3: "THE GOOD NEWS" (AUGUST 8, 2010)

Mad Men might be clever and stylish, but it can also be incredibly sad. This episode, all about divorce and death, is a case in point. Don decides to travel to Acapulco for the New Year's holiday but stops by Los Angeles to see Anna Draper. He learns that she is dying of cancer, though she doesn't know it herself. Bummed out, he returns to New York instead of going to Mexico, then ends up in the nearly deserted offices of SCDP. He meets up with Lane, who has just received a kiss-off letter from his snotty wife. The two lonely guys get drunk and attend a screening of *Godzilla* in a seedy theater, then top off the evening with dinner and hookers, Don's present to the newly alone Lane.

EPISODE 4.4: "THE REJECTED" (AUGUST 15, 2010)

Roger and Don attempt to placate an annoying Lee Garner Jr. Pete is told to drop the Clearasil account, but when he tries to tell his father-in-law, he receives news that Trudy is pregnant. He soon parlays the situation into a demand that the entire Vick's chemical advertising business be moved to SCDP. Megan (the new SCDP receptionist) participates in Faye Miller's focus group for Ponds. Meanwhile, Allison—all teary-eyed over Don—bolts from the group. Later, she angrily throws an ornament at Don when he calmly agrees to help her get another job and move on. Old Mrs. Blankenship becomes Don's new secretary, which should prevent such problems in the future. Don, meanwhile, continues to play old-fashioned artist vs. newfangled scientist in his skepticism toward Faye's work. Joyce, a photo editor for *Life* magazine, becomes Peggy's new pal and introduces her to a bohemian world of pot-smoking artists, including Abe, a writer/journalist.

EPISODE 4.5: "THE CHRYSANTHEMUM AND THE SWORD" (AUGUST 22, 2010)

SCDP tries to woo the business of Honda Motorcycles, almost making Roger, still remembering WWII, go apoplectic. They fail, but Don makes a very positive impression (aided by his reading of *The Chrysanthemum and the Sword*) that leaves hope of getting the Honda auto business in the future. Ted Chaough, head of a rival agency, announces that he is in Don's rearview mirror. Don scoffs. He also begins to make some progress with Faye, with the help of a bottle of sake sent him by Chaough as a taunt. Sally cuts her hair and is later caught masturbating, causing her to be sent to a child psychiatrist.

EPISODE 4.6: "WALDORF STORIES" (AUGUST 29, 2010)

Danny Siegel, Jane's lame cousin, comes to SCDP seeking work. He has only one useful idea, but most of his portfolio is plagiarized. Don scores a win at the CLIO Awards for TV advertising for his Glo-Coat commercial, then returns drunk from the affair to woo Life Cereal, sealing the deal with them with a slogan he himself stole from Danny. So Danny eventually gets hired. Drunk Don woos some women as well and misses an appointment with his children. A flashback to Don's first meeting with Roger (who is buying a coat for Joan) when Don was still selling fur coats; Don hopes to parlay the meeting into a job, but Roger initially blows him off. Peggy's initial relations with new art director Stan Rizzo are a bit problematic. Ken Cosgrove is hired to join SCDP; Pete isn't happy but eventually assents.

EPISODE 4.7: "THE SUITCASE" (SEPTEMBER 5, 2010)

In an episode that marks the exact halfway point in *Mad Men*'s ninety-two-episode arc (giving it roughly the same number of entries as the finished works in Balzac's *Comédie Humaine*), we see perhaps the best episode of the fourth season, even if (like most of the season) it may be overly busy. Peggy, Stan, and Don struggle with Samsonite luggage. Don gets a viable idea inspired by Muhammad Ali's stunning first-round knockout of Sonny Liston on May 25, 1965, in a title defense that was the first fight by Ali under that name after he had wrested the title from Liston as Cassius Clay back in 1964. Duck, now fully descended into the sauce, loses his job and tries to lure Peggy into joining him as a partner and creative director at their own new firm. She knows better. Duck is an awful human being. Duck bests Don in a drunken brawl. Peggy breaks up with her boyfriend in a squabble concerning a conflict between her work and his plans for her birthday. Tensions flare between her and Don; she points out that his famous Glo-Coat ad was developed from her idea. Don gets the expected (but still sad) word of Anna's death from Stephanie. In a moment of genuine contact between them, he tells Peggy that the only person who truly knew him has died.

EPISODE 4.8: "THE SUMMER MAN" (SEPTEMBER 12, 2010)

Don exercises his writing skills (despite his verbal brilliance, he has never written anything longer than 250 words in his life) by keeping a diary. The mad men battle a vending machine; Joan battles Joey, whose sexist response leads Peggy to fire him. Henry and Betty run into Don while he is having dinner with Bethany. Henry might be a candidate to direct Congressman John Lindsay's possible presidential campaign. Don finally has a date with Faye. Don is not invited to Gene's second birthday party, though he is invited to clear his shit out of the garage, which is supposed to be *his* garage. He attends the party anyway. And deposits his shit in a dumpster.

EPISODE 4.9: "THE BEAUTIFUL GIRLS" (SEPTEMBER 19, 2010)

Don beds Faye. Roger and Joan have sex, fueled by the adrenaline from getting mugged. Abe tries to get Peggy excited about civil rights; she seems more interested in women's rights but is nevertheless interested. An idealist, she is concerned that Fillmore Auto Parts, the key client in this episode, is run by racists. Don says it is their job to get men to like Fillmore, not to get Fillmore to like Negroes. Sally runs away from home and joins Don, saying she wants to live with him. In a key moment, Faye proves totally incapable of dealing with the girl, while Megan emerges from the shadows to save the day, comforting Sally with natural ease. Miss Blankenship's death at her desk becomes a moment of black comedy as her coworkers spirit her body out of the office before it can upset the visiting clients from Secor Laxative.

EPISODE 4.10: "HANDS AND KNEES"
(SEPTEMBER 26, 2010)

Another filler with almost too many events for forty-five minutes of television. Pete's attempt to land the North American Aviation (NAA) account means that the principals will need security clearances. Don, thanks to an error by Megan, is on the list of individuals to be checked. The resultant checks give Don a panic attack. Faye is on hand to help him through and takes the news well when he confesses his identity switch to her, seemingly taking their relationship to a new level. It is, however, Megan who delivers the Beatles tickets that will win points for him with Sally, even though he threatens to wear earplugs to the concert, reminding us of how out of tune (literally) Don is with certain elements of the sixties. Pete reluctantly bounces NAA to save Don. Roger gets shocking news: Lucky Strike is pulling its business, and Joan is pregnant—by Roger. He arranges for her to have an abortion, but she backs out.

EPISODE 4.11: "CHINESE WALL" (OCTOBER 3, 2010)

The rest of SCDP finally learns of Lucky Strike's departure, while Roger feigns shock. Distraught, he seeks solace from Joan but receives little. The firm scrambles to find a way to make up for the loss, with little success. Don suggests to Faye that she could help by supplying inside information gained from her clients, but she refuses, citing ethics. Later, she decides to comply, but by this time Don has already had an assignation with Megan, and anyone who is paying attention can see that his affections are already shifting away from his string of blondes toward his new French Canadian secretary. Amid all this, Trudy gives birth to a baby girl and Peggy renews her relationship with Abe. She also makes a successful presentation to Playtex, despite having lipstick on her teeth, as signaled hilariously by the Playtex rep, who she thinks is making a clumsily vulgar overture. LOL.

EPISODE 4.12: "BLOWING SMOKE" (OCTOBER 10, 2010)

Don runs into his old girlfriend Midge, now a starving artist and heroin addict. He buys one of her paintings to try to help her out. Unable to find a tobacco account to replace Lucky Strike, Don makes a preemptive strike of his own, taking out a full-page ad in the *New York Times* announcing that SCDP will no longer work with tobacco companies due to ethical concerns about marketing health-destroying products. The other partners at SCDP are displeased, though the ad begins to garner positive attention, including from the prestigious American Cancer Society. Don also gets a congratulatory call from "Sen. Robert Kennedy," who turns out to be Ted Chaough punking him. SCDP begins to reduce its staff. The partners have to put up cash to keep the company afloat, so Don pays Pete's share.

EPISODE 4.13: "TOMORROWLAND" (OCTOBER 17, 2010)

Season 4 ends with a flurry of new beginnings, the most important of which is Don's seemingly sudden engagement to Megan during a trip to Disneyland, on which she has come along to help watch his kids, who are with him on the part-business, part-personal trip. Of course, the second half of Season 4 has actually carefully laid the groundwork for this, though it still comes as a pretty big surprise to Faye, and even to Betty. Peggy's complex reaction is interesting as well, though Joan assures her that the event is pure cliché. Don's successful presentation to the American Cancer Society potentially opens new business opportunities. Peggy and Ken, meanwhile, snag some actual new business, winning the Topaz Pantyhose account. The Francises finally move out of Don's Ossining house for a new home in Rye, which will allow him to sell it at a profit.

EPISODE 5.1–2: "A LITTLE KISS" (MARCH 25, 2012)

After a year and a half off the air, *Mad Men* returned with a vengeance with a double-length episode. Don and Megan are now married and living in their stylish new Manhattan apartment. Married life seems to agree with Don; he seems a kinder and gentler sort as he approaches his ostensible fortieth birthday (though Dick Whitman was apparently six months older than the original Don Draper whose birthday is actually being celebrated). The surprise birthday party orchestrated by Megan (and which ruins the white carpet in their new apartment) is the central event of the episode, punctuated by her sexy performance of "Zou Bisou Bisou." Don is mortified, just as he was with Betty's sexy new bathing suit. He doesn't like his women displaying their sexiness publicly. Megan doesn't appreciate the reaction, though her efforts to clean up after the party end in a nice makeup. Joan now has a baby boy, which she seeks to pass of as Greg's. Peggy and Stan struggle to sell Heinz beans. Pete struggles to regain the Mohawk Airlines account, with some unwelcome help from Roger. Bert and Abe argue about Vietnam. A rival firm is embarrassed when some of its employees dump water on civil rights protestors from their office window. SCDP's efforts to make hay from the event end up in a barrage of applications from potential black secretaries.

EPISODE 5.3: "TEA LEAVES" (APRIL 1, 2012)

It is early summer 1966. Don and Harry try to sign the Rolling Stones to record a jingle for Heinz beans, showing how clueless they really are about the landscape of 1960s rock music. The motif might be a veiled allusion to the 1967 album *The Who Sell Out*, which is filled with mock advertisements, including a song entitled "Heinz Baked Beans," which is in fact featured in the album's title art. Betty has a health scare but is mostly just being overweight. Pete reels in Mohawk Airlines (trampling Roger along the way), and Don (on Peggy's recommendation) hires Michael Ginsberg to write their copy.

EPISODE 5.4: "MYSTERY DATE" (APRIL 8, 2012)

Don is plagued by a cold and fever that send him into a hallucination that seems derived from film noir. He is seemingly seduced by and then murders an old flame. New flame Megan is still on hand to take care of him, though. Meanwhile, the Speck murders of eight young Chicago nurses loom over the episode. Sharing a moment with Dawn, Peggy relates how she was "discovered" as a copywriting talent, comparing herself with Esther Blodgett, the rising star of *A Star Is Born* (1937). Peggy, following in Don's footsteps as usual, gets more and more into film as the series proceeds. Greg returns home for a visit and announces that he has volunteered for a second year in Vietnam, where his position makes him feel important. Joan tells him, fine, go, but don't come back.

EPISODE 5.5: "SIGNAL 30" (APRIL 15, 2012)

Pete decides to learn to drive. He lusts (unsuccessfully) over a high-school girl in his driver's ed class. Lane makes a British contact he hopes will win them the advertising business for Jaguar. The resultant scramble (in which Pete, Roger, and Don take the potential client to a classy whorehouse without Lane's knowledge) leads to fisticuffs between Pete and Lane, with Lane victorious. The Drapers and Cosgroves attend a dinner at Pete and Trudy's new suburban house; Don exercises his working-class muscles in fixing their leaky faucet. While he's in his undershirt, the admiring wives gawk, awed by his raw masculine power. Even Megan is impressed enough to have sex with him in the car on the way home. Ken's work as a science-fiction writer (pen name Ben Hargrove) is beginning to bear fruit, so much so that Bert warns him to concentrate on his work for SCDP instead. So he switches genres and pen names and writes a suburban satire about a man who is suspiciously similar to Pete. The University of Texas sniper Charles Whitman lurks in the background, though Don (interestingly enough, given his own real surname) has to correct another character who refers to the sniper as "Whitmore."

EPISODE 5.6: "FAR AWAY PLACES" (APRIL 22, 2012)

Abe invites Peggy to go see *The Naked Prey* (1965), saying that the Cornel Wilde vehicle sounds sexy. Peggy declines, wanting to concentrate on Heinz beans. When Raymond the Heinz rep doesn't like her ideas, she lights into him à la Don. He asks that she be removed from the account. Upset, she goes to see the film on her own. After a stranger offers her a toke, she offers him a hand. Roger tries LSD, and he likes it, especially his vision of being a participant in the 1919 World Series. In the aftermath, he agrees to part ways with Jane. Don takes Megan to Howard Johnson's on a research mission; they get into a fight, and he leaves her there. She makes her way home on her own, leaving a distraught Don looking for her. Tensions seem to be rising more and more between them. Bert complains that Don needs to get his act together and concentrate on work.

EPISODE 5.7: "AT THE CODFISH BALL" (APRIL 29, 2012)

Sally and Bobby stay with Don and Megan after their babysitting grandmother descends into the film noir classic *Detour* and trips over an extended phone cord (as Sally surreptitiously talks with Glen) and breaks her ankle. Megan's parents visit. Her father is a leftist professor/Marxist; her mother is Julia Ormond. They don't get along well, but the mom fleetingly gets on great with Roger. Professor Calvet doesn't approve of Don's capitalist ways, but he supports his daughter's dreams. While in New York, the dad has a disappointing response from a potential publisher for his new book, as if leftist intellectuals otherwise had no trouble getting published in the 1960s. Don wins an award from the American Cancer Society for his anti-smoking letter, but he also wins no new business from the bigwigs on the ACS board because they're afraid he'll turn on them like he did on Lucky Strike. After a client requests music that sounds like the Beatles, Don (still trying to grasp the rock revolution of the decade) asks Megan: "When did music become so important?"

EPISODE 5.8: "LADY LAZARUS" (MAY 6, 2012)

As usual, Pete encounters insurance salesman Howard Dawes on the commuter train. This time there's a twist, though, as Pete ends up having a sexual encounter with Dawes's neglected wife, Beth. There seems to be a genuine connection, but she doesn't want to begin an affair. Megan, pursuing her acting dream, goes on a secret audition, telling Peggy she is going out with Don. When Don calls Peggy looking for Megan, it looks bad. Don and Megan gang up on Raymond to save the Heinz beans account using a brilliant original ad idea produced by Megan. Then they plan to try their team act on Cool Whip, but Megan decides she wants to leave the ad business. Peggy steps in but doesn't perform well as Megan's replacement. In an attempt to remedy Don's cluelessness, Megan gives him a copy of *Revolver*, perhaps the greatest of Beatles albums. She recommends the acclaimed track "Tomorrow Never Knows," which Don plays. A song filled with references to death, it's an ominous choice. Don isn't impressed, turning it off before it has played through. *Revolver*, incidentally, was released on August 5, 1966, so it was still new. A radio broadcast embedded in this episode identifies it as set in October 1966, just as nearly all *Mad Men* episodes can be placed fairly precisely in time.

EPISODE 5.9: "DARK SHADOWS" (MAY 13, 2012)

Roger bribes both Jane and Ginsberg in an attempt to enlist their Jewishness as part of his effort to land the Manischewitz wine account. Ginsberg's ad idea for the product is brilliant. Jane's participation costs Roger big as he has to buy her a new apartment, which he then "sullies" by having sex with her in it. Betty struggles to lose the weight she has gained. Ginsberg comes up with a clever idea for the Pepsi product Sno Ball, but Don pitches his own idea instead. Thanksgiving dinner arrives, but it brings no feast for Betty. She attempts to fuel dissent between Don and Megan by telling Sally about Anna. She's not entirely successful, but there are definitely signs of strife in Don's new marriage, as indicated by the episode title (which derives from the classic Gothic soap opera that premiered in June 1966, just a few months earlier than the events of the episode).

EPISODE 5.10: "CHRISTMAS WALTZ" (MAY 20, 2012)

Another Christmas episode with very little Christmas in it, except for Lane's attempts surreptitiously to wrangle a Christmas bonus out of SCDP to help him get out of hot water with the British tax authorities. He ends up forging Don's signature on a check, thinking he will be able to return the money via his bonus, which never materializes. Megan gets Don to attend an anti-consumerist play—he reacts badly, declaring that consumerism is simply a natural result of the pursuit of happiness. Paul resurfaces, now as a Hare Krishna; he has written a script for a *Star Trek* episode, which he hopes Harry Crane can market to NBC. Harry express-es doubt that *Star Trek*, then struggling for ratings in its first season, would be able to stay on the air long enough to use the script. The script, apparently, is awful. Despite the efforts of Mother Lakshmi, Harry tells Paul the script is excellent but that *Star Trek* just isn't buying scripts at the moment. So he gives Paul money and a plane ticket and urges him to travel to California, land of new beginnings. SCDP has another shot at Jaguar. Don and Joan test drive a Jaguar and have a moment of connec-tion.

EPISODE 5.11: "THE OTHER WOMAN" (MAY 27, 2012)

One of *Mad Men*'s more shocking episodes. Though Don objects, the other partners go around him to cut a deal with Joan that offers her a partnership with a 5 percent stake in SCDP in exchange for the granting of her sexual favors to lowlife Herb Rennet, a car dealership owner in a position to influence Jaguar to take its business to SCDP. All of the partners, of course, are in the business of selling themselves, but this particular moment makes the prostitution that lies at the heart of their work particularly overt. Don makes a brilliant pitch to Jaguar. SCDP wins the account, though it is unclear how much Joan's contribution helped. In the meantime, Peggy, tired of feeling unappreciated, shocks Don by re-signing to take an offer to work for Ted.

EPISODE 5.12: "COMMISSIONS AND FEES" (JUNE 3, 2012)

SCDP works on the Jaguar account. Feeling cocky, they (led by Don) go after Dow Chemical as well. Learning of Lane's forged check, Don de-mands the Brit's resignation. Lane decides to kill himself via the carbon monoxide from the exhaust of his new Jaguar, but (in one of the series' great moments of black comedy) the damn thing won't start, displaying the very unreliability that makes advertising it a challenge. So Lane hangs himself in his office, later to be discovered by his coworkers. Sally comes to stay with her dad, while her mom and stepdad go on a ski trip, but Dad is too distracted by work to spend time with her. While in Manhattan, Sally (with Megan also busy with her own work as an actress) manages to hook up with Glen Bishop, then has her first period and flees back to her mom. Don takes Glen back to his school and even lets him drive on the way—the creepy kid who understands Betty with the creepy adult who does not.

EPISODE 5.13: "THE PHANTOM" (JUNE 10, 2012)

Profits are up at SCDP, but loneliness and alienation reign. Megan's friend wants to audition for a commercial shot by SCDP and asks Megan to enlist Don's help. Instead, Megan tries to get the audition for herself, but Don refuses to help, furthering the growing gap between the Drapers. Marie Calvet visits again and again hooks up with Roger, though she declines his request for her to look after him while he drops acid. As usual, lots of things going on, but the highlight of the episode is the final montage segment, showing a series of characters, lonely and alone, culminating in a scene in which Don goes into a bar, looking just as dashing as the James Bond background music. A woman approaches him, ostensibly on behalf of her girlfriend, and asks if he is alone. It's both a profound and a trivial question because, of course, Don is *always* alone, no matter what.

EPISODE 6.1–2: "THE DOORWAY" (APRIL 7, 2013)

This amazing double-length season-opener is one of our favorite episodes of the entire series. It begins with a teaser scene designed to make it look as if Don might have just had a life-threatening heart attack, then cuts to Don reading Dante on the beach in Hawaii, then builds up a whole network of allusions to death in general, which runs throughout the episode like a meme. Don, for example, constructs an ad for the Royal Hawaiian hotel (his reason for being in Hawaii in the first place) that is (presumably inadvertently) shot through with death imagery of a kind the hotel's reps understandably find highly unacceptable. Peggy struggles with an ad campaign as well, as news from Vietnam torpedoes a brilliant idea she had constructed for hawking Koss headphones. Lot of other things are going on in this intricately constructed episode as well, including the buildup to Peggy's affair with Ted and Don's affair with downstairs neighbor Sylvia Rosen, another in the long line of dark-haired beauties that grab Draper's heart.

EPISODE 6.3: "COLLABORATORS" (APRIL 14, 2013)

Something of a lull, this episode is still chock full of material. Herb, the sleazy Jaguar dealer once again rears his ugly head, creeping out Joan and inspiring Don to deliver his worst pitch ever, presumably on purpose and with delicious malice. Pete gets caught with his hand in a neighbor's cookie jar, drawing a stern response from the usually bubbly Trudy. Don continues his affair with Sylvia, with her Catholic guilt looming in the background and her Jewish husband clueless. Megan is also oblivious, as her chat with Sylvia reveals, while Sylvia's difficulty in untangling Megan's revelations about her real life and her role on a soap opera emphasize just how soapy *Mad Men* can be. Don's whorehouse childhood looms as well, illuminating his problematic attitude toward women.

EPISODE 6.4: "TO HAVE AND TO HOLD" (APRIL 21, 2013)

Don seems to hit a low point with the hypocrisy of his negative reaction to the fact that his actress wife, Megan, has a love scene at work, after which he rushes off for an assignation with his own married girlfriend. Remember, though: no scene in *Mad Men* can be viewed in isolation—each scene plays off others. Don watches Megan's love scene from the wings, which mirrors his earlier flashback to childhood where he watched through a keyhole while his stepmother had sex with the manager of the bordello in which they were staying after the death of his father. Megan and the stepmother are even lying in the same position on the bed. (The stepmother, of course, was pregnant, whereas Megan isn't, though she just had a miscarriage.) Little wonder that Don, watching Megan, thinks she looks like a whore. So, sure, he was being hypocritical and unfair to Megan. But he was also being vulnerable, reminding us of just how scarred he is from his nightmarish childhood. Prostitution, of course, is now a major theme of the show, as when Don et al. rush off for a secret rendezvous with Heinz Ketchup, first at Pete's tawdry love nest, then at a hotel, just hoping to sell themselves. (And later, of course, he listens outside the door of that hotel as Peggy, always his protégée, similarly prostitutes herself [using verbiage learned from Don], just as he had lurked outside the door at the bordello.) The intricate structure of this show is amazing, as is the fact that it features both Ray Wise (as a Dow Chemical exec trying to cope with anti–Vietnam War protestors) and Marley Shelton (as Joan's old pal who now sells cosmetics for Mary Kay) in secondary guest roles.

EPISODE 6.5: "THE FLOOD" (APRIL 28, 2013)

The Martin Luther King episode, in which everyone is shocked and stunned by King's April 4, 1968, assassination and feels that they must offer special condolences to Don's secretary, Dawn. Megan announces that she is tired of her father's Marxist bullshit when he suggests that the assassination might at least have the positive effect of hastening the decay of capitalism. She announces that "the bottle" plays the same role for Don as Marx does for her father, though she is later moved to tears by his speech about loving his children. Don has some rare dad time with Bobby, including a trip to the theater to see *Planet of the Apes*, which opened one day earlier. In addition to the dates, the film, of course, is the perfect gloss on the episode , with the combined racial allegory and hints of approaching apocalyptic doom, rhyming not only with the general spirit of 1968, but with the sense that Don seems to be approaching some sort of meltdown . . .

EPISODE 6.6: "FOR IMMEDIATE RELEASE" (MAY 5, 2013)

Bert, Pete, and Joan concoct a scheme to take SCDP public without telling Don (or, presumably, Roger). Don, in turn, devises a merger with rival firm CGC without consulting them. There are lots of secrets and schemes in *Mad Men*, but these do not seem believable, even if they reinforce the sense that SCDP is careening madly from one crisis to another without direction, just like the capitalist system it so neatly allegorizes. And there are more crises to come, especially as the stunning new account that will save the day involves developing an ad campaign for the revolutionary new Chevy XP-887, better known as the Chevy

Vega. Ouch. But it's a mesmerizing episode, with lots of delicious ironies, as when Abe predicts that the worst that can happen in the coming
months of American politics is that Bobby Kennedy will be elected president. And Jon Hamm is at his eyebrow-arching best, trundling through
the episode conveying Don's growing sense of astonishment and disbelief that everyone he meets seems to be an even bigger fake than he is.
Henceforth, whenever we want to call bullshit on someone, we should
look them square in the eye and say, "I love puppies."

EPISODE 6.7: "MAN WITH A PLAN" (MAY 12, 2013)

Don's world is spiraling out of control. So, just to find something that
makes him feel in charge, he takes refuge by dominating his mistress
Sylvia in a hotel room and abusing his weaker, nice-guy doppelgänger at
work, Ted. (Such doppelgängers proliferate at this point, including his
nefarious double Bob Benson.) Then Sylvia (clearly a sort of figure of the
mother Don never had) kicks Don to the curb, leaving him feeling lost
and helpless. To top matters off, the mild-mannered Ted exerts his masculine power by piloting his own plane, while Don squirms helplessly in
the passenger seat, trying to read *The Last Picture Show*. The future isn't
looking all that great for Don . . .

EPISODE 6.8: "THE CRASH" (MAY 19, 2013)

One of the greatest of all *Mad Men* episodes, possibly because most of
the principals at SCDP-CGC spend a weekend at work hopped up on Dr.
Feelgood's vitamin formula, giving it all a surreal quality. Meanwhile, we
see Don's kids watching *The Prisoner*, which debuted in the United
States on CBS on June 1, 1968, three days before Bobby Kennedy's
assassination. (They are possibly watching episode 4 of *The Prisoner*, in
which No. 6 gets drugged and goes all wacky, which would be perfect.)
The Prisoner certainly has its own surreal moments, and Don is feeling
more and more trapped in his life (and apparently finally beginning to
lose it altogether). So the classic series functions as an interesting gloss
on *Mad Men*. Meanwhile, Don's work seems to be triggering more and
more flashbacks about growing up in a whorehouse. The link between

prostitution and advertising gathers steam. In this same eventful episode, an ample black woman burgles the Draper residence while Sally is left alone with the boys, ominously reading *Rosemary's Baby*. That the burglar claims to be Don's mother nicely deconstructs the "Mammy" stereotype, in particular the claim by many whites that their black servants are really members of the family. It also causes Bobby hilariously to wonder (in a typical moment of *Mad Men's* black humor) if he and his siblings are Negroes. The episode also reveals, via the oatmeal ad, that Don's advertising ideas have been inspired by his troubled childhood at least since 1958 or so—in other words, all along. The woman in the oatmeal ad (the "mother" who "knows what you need") is clearly modeled on Aimee, the prostitute from his childhood. This episode also more clearly establishes Sylvia's status as a mother figure, thus helping to explain his difficulty in letting her go.

EPISODE 6.9: "THE BETTER HALF" (MAY 26, 2013)

This episode seems a bit like a breather after the craziness of 6.8, but then a "breather" episode of *Mad Men* has more packed into it than a whole season of most TV shows. The emotional highlight is Don's tryst with Betty (who now finally looks like January Jones again), but that was pretty inevitable. It also includes some interesting pillow talk about closeness, connection, and sex. Another favorite moment, actually, has Megan trying to tell Don about the experience of playing twins on her soap opera. "They're like two halves of the same person," she tells him. "They want the same things, but they go about it differently." And this, of course, shortly after Peggy has told Don that he and Ted are sometimes "the same person," except that they have different styles of trying to reach their goals. That might be a fairly heavy-handed parallel, except that it is enhanced by the fact that we don't know if Don himself even notices the parallel, because he is not the greatest listener (and his eyes generally start to glaze over the minute Megan starts talking). Meanwhile, the parallel radiates to all the other doublings in an episode in which Don has two wives; Bobby (for a fleeting moment) has two parents; Peggy has two would-be boyfriends, until she accidentally (or was it a physical version of a Freudian slip) stabs Abe in one of those Gothic moments that punctuate the show (lawn mower to the foot, anyone?); and Roger tries to be a father figure to two different little boys but is rebuffed by both their mothers, in an episode in which the basic pathos of his character comes to the fore. And then there's Bob Benson, who is getting *really* friendly with Joan, but who continues to do only nice things for everyone and to have only good things to say about everyone, even Pete. Yet he also manages to be creepy and unlikeable, maybe because he tries so hard that you just have to suspect ulterior motives. Anyway, this was another of those *Mad Men* episodes that just seems better and better and richer and richer the more you think about it.

EPISODE 6.10: "A TALE OF TWO CITIES" (JUNE 2, 2013)

Don and Roger head to L.A. to try to drum up business, especially from Carnation and their new Instant Breakfast product. Roger openly declares that New York is the center of the universe and L.A. is just a fancy Hicksville. His visit to L.A. thus becomes something like Woody Allen's trip in *Annie Hall*. The two cities of the title might thus seem to be New York and L.A., or even New York and Detroit, where the newly minted SC&P (Sterling Cooper and Partners) carries on a dual operation, but the real action is in Chicago (where the riots surrounding the Democratic Convention are apparently, per the episode title, supposed to remind us of the French Revolution). It is mostly off camera, though. The real on-camera drama is Joan and her attempt to get the respect she is due, while she continues to be in the weird position of being the one person the other characters know they can rely on in a crunch but who otherwise continues to be treated like a dumb redhead. Meanwhile, Roger and Don attend a stereotypical sixties Hollywood party, where we get to see good ol' Danny Siegel, now a rising Hollywood producer, punch Roger where it hurts most while apparently channeling Paul Simon's Tony Lacey from *Annie Hall*. Groovy. Don then watches himself drown in the pool, high on hashish, before being brought back to life by Roger. Note that the ending music is the Big Brother and the Holding Company recording of "Piece of My Heart," which is incredibly appropriate, not only because of the psychedelic tenor of the episode (even Pete Campbell sparks one up), but because it appeared on the album *Cheap Thrills* (again appropriate to *Mad Men*) and was released in August of 1968, the month of this episode itself. It was also their last album with Janis Joplin on vocals, since she left the group almost immediately afterward, thus reinforcing the things-fall-apart tenor of this entire season.

EPISODE 6.11: "FAVORS" (JUNE 9, 2013)

Peggy battles a rat, Mitchell Rosen battles the draft board, and Pete battles Bob, though he puts up no fight at all against his homophobia. The juice wars continue. The firm struggles to land Sunkist and Ocean Spray. Ted petulantly declares, "I don't want his juice. I want my juice." He wants his own juice, not Don's juice. Don continues to battle Ted, but the latter helps the former out in his effort to help out Mitchell (and thus Sylvia), lessening their tension. Sally catches Don in flagrante with Sylvia. Don, so good at convincing others, comes up with the lamest explanation ever, claiming he was "comforting" Sylvia.

EPISODE 6.12: "THE QUALITY OF MERCY" (JUNE 16, 2013)

Another amazing, incredibly dense *Mad Men* episode, with Shakespeare (via the title from *The Merchant of Venice*) added into the intertextual mix, along with a heavy dose of *Rosemary's Baby* (which was prefigured when we saw Sally reading the novel back in 6.8). Meanwhile, Don both begins and ends in a fetal position, suggesting his ongoing downward spiral; Bob's background as an inbred hillbilly fancy-pants manservant is revealed; and Ted and Peggy get all giggly—until Don messes it up. The descent into darkness continues, yet Don delivers the funniest line in the whole series with his "I mean, not with Peggy." Meanwhile, this was the first episode all season that the exact date couldn't be pinned down by an external reference. However, given the arc of the season (and the hilarious Nixon anti-crime ad on TV, suggesting that the election is approaching), we can assume it is October.

EPISODE 6.13: "IN CARE OF" (JUNE 23, 2013)

The sixth season ends with a bang. Don tries to lure the Hershey's Chocolate account with a nostalgic sentimental story about warm memories of its product from his childhood, then has a change of heart and confesses that it was all lies and that his childhood was actually a living hell (though he still enjoyed the occasional Hershey bar). Meanwhile, everybody else ends up scrambling to try to get to California, the result being that Ted goes (in order to escape his entanglement with Peggy and salvage his marriage) and Megan goes (having made professional arrangements because she thought Don was going). Don stays behind. Then he is put on mandatory leave by the firm after his Hershey's performance, which they believe suggests that he has become dangerously unstable. Duck is an awful human being. Don takes his three kids to see the Pennsylvania whorehouse where he grew up, seemingly opening a new era of honesty and transparency.

EPISODE 7.1: "TIME ZONES" (APRIL 13, 2014)

Don, still in exile from SC&P, visits Megan in California, where she has gone native, sashaying about in micro-skirts and living in a cool canyon house with coyote cries in the background. Pete is trying to go all California as well but isn't quite as successful in pulling it off. Joan tries to break into accounts work. Roger has a new hippie girlfriend in whose bed "anyone is welcome." Peggy's new life as a slumlord turns out to be a real pain, as is new creative director Lou Avery. Don charms a comely widow on a flight back to New York, where he keeps his hand in the ad game by feeding ideas to Freddie, now working freelance. He's still Don, but he isn't doing well, all in all.

EPISODE 7.2: "A DAY'S WORK" (APRIL 20, 2014)

Not one of *Mad Men*'s more scintillating episodes, but the SC&P conference call between New York and California featuring clunky 1960s technology is funny. Valentine's Day pisses off Peggy. Everyone tries to get rid of their black secretaries. Pete can't get no respect. Jim and Roger begin to clash big time. Sally discovers her father's exile and then tells him she loves him, somewhat to his surprise.

THE EPISODES

275

EPISODE 7.3: "FIELD TRIP" (APRIL 27, 2014)

Megan's behavior becomes erratic, causing her agent to appeal to Don to stabilize her. So he heads to California, despite needing some steadying himself. There, he confesses to Megan that he is "on leave." She isn't pleased that he chose to stay in New York anyway and tells him it's over. Jim withdraws Peggy's *Rosemary's Baby* aspirin ad from consideration for a Clio, adding to her general miseries. Harry brags about the virtues of SC&P's nonexistent computer. Jim declares Harry the most dishonest man he has ever worked with. Back in New York, Don begins to consider other job offers but manages to convince Roger to invite him back in to SC&P instead. He has less success with Megan. His triumphant return to SC&P is not so triumphant. Don's presence makes everyone uncomfortable, except Ginsberg who is oblivious to office politics (and maybe life in general . . . more to come).

EPISODE 7.4: "THE MONOLITH" (MAY 4, 2014)

This episode is built around Stanley Kubrick's *2001: A Space Odyssey*, as signaled by the fact that the title is a clear reference to the large monoliths that periodically appear to announce the onset of a new leap forward in human evolution. These monoliths are referenced by several visual echoes that signal that the 1960s was a major turning point in American history, including the importance and function of technology. Here, SC&P acquires a massive new computer that echoes the film's HAL 9000 and suggests a threat to the traditional, nostalgia-driven advertising strategies preferred by Don. Meanwhile, Don has a weird encounter with the guy installing the computer, providing another hint that he might have a few screws loose.

EPISODE 7.5: "THE RUNAWAYS" (MAY 11, 2014)

This episode continues the *2001* references when Ginsberg watches Lou Avery conferring with Cutler inside the sealed glass room that contains the new computer. Unable to hear, Ginsberg sees the lips of the two men moving, and he attempts to read their lips, much in the way HAL attempts to read the lips of two astronauts who are plotting against him in *2001*. Eventually, the perceived threat posed by the computer will drive Ginsberg into insanity and weird self-mutilation. The odd moment of lip-reading complicates the reference to *2001* by placing the computer-phobic human Ginsberg in the position of the film's human-phobic computer. Ginsberg's reaction to the computer, which involves a belief that the computer plans to turn them all into "homos" and ultimately involves cutting off his own nipple (to open the "valve") and presenting it to Peggy in a gift box, seems a bit extreme. But Ginsberg, born in a concentration camp and then orphaned (though at one point in the series he claims to be from Mars), has had an extreme life and perhaps has good reason to be paranoid.

EPISODE 7.6: "THE STRATEGY" (MAY 18, 2014)

Don joins Peggy's Burger Chef team, and it is clear that she feels threatened, while at the same time wanting to take advantage of his still-formidable abilities. Their campaign, meanwhile, helps to mark the rise of fast food as a key element of day-to-day American culture. Bob proposes to Joan so she can be his show wife and help him in his new career at GM. She declines. Harry's computer-fueled stock is on the rise at SC&P, which doesn't say much for SC&P.

EPISODE 7.7: "WATERLOO" (MAY 25, 2014)

The first half of the final season ends with a bang. The show's use of historical events as a backdrop culminates in the Apollo 11 moon landing (July 20, 1969). Don lets Peggy take the lead in a pitch that wins the Burger Chef account, and Bert Cooper dies, only to be resurrected in a final musical number that appears to be another of Don's weird visions but could be interpreted in all sorts of ways. Cooper's posthumous soft-shoe performance of "The Best Things in Life Are Free" suggests that, in death, he has disavowed the Ayn Rand ethos that drove him in life. Meanwhile, Roger saves Don's bacon by engineering the sale of 51 percent of the company to McCann Erickson, with the stipulation that Don, about to be ousted from the firm altogether, is included in the deal.

EPISODE 7.8: "SEVERANCE" (APRIL 5, 2015)

Richer than ever and back on top professionally, but with another divorce under way, Don is in full-on swinging-bachelor mode. The same might be said for Roger, big new mustache and all. Ted goes the 'stache route as well. Johnny Mathis (no, not *that* Johnny Mathis) tries to set Peggy up with his brother-in-law. Don, continuing his recent string of strange visions (death seems to be a key focus), has a weird dream about Rachel Katz (nee Menken), who then turns out to have just died. The reconstituted Sterling Cooper dumps one-eyed Ken Cosgrove, who then lands on his feet as head of advertising at Dow Chemical, where he plans to torment his old employers. Joan has perhaps her grossest encounter yet with sexist louts, this time from the firm's new owners at McCann. Don bags Mildred Pierce in an alley.

EPISODE 7.9: "NEW BUSINESS" (APRIL 12, 2015)

Don continues his pursuit of Diana the Tragic Waitress. He also pays Megan a cool $1 million to get the divorce over with and assuage his guilt, not knowing that Megan's mom has just made off with all of his furniture, then boffed Roger in the subsequently empty apartment. Harry Crane tries (really ineptly) to hit on the newly single Megan, attempting to use his show-biz connections as a lure. Mimi Rogers appears as an ambitious female photographer who hits on both Peggy and Stan in pursuit of more business opportunities from the firm.

EPISODE 7.10: "THE FORECAST" (APRIL 19, 2015)

McCann Erickson's noninterference pledge already begins to wane as they demand that SC&P produce a forecast of its future vision. Roger Sterling assigns the task to Don after Ted wriggles out of it. Don takes the task surprisingly seriously, showing some disturbing signs of going all corporate. Glen Bishop, who keeps resurfacing like a bad penny, shows up once again, now preparing to ship out for Vietnam. Of course, he makes one last pass at Betty. Joan meets an older rich guy, and romance, though problematic, begins to bloom. Peggy is getting increasingly snarky. Don finally sells his posh penthouse, then has a moment of seller's remorse as the episode ends.

EPISODE 7.11: "TIME & LIFE" (APRIL 26, 2015)

Some bonding between Stan and Peggy, who confesses that she had a child. Other things happen. Mostly though, McCann Erickson makes its move to absorb SC&P altogether. Don's lame plan to escape by moving their whole operation out of California is quickly shot down. So one last effort to dramatize the romance of business fizzles pretty badly. Most of the principals are now in position to become total sell-outs, having "died and gone to advertising heaven" via big-time job offers at McCann. Apparently the series is moving toward the *shocking* final revelation that capitalism is mostly evil and corporations are mostly villains.

EPISODE 7.12: "LOST HORIZON" (MAY 3, 2015)

The awfulness of McCann continues to dominate, as Joan experiences sexual harassment and sexism in general. The new firm, a kind of monolith, gives her an ultimatum: "put out or get out." Peggy nevertheless rolls into the new offices determined to take on the world, after receiving some surprisingly sage advice during a moment of bonding with Roger as they prepare to exit the offices of SC&P, now an abandoned wasteland. Don, meanwhile, cannot handle the corporate routinization at McCann. He bolts mid-meeting and heads west on a road trip, apparently accompanied by Bert Cooper's ghost.

EPISODE 7.13: "THE MILK AND HONEY ROUTE" (MAY 10, 2015)

Don's *On the Road*–style trip continues as his car breaks down in a small town. He shares war stories with some local vets and later they beat him up when they suspect (wrongly) that he robbed them. His car gets fixed, but he gives it to a young local con man who clearly reminds him of himself. It's as if Don is preparing for the end, as is Betty, who learns that she has terminal lung cancer. Things are really looking up for Pete, however, as he is suddenly set to regain his wife and child and to move to a posh new job.

EPISODE 7.14: "PERSON TO PERSON" (MAY 17, 2015)

This last episode is all about endings—including Betty's gracious move toward death. Some of the endings are conventional romantic ones, like when both Roger (with Megan's mother) and Peggy (with Stan) find true love. Joan's romance with Richard ends, however, as does her association with McCann. She prepares for a new beginning with her own film production company and a fat account from Ken. Pete prepares for a new life with Lear Jet and seems to be riding high, even if he has to move to Wichita. Don (of course) has the most enigmatic ending. He finally makes his way to California, but from there it is unclear whether he has found New Age–style peace. Ambiguous or clear, depending on one's interpretation, Don either created the famous hippie-infused Coke commercial . . . or didn't.

BIBLIOGRAPHY

Akass, Kim, and Janet McCabe. "*The Best of Everything:* The Limits of Being a Working-Class Girl in *Mad Men*." In *Mad Men: Dream Come True TV*, ed. Gary R. Edgerton, 177–92. London: I. B. Tauris, 2011.

"Alcoholism." *CQ Almanac.* Washington, DC: Congressional Quarterly, 1970.

Anderson, Tim. "Uneasy Listening: Music, Sound, and Criticizing Camelot in *Mad Men*." In *Mad Men: Dream Come True TV*, ed. Gary R. Edgerton, 72–85. London: I. B. Tauris, 2011.

Baldwin, Matthew, Monica Biernat, and Mark J. Landau. "Remembering the Real Me: Nostalgia Offers a Window to the Intrinsic Self." *Journal of Personality and Social Psychology* 108, no. 1 (2014): 128–47.

Barkman, Ashley Jihee. "Mad Women: Aristotle, Second-Wave Feminism, and the Women of *Mad Men*." In *"Mad Men" and Philosophy: Nothing Is As It Seems*, ed. Rod Carveth and James B. South. Hoboken, NJ: John Wiley and Sons, 2010.

Batchelor, Bob. *The 1900s.* Westport, CT: Greenwood, 2002.

Baudrillard, Jean. *Simulacra and Simulation.* Trans. Sheila Faria Glaser. Ann Arbor: University of Michigan Press, 1995.

Bertha, Mike. "*Mad Men*'s Miracle Mets: The Mets Pennant Is a Metaphor for Don's Fate." *Cut4.* May 5, 2014. http://m.mlb.com/cutfour/2014/05/05/74365558/mad-men-mets-pennant-metaphor-for-don-drapers-fate (accessed June 12, 2014).

Booker, M. Keith. *Joyce, Bakhtin, and the Literary Tradition: Toward a Comparative Cultural Poetics.* Ann Arbor: University of Michigan Press, 1996.

———. *Monsters, Mushroom Clouds, and the Cold War: American Science Fiction and the Roots of Postmodernism, 1946–1964.* Westport, CT: Greenwood, 2001.

Boorstin, Daniel J. *The Americans: The Democratic Experience.* New York: Random House, 1973.

Brick, Howard. *Age of Contradiction: American Thought and Culture in the 1960s.* Ithaca, NY: Cornell University Press, 2000.

Cardwell, Sarah. "Television Aesthetics: Stylistic Analysis and Beyond." In *Television Aesthetics and Style*, ed. Jason Jacobs and Steven Peacock, 23–44. New York: Bloomsbury, 2013.

Carmical, J. H. "Stocks Advance in Heavy Trading." *New York Times.* January 19, 1966.

Cohen, Lizabeth. *A Consumers' Republic: The Politics of Mass Consumption in Postwar America.* New York: Knopf, 2003.

CQ Press. "February." In *Historic Documents of 1972*, 138–217. Washington, DC: CQ Press, 1973.

Cracknell, Andrew. *The Real Madmen: The Renegades of Madison Avenue and the Golden Age of Advertising.* Philadelphia: Running Press, 2011.

Danesi, Marcel. *Popular Culture: Introductory Perspectives*. Lanham, MD: Rowman & Littlefield, 2008.

de Groot, Jerome. "Perpetually Dividing and Suturing the Past and Present: *Mad Men* and the Illusions of History." *Rethinking History* 15, no. 2 (2011): 269–85.

Della Femina, Jerry. *From Those Wonderful Folks Who Gave You Pearl Harbor*. New York: Simon and Schuster, 1970.

Dickstein, Morris. *Gates of Eden: American Culture in the Sixties*. New York: Basic, 1977.

Dougherty, Philip H. "Advertising: An Audition for the Young and Beautiful." *New York Times*. February 24, 1967.

————. "Advertising: Mary Wells Doesn't Scrimp." *New York Times*. October 9, 1969.

Ewen, Stuart. *Captains of Consciousness: Advertising and the Social Roots of the Consumer Culture*. New York: Basic, 2001.

Ewen, Stuart, and Elizabeth Ewen, *Channels of Desire: Mass Images and the Shaping of American Consciousness* New York: McGraw Hill, 1982.

Fowler, Elizabeth M. "Personal Finance: The Typical Consumer." *New York Times*. November 9, 1964.

Frank, Thomas. *The Conquest of Cool: Business Culture, Counterculture, and the Rise of Hip Consumerism*. Chicago: University of Chicago Press, 1998.

Giges, Nancy. "Ad Women: How Agency Life Really Was." *Advertising Age* 79, no. 25 (2008).

Gilman, Richard. "There's a Wave of Pornography Obscenity Sexual Expression." *New York Times*. September 8, 1968.

Gimlin, J. S. "Regulation of the Cigarette Industry." Editorial Research Reports. *Congressional Quarterly Researcher* 2 (1967).

Gleason, Ralph J. "Like a Rolling Stone." *American Scholar* 36, no. 4 (1967): 555–63.

Goodlad, Lauren, Lilya Kaganovsky, and Robert A. Rushing, eds. *"Mad Men," Mad World: Sex, Politics, Style, and the 1960s*. Durham, NC: Duke University Press, 2013.

Goodman, Tim. "'Mad Men' Series Finale: Tim Goodman on a Masterful and Difficult Achievement." *Hollywood Reporter*. May 18, 2015.

Goodrum, Charles, and Helen Dalrymple, *Advertising in America: The First 200 Years*. New York: Harry N. Abrams, 1990.

Gray, Jonathan, and Amanda D. Lotz. *Television Studies*. Malden, MA: Polity, 2012.

Greene, Eric. *"Planet of the Apes" as American Myth: Race, Politics, and Popular Culture*. Middletown, CT: Wesleyan University Press, 1998.

Hampp, Andrew. "The Three-Martini Lunch Is Alive and Well on AMC." *Advertising Age* 78, no. 25 (2007).

Heath, Joseph, and Andrew Potter. *Nation of Rebels: Why Counterculture Became Consumer Culture*. New York: HarperBusiness, 2004.

Hebdige, Dick. *Subculture: The Meaning of Style*. London: Routledge, 1979.

Heidkamp, Bernie. "New 'Mad Men' TV Show Uses the Past to Reveal Racism and Sexism of Today." *Alternet*. August 23, 2007. http://www.alternet.org/story/60278/new_%22mad_men%22_tv_show_uses_the_past_to_reveal_racism_and_sexism_of_today (accessed January 21, 2015).

Heimann, Jim, ed. *Advertising from the "Mad Men" Era*. Köln: Taschen, 2012.

Heller, Steven. "So, What's the Big Idea?" In *Advertising from the "Mad Men" Era*, ed. Jim Heimann, 341–44. Köln: Taschen, 2012.

Hepper, Erica G., et al. "Pancultural Nostalgia: Prototypical Conceptions Across Cultures." *Emotion* 14, no. 4 (2014): 733–47.

Hobsbawm, Eric. *The Age of Empire, 1875–1914*. New York: Pantheon, 1987.

Igla, Jonathan. Audio Commentary. *Mad Men*: Season Four. DVD. Santa Monica, CA: Lionsgate, 2010.

Jacobs, Jason, and Steven Peacock, eds. *Television Aesthetics and Style*. New York: Bloomsbury, 2013.

Jagger, Mick, and Keith Richards. "Sympathy for the Devil." On *Beggars Banquet*. London: London Records, 1968.

Jameson, Fredric. *Archaeologies of the Future: The Desire Called Utopia and Other Science Fictions*. London: Verso, 2005.

———. *Postmodernism, or, The Cultural Logic of Late Capitalism*. Durham, NC: Duke University Press, 1991.

———. *Signatures of the Visible*. London: Routledge, 1992.

Janover, Michael. "Nostalgias." *Critical Horizons* 1, no. 1 (2000): 113–33.

Jenkins, Keith. *Re-thinking History*. Routledge Classics ed. New York: Routledge, 2003.

Jing, Wu. "Nostalgia as Content Creativity: Cultural Industries and Popular Sentiment." *International Journal of Cultural Studies* 9, no. 3 (2006): 359–68.

Juarez, Vanessa. "Mad Men." *Entertainment Weekly*. July 5, 2010.

Katona, George. *The Mass Consumption Society*. New York: McGraw-Hill, 1964.

Klaassen, Abbey, and Lisa Sanders. "AMC Show Puts 'Mad' Back in Mad Ave." *Advertising Age*. April 3, 2006.

Koshetz, Herbert. "Extra Shopping Day This Year Helped Christmas Business." *New York Times*. December 28, 1969.

Kramer, Michael J. *The Republic of Rock: Music and Citizenship in the Sixties Counterculture*. Oxford: Oxford University Press, 2013.

Kreisel, Deanna K. "Mr. Draper Goes to Town." *Kritik*. April 28, 2014. https://deannakreisel.wordpress.com/2014/05/05/mr-draper-goes-to-town/ (accessed December 24, 2015).

Lafargue, Paul. "Marx and Literature." In *Literature and Art: Selections from Their Writings*, by Karl Marx and Frederick Engels, 138–40. New York: International Publishers, 1947.

Lang, Clarence. "Representing the Mad Margins of the Early 1960s: Northern Civil Rights and the Blues Idiom." In *"Mad Men," Mad World: Sex, Politics, Style, and the 1960s*, ed. Lauren M. E. Goodlad, Lilya Kaganovsky, and Robert A. Rushing, 73–91. Durham, NC: Duke University Press, 2013.

Lawrence, Mary Wells. *A Big Life in Advertising*. New York: Knopf, 2002.

Leach, William R. *Country of Exiles: The Destruction of Place in American Life*. New York: Pantheon, 1999.

———. *Land of Desire: Merchants, Power, and the Rise of a New American Culture*. New York: Vintage-Random House, 1994.

Leboe, Jason P., and Tamara L. Ansons. "On Misattributing Good Remembering to a Happy Past: An Investigation into the Cognitive Roots of Nostalgia." *Emotion* 6, no.4 (2006): 596–610.

Lee, Ashley. "Mad Men Creator Matthew Weiner Explains Series Finale, Character Surprises and What's Next." *Hollywood Reporter*. May 20, 2015.

Lippert, Barbara. "It's a Mad, Mad World." *Adweek*. August 16, 2009.

Lowry, Tom. "How *Mad Men* Glammed Up AMC." *BusinessWeek*. July 23, 2008.

Lukács, Georg. *The Historical Novel*. Trans. Hannah Mitchell and Stanley Mitchell. Lincoln: University of Nebraska Press, 1983.

Maas, Jane. *Mad Women: The Other Side of Life on Madison Avenue in the '60s and Beyond*. New York: Thomas Dunne, 2012.

Maerz, Melissa. "The All-American Anti-Hero." *Rolling Stone*. September 17, 2009.

Mitchell, Joni. "Both Sides, Now." Recorded by Judy Collins. On *Wildflowers*. New York: Elektra, 1967.

Morgan, Edward P. *What Really Happened to the 1960s: How Mass Media Culture Failed American Democracy*. Lawrence: University Press of Kansas, 2010.

Moss, Elisabeth. Audio Commentary. *Mad Men*: Season One. DVD. Santa Monica, CA: Lionsgate, 2007.

Munslow, Alun. *Deconstructing History*. New York: Routledge, 1997.

———. "Where Does History Come From?" *Today's History* 52, no. 3 (2002): 18–20.

Naranch, Laurie. "Cash or Credit? Sex and the Pursuit of Happiness." In *"Mad Men" and Politics: Nostalgia and the Remaking of Modern America*, ed. Linda Beail and Lilly J. Goren, 99–115. New York: Bloomsbury Academic, 2015.

Nussbaum, Emily. "Faking It: 'Mad Men's' Don Draper Problem." *New Yorker*. May 20, 2013.

Ogilvy, David. *Confessions of an Advertising Man*. New York: Atheneum, 1963.

———. *Ogilvy on Advertising*. New York: Vintage, 1983.

Panse, Silke, and Dennis Rothermel, eds. *Critique of Judgment in Film and Television*. New York: Palgrave Macmillan, 2014.

Parrott, Billy. *The "Mad Men" Reading List*. New York Public Library. February 27, 2012.

Paskin, Willa. *"Mad Men*, Season 7, Part 1." *Slate*. May 6, 2014.

Polan, Dana. "Maddening Times: *Mad Men* in Its History." In *"Mad Men," Mad World: Sex, Politics, Style, and the 1960s*, ed. Lauren M. E. Goodlad, Lilya Kaganovsky, and Robert A. Rushing, 35–52. Durham, NC: Duke University Press, 2013.

Poniewozik, James. *"Mad Men*, What Have You Done with Peggy Olson?" *Time*. April 29, 2014.

Quimby, Freeman H. "Little Known Facts About the Psychoactive Drugs (Part I—Alcohol)." *Congressional Research Service*. July 22, 1970.

Reinhold, Robert. "80% Success Claimed for Sex Therapy." *New York Times*. April 27, 1970.

Rielly, Edward J. *The 1960s*. Westport, CT: Greenwood, 2003.

Rogin, Michael. *Ronald Reagan the Movie: And Other Episodes in Political Demonology*. Berkeley: University of California Press, 1988.

Romano, Andrew. 2014. "How to End 'Mad Men'? Matthew Weiner Gives Final Season Sneak Peek." *Daily Beast*. March 24, 2014. http://www.thedailybeast.com/articles/2014/03/24/how-to-end-mad-men-matthew-weiner-gives-final-season-sneak-peek.html (accessed March 30, 2014).

Rosin, Hanna. "The Madness of Matthew Weiner." *Atlantic*. April 2014.

Rushing, Robert A. "'It Will Shock You How Much This Never Happened': Antonioni and *Mad Men*." In *"Mad Men," Mad World: Sex, Politics, Style, and the 1960s*, ed. Lauren Goodlad, Lilya Kaganovsky, and Robert A. Rushing, 192–210. Durham, NC: Duke University Press, 2013.

Ryan, Ted. "The Making of 'I'd Like to Buy the World a Coke.'" Coca-Cola Company. January 1, 2012. http://www.coca-colacompany.com/stories/coke-lore-hilltop-story/ (accessed January 24, 2015).

Sagan, Carl. *Cosmos*. New York. Random House, 1980.

Samuel, Lawrence R. *The American Dream: A Cultural History*. Syracuse, NY: Syracuse University Press, 2012.

Schlesinger, Arthur M., Jr. *The Politics of Hope* and *The Bitter Heritage*. Princeton, NJ: Princeton University Press, 2008.

Schwartz, Missy. "Mad Men." *Entertainment Weekly*. June 2, 2008.

Seltzer, Sarah. *"Mad Men* Owed Betty Draper a Better Ending." *Flavorwire*. May 12, 2015. http://flavorwire.com/518377/mad-men-owed-betty-draper-a-better-ending (accessed May 13, 2015).

Shaffer, H. B. "Advertising in a Consumer Society." In *CQ Researcher*. Vol. 1. Washington, DC: CQ Press, 1969.

"Sidelights." *New York Times*. February 15, 1966.

Sloane, Leonard. "Advertising: Ivy League Losing Ground on Madison." *New York Times*. February 25, 1966.

Spielvogel, Carl. "Advertising: Picture for 1960 Looks Bright." *New York Times*. January 3, 1960.

Spring, Dawn. *Advertising in the Age of Persuasion: Building Brand America, 1941–1961*. New York: Palgrave Macmillan, 2011.

Spring, Joel. "Schooling for Consumption." In *Critical Pedagogies of Consumption: Living and Learning in the Shadow of the "Shopocalypse,"* ed. Jennifer A. Sandlin and Peter McLaren, 69–82. New York: Routledge, 2010.

Steinberg, Brian, and Andrew Hampp. "Did the Admen Watch 'Mad Men'?" *Advertising Age*. July 23, 2007.

Strutton, David, and David G. Taylor. "What Would Don Draper Do? Rules for Restoring the Contemporary Agency Mojo." *Business Horizons*. September 2011.

Suderman, Peter. "Boys Behaving Badly." *National Review*. December 3, 2007.

Susman, Warren. *Culture as History: The Transformation of American Society in the Twentieth Century*. New York: Pantheon, 1984.

Thompson, Ethan, and Jason Mittell, eds. *How to Watch Television*. New York: New York University Press, 2013.

Trachta, Ali. "Matthew Weiner Explains Betty Draper, Mad Men's 'Melancholy Dame.'" *LA Weekly*. March 28, 2013.

Tungate, Mark. *Adland: A Global History of Advertising*. London: Kogan Page, 2007.

Twitchell, James B. *Adcult USA: The Triumph of Advertising in American Culture*. New York: Columbia University Press, 1996.

Tyree, J. M. "No Fun: Debunking the 1960s in *Mad Men* and *A Serious Man*." *Film Quarterly* 63, no. 4 (2010): 33–39.

U.S. Senate, Committee on Labor and Public Welfare, Subcommittee on Alcoholism and Narcotics. *Alcoholism and Narcotics: Hearings . . . Ninety-first Congress, First and Second Sessions*. Washington: U.S. Government Printing Office, 1970.

VanDerWerff, Todd. "Mad Men: 'Smoke Gets In Your Eyes.'" *A.V. Club*. November 6, 2013. http://www.avclub.com/tvclub/mad-men-smoke-gets-in-your-eyes-105216 (accessed August 29, 2014).

Vartan, Vartanig G. "Sidelights: Wall St. Debate: The Dow 1,000." *New York Times*. February 15, 1966.

Weiner, Matthew. "The Art of Screenwriting No. 4." Interview by Semi Chellas. *The Paris Review*. Spring 2014.

———. Audio commentary. *Mad Men*: Season Four. DVD. Santa Monica, CA: Lionsgate, 2010.

———. Audio commentary. *Mad Men*: Season Seven Part 1. DVD. Santa Monica, CA: Lionsgate, 2014.

———. "Mad Men Creator on Don Draper's Losses and the End of the Road." Interview by Terry Gross. "Fresh Air." NPR. May 7, 2015. http://www.npr.org/2015/05/07/404904172/mad-men-creator-on-don-drapers-losses-and-the-end-of-the-road (accessed May 9, 2015).

———. "Mad Men's Creator: Don Draper Represents American Society." Interview by Hanna Rosin. *The Atlantic*. March 19, 2014.

———. "Matthew Weiner on 'Mad Men' and Meaning." NPR. April 23, 2013.

———. "Matthew Weiner Talks about *Mad Men's* Next and Final Season." Interview by Denise Martin. *Vulture*. March 11, 2014. http://www.vulture.com/2014/03/matthew-weiner-sets-up-mad-mens-season-7.html (accessed March 11, 2014).

Weinman, Jaime J. "Why We Can't Be Mad at 'Mad Men.'" *Maclean's* 121, no. 30/31 (2008): 78.

White, Mimi. "Mad Women." In *Mad Men: Dream Come True TV*, ed. Gary R. Edgerton, 147–58. London: I. B. Tauris, 2011.

Whitney, Matheson. "Peer Into the Mind of the Man Who Made 'Mad Men.'" *USA Today*. October 26, 2009.

Wicke, Jennifer A. *Advertising Fictions: Literature, Advertisement, and Social Reading*. New York: Columbia University Press, 1988.

Wolf, Jeanne. "*Mad Men* (& Women)." *Saturday Evening Post*. March/April 2014.

Žižek, Slavoj. *The Sublime Object of Ideology*. 2nd ed. London: Verso, 2009.

INDEX

ABOUT THE AUTHORS

M. Keith Booker is professor of English and director of the Program in Comparative Literature and Cultural Studies at the University of Arkansas. He has written or edited more than forty books on literature and popular culture. His books include *Drawn to Television: Prime-Time Animated Series from The Flintstones to Family Guy* (2006) and *Historical Dictionary of American Cinema* (2011).

Bob Batchelor is a cultural historian who has written or edited more than twenty-five books on popular culture, American literature, and communications history. He teaches in the Media, Journalism & Film Department at Miami University. Batchelor is the founding editor of the *Popular Culture Studies Journal* for the Midwest Popular Culture Association and a member of the editorial advisory board of the *Journal of Popular Culture*. Among his books are *John Updike: A Critical Biography* (2013) and *Gatsby: The Cultural History of the Great American Novel* (Rowman & Littlefield, 2014).